# RIGOR
## AND
# ENGAGEMENT
## FOR
# GROWING MINDS

### STRATEGIES THAT ENABLE
### HIGH-ABILITY LEARNERS
### TO FLOURISH IN ALL CLASSROOMS

## BERTIE KINGORE
### AUTHOR

## JEFFERY KINGORE
### DESIGN & PHOTOGRAPHY

**PA Publishing**

Current Publications by
**Bertie Kingore, Ph.D.** —————————

VISIT DR. KINGORE ONLINE!
**www.bertiekingore.com**

*Alphabetters: Thinking Adventures with the Alphabet (Task Cards)*
*Assessment: Timesaving Procedures for Busy Teachers, 4th ed.*
*Assessment Interactive CD-ROM*
*Bertie's Book Notes CD-ROM*
*Centers In Minutes, Vol. 1: Grades K-8 CD-ROM*
*Centers In Minutes, Vol. 2: Literacy Stations, Grades K-4 CD-ROM*
*Developing Portfolios for Authentic Assessment, PreK-3*
*Differentiation: Simplified, Realistic, and Effective*
*Differentiation Interactive CD-ROM*
*Engaging Creative Thinking: Activities to Integrate Creative Problem Solving*
*Integrating Thinking: Strategies that Work!, 2nd ed.*
*Just What I Need! Learning Experiences to Use on Multiple Days in Multiple Ways*
*Kingore Observation Inventory (KOI), 2nd ed.*
*Literature Celebrations: Catalysts for High-Level Book Responses, 2nd ed.*
*Reaching All Learners: Making Differentiation Work!*
*Reading Strategies for Advanced Primary Readers: Texas Reading Initiative Task Force for the Education of Primary Gifted Children*
*Reading Strategies for Advanced Primary Readers: Professional Development Guide*
*Recognizing Gifted Potential: Planned Experiences with the KOI*
*Recognizing Gifted Potential: Professional Development Presentation*
*Teaching Without Nonsense: Translating Research into Effective Practice, 2nd ed.*
*Tiered Learning Stations in Minutes: Increasing Achievement, High-level Thinking, and the Joy of Learning*
*We Care: A Curriculum for Preschool Through Kindergarten, 2nd ed.*

FOR INFORMATION OR ORDERS CONTACT:
**PA PUBLISHING**
PO Box 28056 • Austin, Texas 78755-8056
Phone/fax: 866-335-1460 • E-mail: info@kingore.com

# RIGOR AND ENGAGEMENT FOR GROWING MINDS:
## STRATEGIES THAT ENABLE HIGH-ABILITY LEARNERS TO FLOURISH IN MIXED-ABILITY CLASSROOMS

Copyright © 2013  Bertie Kingore

Published by **PA Publishing**
Printed in the United States of America

ISBN: **0-9787042-8-2**
ISBN: **978-0-9787042-8-5**

## DEDICATION

*No one makes it alone.*

This book is dedicated to two of the three musketeers:

Richard Kingore

and

Jeffery Kingore.

You urge me to speak and make it possible to work hard and play hard.

## ACKNOWLEDGEMENTS

My family is my team of encouragers fueling my passion for life.
The five of you are always with me.

Special thanks to J. Scott, Glenda Higbee, Matthew Kingore,
Pam DePinto, and Jill Dowling Armstrong for your thoughtful
work, candor, reflections, and support.

# CONTENTS

# LIST OF FIGURES

# REPRODUCIBLE PAGES AND CD CONTENTS

# FOREWORD
## BY SUSAN WINEBRENNER

For decades, many educators have believed that the strategies used to challenge and engage gifted students could and should benefit *all* students, not because all students are academically gifted, but because all deserve the very best teaching and learning experiences. These include: higher order thinking, inquiry and in-depth study, using primary sources of information, flexible grouping by interest and learning strengths, and meaningful choices regarding content and process.

Bertie Kingore has verified those claims with this wonderful book. What amazing timing! Now IS the time for all educators and parents of gifted and high ability learners to recapture the essence of what gifted education has always tried to provide: truly challenging, personally-relevant learning experiences. With this book, all students can be supported in their efforts to interact with real-life problems in real-life situations.

Many teachers have asked me, "What if the learning options I am offering my gifted students make some other students *feel badly?*" Dr. Kingore's obvious answer is to integrate the most exciting and desirable learning elements into everyone's learning experiences, albeit at graduated levels of challenge. Engagement is guaranteed when students are actively interacting with a topic that interests them. Capture their interest, and you can use any number of required cognitive skills to keep them engaged until their learning is assessable. This book provides a sumptuous feast of specific techniques to ensure the success of your efforts to do just that!

The magic word is RIGOR! The narrowed teaching and learning approach of the past that focuses on discrete skills for documenting minimal competencies is finally giving way to re-enfranchising students' potential for authentic learning.

To provide support for students who have not had much previous experience in higher-level learning, Dr. Kingore demonstrates in detail ways to provide the scaffolding and support they need when they are interacting with challenging content. To continuously challenge learners, this book clearly describes how to manage self-selected, personally-relevant projects that allow students to demonstrate competence with the Common Core State Standards in advanced and rigorous ways.

Finally, the author addresses the issues surrounding assessment and describes how increasing rigor and relevance in all classroom activities allows all students to experience continuous learning at their highest capability levels.

As you wonder how you can participate effectively in this long-awaited paradigm shift in education, *Rigor and Engagement for Growing Minds* becomes your most user-friendly tool in achieving that goal. I know you will enjoy the experience and your students will be re-invigorated to work at their top levels of challenge. Everyone wins!

–Susan Winebrenner, M.S.

# INTRODUCTION

*Rigor*

Rigor—the very word worries some educators. As I work with teachers, many share with me concerns about additional pressures and making learning harder when even high-ability students are struggling in some classrooms. The good news is that rigor does not necessarily mean more hard work for teachers or students. Rigor is concerned with the quality of learning. As I developed the content in this book, we learned together that when rigor is relevant and realistic with real-world connections, high-ability students become more engaged in learning and demonstrate real commitment to their more authentic projects. This book is designed to enable high-ability learners and you, their educators, to be successful and flourish.

The language of rigor and engagement (as well as concerns for the lack of each) has circulated throughout education for decades. At least as early as the 1970's, gifted educators voiced the need for rigor in instruction. By the 1980's, Sandra Kaplan's work in depth and complexity influenced curriculum development in many states. In the 1980's and 1990's, Jerome Harste advanced the crucial role of nonfiction and inquiry for higher achievement and the development of more critically literate students. Today, we are immersed in a great discussion of rigor and engagement that permeates the globe. The potential difference in this current focus is the coming together of the Common Core of State Standards, the work of well-funded foundations for the improvement of instruction (including the foundations of Bill and Melinda Gates and George Lucas), and national incentives such as the Race for the Top.

Rigor is much more than the latest buzzword. Students embrace interactive, authentic learning experiences that help reset their learning attitude and lead them to accept more rigorous challenges to maximize their future potential beyond minimum competencies. Schools must reset learning priorities

Kingore, B. (2013). *Rigor and Engagement for Growing Minds.* Austin, TX: PA Publishing.

from testing minimum competency to the implementation of more relevant, real-world, rigorous expectations affecting students' roles and successes in college and the workforce.

The content of *Rigor and Engagement for Growing Minds: Strategies that Enable High-Ability Learners to Flourish in All Classrooms* emphasizes realistic, practical applications that effectively promote rigor and engagement in learning environments. The word rigor is used as an acrostic to organize the contents of this book and to clarify the five instructional priorities required in a rigorous learning environment. The current focus of education and standards involves understanding how instruction influences students' future, including their academic lives and careers. Hence, the main objective of this book is to explore the instructional practices that enable students to progress toward autonomy, future competency, and success. In a rigorous learning environment, educators:

> **R**ecognize realistic and relevant high-level expectations;
> **I**ntegrate complexity and depth in content, process, and product;
> **G**enerate cognitive skills;
> **O**rchestrate support systems and scaffold success; and
> **R**efine assessments to guide instruction and benefit learners.

## AN AMBIGUOUS TITLE

The title of this book is ambiguous to foster a dual purpose. *Growing* can be interpreted as a verb or as an adjective.

Specifically, rigor and engagement should grow or produce more cognitively rich mental activity, but simultaneously, increasing rigor and engagement enriches students' growing minds.

*Growing* is intended as a verb to emphasize the roles of educators in developing and nurturing mental growth.
* What should schools do to promote and support the mental, emotional, physical, and social development of today's youth?
* What should educators do to enable all students to experience continuous learning and develop their highest potential?

*Growing* is dualistically intended as an adjective to describe the minds of learners. The minds of today's digital youth are growing and changing in remarkable ways. Students are the reason for educational settings. Their minds are our future.

## TERMINOLOGY

### RIGOR

In today's learning environments, rigor is a term of major interest that is frequently ill-defined. Throughout this work, *rigor* refers to academic applications and expectations relative to students with high-ability or high potential. The following definition is most appropriate to stimulate high-ability learners.

Advanced achievement levels require a rigorous learning environment where students:
* Engage in high-level learning processes;
* Receive support to learn concepts and skills on and beyond grade-level, at a pace commensurate with their capabilities; and

- Demonstrate their understanding through high-end products evidencing relevant, sophisticated content.

## ENGAGEMENT

Engagement means that students are actively participating in the learning process. You can observe their alert attention as they discuss, interact, move, write content notes, explain, experiment, perform, problem solve, ask questions, and even draw to illustrate, symbolize, or graphically represent a point. Ideally, students who are demonstrating high-levels of engagement are actively functioning in a state of flow– Csikszentmihalyi's (1993) concept of the intrinsic motivation you experience when physically, mentally, and emotionally absorbed in a task with promising success. Csikszentmihalyi identifies the conditions necessary to achieve a state of flow as clear and attainable goals, concentration, a balance between high challenge and skill level, and clear and immediate feedback.

## HIGH-ABILITY

As many states have chosen to do, I use the term high-ability because it is more inclusive. High-ability connotes academically advanced learners, high-potential students, identified gifted students, and students with gifted potential who have not been formally identified. All of these learners require pace and level acceleration in their instructional services to experience continuous learning. They need teachers who care about students with advanced potential, are knowledgeable about appropriate applications of academic rigor, and are quite skilled in differentiation practices.

## DIFFERENTIATION

Differentiation requires assessing students' readiness levels and then responding to that assessment by customizing instruction to enable each student to experience continuous learning at their highest pace and level. Rigor is a complementary component of differentiation. Educators who promote rigor in differentiated learning environments are more likely to secure higher student achievement.

# FEATURES IN THE BOOK

## VOICE

Rather than the more formal third person voice, I use first person in this book. This work is quite personal and relevant to me. I share a research base for decision-making but do so through personal observations, convictions, and experiences in classrooms across the United States and Canada.

## TECHNIQUES AND LEARNING EXPERIENCES

All of the learning experiences and techniques shared in this book have been field-tested over the last six years with in-service educators working with a wide range of economic and cultural populations. Those teachers' suggestions and adaptations enable you to have confidence when selecting among the methods most applicable to your situation.

## RESOURCES

As the quantity of resources in the References section indicates, this work applies an extensive research base. While I remain

Kingore, B. (2013). *Rigor and Engagement for Growing Minds.* Austin, TX: PA Publishing.

concerned about interrupting comprehension and flow of text, I note research references extensively throughout this book. Today's educators want to know the research-base for information and recommended applications to guide instructional decisions and further their continued research review.

## WEBSITES

In this digital age, I am wary of sharing websites that may rapidly change or disappear. However, in this text, I do suggest a handful of websites I believe have potential for long-term applications and are too valuable to ignore. All of these sites are active at the time of publication and provide a sampling of the resources available for educators' and students' pursuit of high-level information.

Appendix B includes the addresses of all of the websites cited in the book. Nearly all of the sites have hyperlinks to related sites to expend the value of the information.

## STANDARDS

Inasmuch as the Common Core of State Standards (CCSS, 2010) permeates education and best practices, connections to the CCSS are made throughout this book. The CCSS is considered more rigorous than previous standards but requires the additional and more complex differentiation of curriculum and instruction recommended in this book to be responsive to high-ability students

## TECHNOLOGY

Technology is inherently engaging to students and helps students as well as teachers promote hands-on learning and relevant connections. Multiple examples applying technology to instruction are integrated throughout the book. Technology is particularly important to high-ability students as it enables them to participate in virtual teams and communicate with long-distance peers and adults working on similar interests and projects.

## REAL-WORLD APPLICATIONS

Connecting instruction to authentic, real-world applications is a dominant feature of academic rigor and the CCSS. In Chapter 2, explore multiple examples that compare traditional learning assignments and more relevant, real-world applications. Select among the suggestions for more authentic products to engage students of all ages.

## ASSESSMENT

Assessment and instruction need to work in tandem. While Chapter 6 is dedicated to assessment in a rigorous learning environment, a wide selection of rubrics and other assessment tools are integrated and modeled throughout this work. The main focus of the assessment examples is to share practical tools and procedures you can immediately use in classrooms to determine instant, valid, and actionable data about students' learning.

## ICON FOR IMMEDIATE APPLICATIONS

This icon signals learning experiences with immediate applications. These

Kingore, B. (2013). *Rigor and Engagement for Growing Minds.* Austin, TX: PA Publishing.

tasks are designed to absolutely minimize the intensity of your preparation; they do not lessen the mental time, high-level thinking, or engagement required of students. Subtitles identify each Get Going application to facilitate scanning for applications relevant to your instructional situation and student population.

These techniques and learning experiences provide ready-to-use, highly effective instructional opportunities to promote engaging learning experiences and high-level thinking in a rigorous learning environment. Many of these learning experiences are also effective choices for flexible group interactions and problem solving opportunities.

### BULLETS AND SUBTITLES FOR QUICK SELECTION

The text is interspersed with subtitles as well as bulleted lists to enable you to efficiently skim. You can quickly access and select the ideas most useful to you. When you want to revisit an idea, these features will help you relocate that information.

### GRAPHICS AND VISUAL TOOLS

Many students today respond positively to visual tools and graphics. A large number of graphic organizers and other visual tools are used to attract students' interest, guide the organization of complex information, and help students visualize concepts. Graphics discourage simple thinking and the possibility of students copying text because graphic organizers require students to cognitively process information at a deeper level and recompose it in a different form.

### REFLECTION DEVICE

Teachers improve their instruction by reflecting on best practices and their own applications. Reflection pages conclude each chapter to invite you to unpack your thinking about rigor and its applications. The reflections facilitate your decision-making regarding your priorities and procedures when implementing more rigorous instruction. The reflections also provide suggestions for networking with others to discuss key elements and pose questions about concepts, processes, and connections to the content. The intent is to trigger grand professional conversations about best practices to further students' deeper understanding and lifelong learning. As we engage in reflection, we model and practice the collaboration and skills identified as essential for students committed to growing and changing as learners.

## FEATURES ON THE CD

The CD provides ready-to-use applications intended to help minimize preparation time as you implement and expand instruction for rigor and engagement. The templates allow students and teachers to complete their own applications. Student examples of completed forms and graphics are not included on the CD as those are only intended as sample applications.

### • CUSTOMIZABLE APPLICATIONS

Customizable versions of figures and templates are often provided. The graphics included for customizing are those that educators may want to adapt for their unique learning environment.

Kingore, B. (2013). *Rigor and Engagement for Growing Minds*. Austin, TX: PA Publishing.

- **REFLECTIONS**

The reflection pages for all chapters are provided to facilitate reproducing them for group applications. Invite members of a faculty to individually complete a copy of a reflection before a discussion ensues.

## AN OPEN NOTE TO MY COLLEAGUES IN SCHOOLS ACROSS THE UNITED STATES AND CANADA

> *Never doubt that a small group of thoughtful citizens can change the world. Indeed, it is the only thing that ever has.*
>
> –Margaret Mead
> American cultural anthropologist

Some of what I learned working with you is:

- You do change the world, one student at a time.
- You care about students and want to be a part of expanding their future promise.
- You want to implement academic rigor and support students so they experience continuous learning.
- You acknowledge student differences to guide your instruction, not label kids.
- You need support and guidance for your professional growth just as students need your support and guidance to flourish.
- You deserve validation for all you endeavor to accomplish to help students.
- You understand the value of standards but seek to integrate them into the curriculum rather that teach standards as separate entities.
- You value a research base for making instructional decisions and seek help translating valued research into effective classroom practices.
- You worry how to accomplish everything expected in today's high-stakes educational settings.
- You muse about sorely needing more realistic, effective ways to resolve these problems and live up to the promise of high standards instead of just being told to implement rigorous instruction.
- You inspire students. You deserve to be inspired.

This book is a response to your ever-expanding talents as educators as well as your concerns, questions, and personal commitment to change. I continue to thank you for caring enough to teach, and I invite you to use this book to select great ideas for challenging great students through rigor and engagement.

I have been involved with this content, developing this book for over six years. During the last ten months, however, my writing evolved to a state of flow. Characteristic of Csikszentmihalyi's concept of flow, my absorption with this content became almost addictive as I experienced the joy of resolving and composing a topic so dear to me and so interesting to other educators. The only conceivable way to exceed this flow experience is if this content proves to be rewarding and useful to you.

I am honored to continue our professional learning quest together.

*Bertie Kingore*

Kingore, B. (2013). *Rigor and Engagement for Growing Minds*. Austin, TX: PA Publishing.

# CHAPTER 1
# UNDERSTANDING RIGOR: WHAT IT IS AND IS NOT

Current national initiatives in education demand increased rigor and engagement in learning environments and outcomes. Simultaneously, educators endeavor to encourage students' deeper thoughts with a greater emphasis on interpretation, persuasion, and analysis. Through rigor and engagement, teachers want to promote a rigorous learning environment for all children while stimulating advanced achievement for high-ability students and students with potential for high-ability. This target, however, is hindered by the prevailing emphasis on minimum competency which pushes support for high-achieving students into the background of our national, state, and local conversation (Plucker, Burroughs, & Song, 2010). Inasmuch as the core curriculum seldom challenges advanced students, high-ability learners may acquire negative attitudes, such as: "School is boring," and "There is little need to think or pay attention in class as we already know the content."

During a recent professional development session, a secondary teacher shared this concern: "I can't initiate more rigorous instruction. My gifted students will not work on difficult tasks. My special education students try harder than my gifted students." Unfortunately, it is true some advanced students have learned habits of mind that are counterproductive, but it is time to help students reset their learning attitude from: "What is the minimum I must do to get an A?" to "What helps me learn and make connections at increasingly complex levels?" Simultaneously, schools must reset learning priorities from minimum competency to implementation of more rigorous expectations.

Rigor is a frequently used, sometimes abused, goal in contemporary learning environments. The process of increasing rigor is connected to how people define the term. Since Webster's Unabridged Dictionary includes several definitions which characterize rigor as strictness, severity, harshness, and

Kingore, B. (2013). *Rigor and Engagement for Growing Minds.* Austin, TX: PA Publishing.

inflexibility, practitioners may misinterpret rigor to mean making learning experiences harder and more stringent for students. However, when the word *rigor* is used in an educational context, it refers to *academic rigor.* In a rigorous learning environment, educators exhibit a greater concern for quality than quantity and conceptual thinking rather than memorization because it is the quality of students' thinking and responses that defines rigorous learning (Daggett, 2007). With developmentally appropriate applications, academic rigor is relevant at any grade level and in any content area.

In reality, the concept of rigor is relative and variable, dependent on a student's background, readiness, and effort to succeed: the greater a student's expertise and motivation, the greater the degree of rigor appropriate to the learner. In reality then, rigor is not one standard in a classroom; rather, it is a variable that increases in response to students' progress. Figure 1.1 presents a comparison to clarify what the concept of rigor intends versus what some might misconstrue rigor to be.

Relevant and realistic rigor emerges from authentic rather than synthetic learning experiences and promotes connections of core knowledge to real-world applications. It implies more academically challenging learning experiences in which educators emphasize content depth with high-level thinking and endeavor to avoid redundant practice. Responding to Vygotsky's (1962) definition of the levels required to ensure learning, educators aim instruction at a zone of proximal development—slightly above students' comfort level but not extending to the counterproductive level of frustration. When that optimal match between child and challenge is achieved, students can experience continuous learning on and beyond grade level. To ensure continuous learning, tier your instruction so students are frequently instructed in small groups to experience concepts and skills at levels of complexity matched to their readiness. Rather than the more stagnate ability-level groups of the past, tiered groups are flexible with fluid group memberships that change in response to instructional objectives and students' needs. The intent of tiered grouping is to accommodate the unique diversity of learners rather than to divide students into leveled groups.

Rigor addresses the need to foster high expectations for all students. Through their efforts, students are expected to achieve and potentially excel beyond minimum competency. Particularly for advanced students, however, higher expectations require that students access text and learning experiences beyond grade level. Advanced students need to be encouraged to select more difficult tasks and extend their learning beyond minimum requirements in order to maximize their learning potential.

Thus, rigor is a vital component of a differentiated learning environment. Rather than *one more thing* to add to our crowded curriculum, rigor intends to promote a more effective way to achieve high standards and learning success. Thus, rigor concerns the quality of learning more than the quantity of what is learned. Academic rigor matches current skill objectives to targets for students' future success in college, in the work force, and as productive citizens.

FIGURE 1.1:
# RIGOR: WHAT IT IS AND IS NOT

| IT IS: | IT IS NOT: |
|---|---|
| 1. Relevant and realistic with real-world connections | 1. Synthetic, graded learning assignments required at specified junctures of learning |
| 2. Academic challenges that promote deeper meaning | 2. Difficult tasks for the sake of being "rigorous" |
| 3. In-depth thinking about the content | 3. Continued practice at levels already mastered |
| 4. A response to zones of proximal development | 4. Instruction at students' frustration levels |
| 5. Continuous learning for all students | 5. Limited to mastery of grade-level standards and core curriculum |
| 6. Tiered instruction as well as flexible learning groups | 6. Stagnate ability grouping |
| 7. An expectation for all students to excel at higher levels | 7. Labeling who can and cannot achieve |
| 8. Students' industrious effort beyond minimum competency | 8. Students completing grade level work in a timely and attractive manner |
| 9. A vital component of differentiation | 9. Something extra to incorporate into the curriculum |
| 10. The quality of learning | 10. The quantity of what is learned |
| 11. Future-directed: "How can we adapt current instruction so students develop the skills and thinking abilities needed to succeed in future roles?" | 11. Present-oriented: "Which current learning standards and core curriculum concepts do students need to master to advance to the next grade level?" |

Understanding Rigor

Kingore, B. (2013). *Rigor and Engagement for Growing Minds*. Austin, TX: PA Publishing.

Incorporating effective differentiation strategies to stimulate students' learning is part of the mission of most school systems. For two decades, educators have worked to implement differentiation of content, process, and product to enable all students to reach higher levels of achievement. Rigor is a complementary component of differentiation. Educators who promote rigor in differentiated learning environments are more likely to get the higher achievement they expect.

> **RIGOR REQUIRES THAT STUDENTS:**
>
> **K**now (factually),
>
> **U**nderstand (conceptually), and
>
> Are able to **D**o (skillfully).
>
> –Erickson (2007)

The process of increasing rigor requires what Erickson (2007) refers to as KUD: Know, Understand, and able to Do. Educators must know and communicate what rigor is, understand its impact on instruction, and be able to implement practices appropriate to fostering a rigorous learning environment. Hence, the process of increasing rigor requires educators to define rigor and identify the specific instructional elements of rigor that enable students to be more engaged and successful in high-level learning cultures. To promote rigor, educators must develop ways to incorporate rigorous elements that differentiate instruction, elicit high-level responses, develop students' autonomy, and increase responsibility for continuous learning. This chapter defines rigor as well as identifies the skills and instructional priorities that are present in a rigorous learning environment. Subsequent chapters explore specific, timesaving applications of rigor in effective learning environments.

## DEFINING RIGOR

Rigor and engagement are significant for all students but differ by degree when nurturing advanced and potentially high-ability children. A rigorous learning environment should require that all students are engaged, supported, and expected to demonstrate high-level understanding. Additionally, advanced learners benefit from an increased pace of instruction, in-depth content, and more complex levels of process and product (NAGC, 2010; Sousa, 2009). Thus, the following definition of rigor and engagement is most appropriate to stimulate high-ability learners.

> **RIGOR FOR HIGH-ABILITY LEARNERS**
> Advanced levels of achievement require a rigorous learning environment where students:
> * Engage in high-level learning processes;
> * Receive support to learn concepts and skills on and beyond grade-level, at a pace commensurate with their capabilities; and
> * Demonstrate their understanding through high-end products evidencing relevant, sophisticated content.

Kingore, B. (2013). *Rigor and Engagement for Growing Minds.* Austin, TX: PA Publishing.

Examining each component of this definition helps to elaborate its implications.

### ENGAGE IN HIGH-LEVEL PROCESSES.

Process skills are a means of learning and essential to conducting objective inquiry and forming conclusions. High-level learning processes include critical and creative thinking, observation, complex and in-depth information processing, and sophisticated communication characterized by academic vocabulary. The application of simple process skills may foster grade-level mastery rather than accelerated learning.

### RECEIVE SUPPORT.

High-ability learners flourish when provided the support of adults and peers who help actualize students' potential for advanced levels of achievement. A supportive environment enables them to access beyond-grade-level information while encouraging them to pursue the unique critical and creative thinking and diverse ideas characteristic of both change and advanced levels of achievement.

### DEMONSTRATE UNDERSTANDING.

Applications of deeper understanding are crucial. Research substantiates that knowledge and understanding must be applied and demonstrated if long-term memory is a goal (Sousa & Tomlinson, 2010; Willis, 2011; Wolfe, 2010). In a rigorous learning environment, learning experiences and products are more than *something to do* when direct instruction is completed. Culminating task discussions and products should substantiate that students have changed in the quality and quantity of their learning. High-ability students benefit from opportunities to engage in relevant research and transdisciplinary projects that challenge them to develop professional-level, real-world concepts and products.

When the instruction of high-ability students is devoid of consistent rigor and engagement, educators risk lower achievement and limited success for these students. Figure 1.2 synthesizes the potentially negative consequences confirmed by research if schools fail to address the needs of high-ability students.

## A RIGOROUS LEARNING ENVIRONMENT

A rigorous learning environment is required to address the learning capabilities of high-ability learners. When high-potential students are denied an appropriate pace and level of instruction, they may develop habits of mind that are counterproductive to advanced levels of achievement by concluding that school is easy, not requiring active attention or effort. Some develop a habit of working the night before an assignment is due, hurriedly completing products that are good enough to get the grade they prefer, rather than working to benefit from a learning opportunity for their own growth and advancement. They frequently seem to settle for simple tasks that do not require perseverance. Simple learning experiences deny advanced students the pride of accomplishment that results when students struggle to meet a challenge that would enable them to excel and extend personal learning. Some high-ability students continuously

Kingore, B. (2013). *Rigor and Engagement for Growing Minds.* Austin, TX: PA Publishing.

## FIGURE 1.2:
# WHAT CAN HAPPEN IF WE FAIL TO NURTURE ADVANCED POTENTIAL?

Without appropriate rigor and engagement, high-ability students may exhibit one or combinations of the following less-productive learning outcomes.

- Underdevelopment of academic habits of mind; less need for the struggle or persistence that promotes advanced learning
- Lower achievement gains; limited progress relative to potential
- Deterioration of potential skills and decreased enthusiasm for learning
- Patterns of underachievement, lower performance, and/or behavior issues
- Boredom
- Hidden abilities
- Decreased personal satisfaction and self-esteem
- A fixed mindset
- Less productive and engaged lives

Colangelo, Assouline, & Gross, 2004; Dweck, 2006; Ford & Harris, 1999; Slocumb & Payne, 2011; Sousa, 2009; Tomlinson, 2003; Willis, 2010.

express that school is boring; some deny their advanced potential in order to better fit into the peer group; others demonstrate behaviors that attract the attention of the peer group but do not forward high achievement. An environment of minimum competencies rather than rigor and engagement fosters less productive futures in school and professions.

The ultimate goal of education should be the same for all learners: to enable each student to experience continuous learning. That goal statement seems simple, yet it has proven most difficult to implement in learning environments. Continuous learning necessitates changes in the pace and level of instruction. It requires educators to pre-assess students, determine their levels of readiness, and then activate a pace and level of learning opportunities appropriate to each student. The obvious result when teachers assess students in today's complex world is that the assessments document that students demonstrate different learning levels and capabilities. When students are assessed to be struggling with learning requirements, teachers vary instruction to build upon what students know, support their best ways to learn, and promote growth toward competency. When students are assessed at a level commensurate with the core curriculum, teachers proceed with a pace and level appropriate to grade-level expectations. However, when students are assessed to have mastered basic content, teachers must accelerate instructional pace and level to exceed core learning targets or those students will not be challenged to continue to learn. Inasmuch as high-ability learners frequently require a faster pace of instruction and higher levels of content, process, and product, rigorous learning environments are vital.

Kingore, B. (2013). *Rigor and Engagement for Growing Minds.* Austin, TX: PA Publishing.

Rigor needs to be appropriately implemented in curriculum content and instructional practices across grade levels. Educators do not lower expectations for any student, they extend learning opportunities to levels that ensure continuous learning for all students—including high-ability learners.

*Continuous Learning*

•

*The ultimate goal of education should be to enable each student to experience continuous learning.*

real-world issues relevant to today and the future. Hence, a rigorous learning environment requires an emphasis on the following student skills: cognitive skills, self-management, communication, group interaction, creative thinking, and an increased awareness of the globalized and environmental demands of school, college, work cultures, and citizenry.

## THE SKILLS OF RIGOROUS INSTRUCTION

*COGNITIVE SKILLS*

Specific skills are crucial in learning environments that successfully respond to the demands of contemporary societies. Observing that schools are still mired in the kinds of educational content and methods that responded to the industrial age, Wagner believes that children today get more relevant skills outside of school from extracurricular activities and social networking—if they are fortunate enough to experience those opportunities (2010).

Rigor requires the sort of mental activity that enables advanced students to:

✓ Scrutinize, evaluate, and assimilate text and ideas coherently;

✓ Substantiate precise, strategic thinking; and

✓ Engage in reflective thought, critical analysis, problem solving, and decision-making.

One of the reasons school systems embrace academic rigor is to expedite instructional changes for high-level learning and future success. Particularly for high-ability students, academic rigor intends to expand students' capacity to comprehend and respond to complex text and ideas that are relevant, thought provoking, and emotionally stimulating. Rather than accumulate the correct answers from the past, rigor should be more concerned with challenging advanced students to pose essential questions, examine ambiguity, and engage in problem-solving

All students benefit from high-level thinking applications; additionally, advanced students benefit from high-level thinking applications that incorporate a greater degree of complexity and depth. High-level thinking for most students is more concrete and progresses toward abstract thinking applications as appropriate. High-ability students think more abstractly much of the time and should experience extensive opportunities for abstract thinking that involves open-ended problems related to change, issues, and ethics. Rather

Understanding Rigor

Kingore, B. (2013). *Rigor and Engagement for Growing Minds.* Austin, TX: PA Publishing.

than memorizing every detail, students need a structure of knowing. They need to know how to think and develop generalizations relating to transdisciplinary situations. They need the ability to ask essential questions and think about concepts in innovative ways because the answers of the past may not solve future problems.

## SELF-MANAGEMENT SKILLS

Academic rigor depends upon students who:

✓ Accept responsibility for their own behavior;

✓ Respect and practice codes of behavior in different situations;

✓ Make informed choices affecting self and others;

✓ Manage time appropriately; and

✓ Strive for autonomy.

Educators dare not instigate a generation of students who require others to always tell them what to do as well as when and how to do it.

Adult worlds expect peers to be competent self-managers capable of task completion without significant urging or input from others. Hence, students benefit from learning environments that model self-management skills and high expectations that promote autonomy and the enhanced productivity that results from effort. While some students experience self-management skills modeled at home, all students can be guaranteed opportunities to develop self-management skills when facilitated in school environments.

## COMMUNICATION SKILLS

Rigor demands increasingly sophisticated communication skills that enable students to:

✓ Communicate clearly, logically, and concisely;

✓ Incorporate precise word choices;

✓ Develop an extensive academic and content-related vocabulary; and

✓ Engage in active listening to understand and appropriately respond to the ideas of others.

Continued success depends upon students' abilities to skillfully and concisely communicate through verbal skills, written skills, presentation skills, and technology skills. In present and future environments, students must be able to express their thinking with a clear focus and voice while effectively engaging in discussions whether in person, in writing, or when globally connected via high-speed technology links. Business professionals express concern about young people who do not know how to speak and write clearly, logically, and concisely; they perceive those communication skills as a greater problem than the spelling and mechanics schools spend so much time teaching and testing (Wagner, 2010).

Communication skills are directly related to vocabulary, and advanced vocabulary is required for complex cognitive processing and comprehension (Marzano, 2006; Sousa,

2009). Furthermore, professional environments expect peers to use and understand content-related vocabulary at sophisticated levels. Advanced students also benefit from guidance to develop active listening and interactive communication skills, enabling them to more diplomatically respond to others whose ideas differ or are flawed.

## COLLABORATION SKILLS

In rigorous learning environments, all students collaborate to refine understanding and pursue problem solving in flexible groups in which they:

✓ Respect and cooperate with team members;

✓ Accept a variety of roles in a group;

✓ Practice negotiation and conflict resolution; and

✓ Gain, evaluate, and present complex information through listening and speaking with others.

Group collaboration skills are prized in the work force and in learning environments. Employers expect workers to interact and communicate effectively with co-workers in their immediate environment or when connected globally (Crockett, Jukes, & Churches, 2011; Wagner, 2010). In school settings, students need to develop the social and communication skills that enable them to benefit from a wide range of peer interactions and collaborations. Students need to see evidence that their contributions to group work are needed and respected.

Students should engage in learning opportunities while working in whole class learning situations, in small groups with age peers, in small groups with intellectual peers, and independently to document academic achievements and pursue individual interest-based learning projects. Beyond cooperative learning techniques, high-ability students need leadership and collaborative skills that enable them to work with others in a class, use technology to participate in virtual teams, and communicate with long-distance peers and adults working on similar interests and projects. They benefit from intellectual peers as well as age peers.

## CREATIVITY AND ADAPTABILITY SKILLS

In today's changing world, students' must:

✓ Respond to existing information with creative thinking that focuses on flexibility, originality, and adaptation;

✓ Extend beyond knowing existing information to constructing new knowledge and ways to learn; and

✓ Generate original problem-solving strategies.

Creative thinking, flexibility, and originality are necessities in our fast-paced world of change. Accessing information is not the issue in today's digital landscape. Information is so readily available that students must learn how to become discerning and creative consumers of information. Students' success in future roles greatly depends on their ability to interpret and apply current and new information to unique situations, problems, and environments (Crockett, Jukes, & Churches, 2011, 3).

Successful students are those who are perceptive, mentally adaptable, innovative, and prepared to actively respond to new ideas and possibilities. The future requires creative thinking and adaptability as students confront problems and opportunities that do not exist today. In his 1984 book *The Third Wave,* Alvin Toffler predicted that the prized literacy of the twenty-first century would not be people who can read and write, but those who can learn, unlearn, and relearn. Daniel Pink (2005), the author of *A Whole New Mind,* observes that increased material abundance heightens the desire for unique products and services. Developing students' capacities for imagination, creativity, and empathy emerge as crucial for maintaining the United States' competitive advantage in the future. Additionally, Willis (2011) asserts that application is greater than facts because fifty percent of the facts we now teach will be modified by the time our students leave school.

Advanced students must synthesize knowledge beyond the disciplines. They benefit from learning environments that exercise higher brain skills by challenging students to ask unique questions, activate imagination, and function as flexible thinkers receptive to change. Inasmuch as today's problems and jobs may not exist in the future, adaptability and creative thinking are timeless and paramount to students' future success.

## KNOWLEDGE OF LEARNING CULTURES

> The focus of education has evolved toward a concern for how instruction influences students' future through:
> ✓ Understanding the culture of school;
> ✓ Understanding the culture of college; and
> ✓ Understanding the culture of the marketplace.

Learning environments incorporate both stated and implied standards that enable people to function. To succeed, students must understand and accommodate their behaviors to the mores and expectations prevalent in the cultures of school, college, the workforce, and professional careers. Understanding the cultures of school environments and the marketplace is a part of the skills students must acquire in order to access preferred jobs and become productive citizens. In specific learning cultures, the requirements of time management, dress codes, diplomacy, work ethics, and autonomy may differ significantly from peer or home environments.

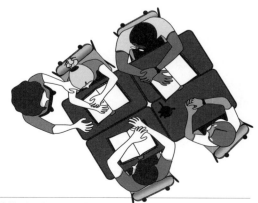

## INSTRUCTIONAL PRIORITIES IN A RIGOROUS LEARNING ENVIRONMENT

Rigor requires action. In a rigorous learning environment, educators demonstrate five instructional priorities that facilitate higher achievement. These instructional priorities enable teachers to implement appropriately rigorous practices to benefit students while promoting high-level learning. In a rigorous learning environment, educators:

*R*ecognize realistic and relevant high-level expectations;

*I*ntegrate complexity and depth in content, process, and product;

*G*enerate cognitive skills;

*O*rchestrate support systems and scaffold success; and

*R*efine assessments to guide instruction and benefit learners.

Each of these instructional priorities is developed in the chapters that follow. The chapters are not hierarchical; approach them in any order that seems most appealing or productive for you. The discussions in each chapter are embellished with a significant number of specific techniques and relevant applications to assist your implementation of rigor.

- The techniques and applications are research-based and field-tested so your implementation will prove worthwhile and successful.

- Most of the examples are timesaving applications because teacher's plates are already full with the demands of the curriculum and standards.

- Most applications use inexpensive, readily available materials because resources are often limited and economy is paramount.

- Some of the applications facilitate a ready-to-go application of rigor by modeling how to vary known learning experiences or techniques to lift the level of challenge or provide more relevant connections.

The ultimate objective of rigor is to enhance students' opportunities for high-level thinking, learning that has value beyond the classroom, personal fulfillment, and success. School-centered learning opportunities must become more authentic to capture today's digital learners. Rigorous learning environments must be relevant to students' goals and dreams as well as address the demands of modern society.

Thinking that students won't try, don't care, and cannot learn is flawed thinking and counterproductive. We believe in students and want to be catalysts to their brighter futures. We want to know that our actions and efforts productively influence lifelong learning. All students can learn; they prove that daily in their sports involvements, technology applications, and accommodations to peer-social demands. Rigorous learning environments build on the

Kingore, B. (2013). *Rigor and Engagement for Growing Minds.* Austin, TX: PA Publishing.

life lessons of students' world outside of school to increase relevancy and engagement in school.

Rather than one more thing to do, rigor is integrated with best practices to foster higher levels of student learning. A valuable point is that rigor does not require starting instruction over; it is furthered by changes in expectations and incorporation of more relevant, engaging instruction to increase the academic mileage of established learning procedures or experiences. Explore these applications characterized by less intensive teacher preparation and inexpensive procedures that empower us (and our sometimes-reluctant and often-overwhelmed colleagues) to successfully increase rigorous instruction.

*Learning Differently*

•

*Student differences should not imply that someone is better than another; they only signal that one person can learn differently than another.*

## RIGOR AND CHALLENGE

Instead of accumulating correct answers from the past, educators in rigorous learning environments should be more concerned with challenging advanced students to pose essential questions, examine the ambiguity of multifaceted materials and different ways of thinking, and engage in problem solving real-world issues relevant to today and the future.

## A PARTING THOUGHT...

Rigor eludes differentiation when we fail to respond with different levels of instruction to students' different levels of readiness. In today's school climate, it seems politically correct to say, "All children are gifted," or "I teach all children as if they were high-ability learners," but what does that imply? Do all students actually learn in the same way, at the same pace, at the same level? Are we debasing the uniqueness of individuals, backgrounds, interests, and learning differences? It is time to respectfully recognize that students differ and exhibit a wide range of capabilities and interests. Differences should not imply that someone is better than another; they only signal that one person can learn differently than another. Adults model the art of education when they respond to those differences so all students, including high-ability learners, experience continuous learning at their highest capabilities. Rigor should guarantee continuous learning at the deeper levels of cognitive processing that foster conceptual understanding.

Kingore, B. (2013). *Rigor and Engagement for Growing Minds.* Austin, TX: PA Publishing.

FIGURE 1.3:
# THINKING REFLECTIVELY

1. **IDEAS**

   Identify two or more ideas you intend to apply immediately.

2. **RIGOROUS WORDS**

   List and explain the three to five words you think are most significant to rigor in your learning environment.

3. **DEFINITION OF RIGOR**

   As an individual or group, write a definition of rigor for your student population to best acknowledge your educational philosophy and expedite best practices in your educational environment.

4. **COMPARING CHARACTERISTICS**

   How are the characteristics of a rigorous learning environment for grade-level students different than rigor for high-ability students?  After completing your similarities, differences, and summary on Figure 1.4, refer to the appendix to compare your perceptions with a completed example.

Kingore, B. (2013). *Rigor and Engagement for Growing Minds.* Austin, TX: PA Publishing.

Understanding Rigor

FIGURE 1.4:

# CHARACTERISTICS OF A RIGOROUS LEARNING ENVIRONMENT

STUDENTS
ACHIEVING
AT GRADE
LEVEL

ALL STUDENTS

HIGH-ABILITY
STUDENTS

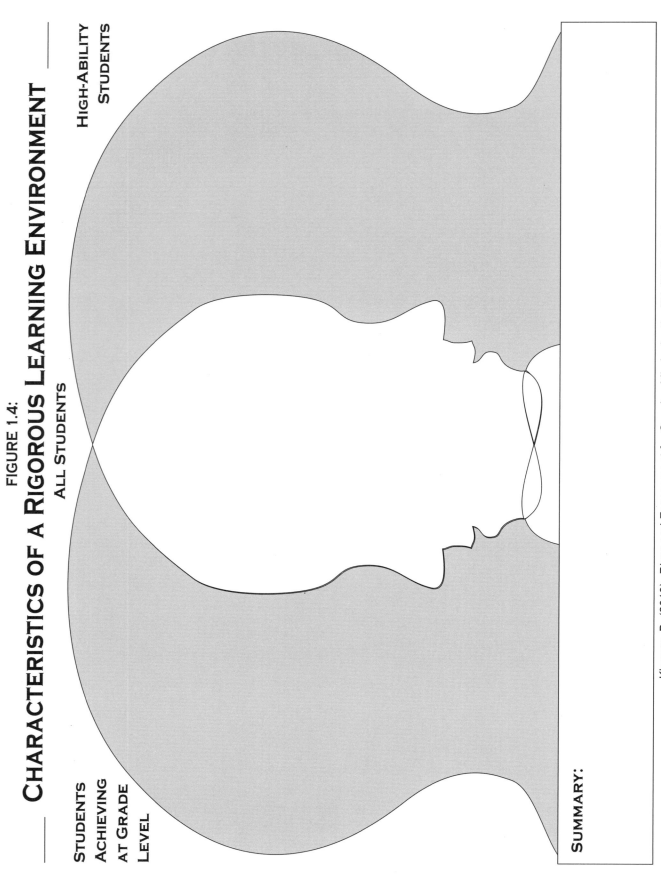

SUMMARY:

Kingore, B. (2013). *Rigor and Engagement for Growing Minds*. Austin, TX: PA Publishing.

# CHAPTER 2
# RECOGNIZING REALISTIC AND RELEVANT HIGH-LEVEL EXPECTATIONS

High-level expectations are an essential objective in education. Educators recognize that realistic and relevant expectations in schools stimulate students' higher expectations for success. Conversely, impracticable and unrealistic expectations breed defeatist responses. Sullo (2009) admonishes that when students perceive that they cannot succeed, they typically seek power in less responsible ways, such as assuming an *I don't care* attitude or becoming a disruption. Realistic and relevant expectations are hierarchical so initial achievements become building blocks to higher-level success.

## REALISTIC EXPECTATIONS

In rigorous learning environments, teachers communicate realistic expectations that challenge students to demonstrate effort to advance their own learning. For example, I wanted students to understand that their effort would result in success, so I guaranteed learning in my classrooms (Figure 2.1).

**FIGURE 2.1:**
**LEARNING GUARANTEE**

I guarantee you will learn in this class! To insure that guarantee, you need to demonstrate three things in class each day:
  ✓ I will think;
  ✓ I will try; and
  ✓ I will participate.

If you bring these three things to class, I guarantee that you will succeed.

Sincerely,

LEARNING GUARANTEE

Kingore, B. (2013). *Rigor and Engagement for Growing Minds*. Austin, TX: PA Publishing.

Kingore, B. (2013). *Rigor and Engagement for Growing Minds.* Austin, TX: PA Publishing.

Early in the year, I told students that I guaranteed they would learn and advance in my class if they demonstrated daily that they would think, try, and participate in the class learning experiences. This technique may seem too simple or even silly, yet it set a tone of shared responsibility and realistic expectations for learning. If a student was not making progress despite thinking, trying, and participating, it removed the burden from the student and became a clear indication to me that I needed to approach this learning situation another way. On the other hand, if a potentially advanced student was performing at grade level rather than working toward higher levels, that student and I would conference to initiate discussions of change.

It is important to ask students to document what they are doing to enable themselves to learn and change as a learner. Cement your learning guarantee with an accountability contract that asks all students to make a commitment to actively pursue continuous learning. Include realistic expectations on the contract that clarify students' role in high-level learning outcomes. Make this process productive and personally relevant by eliciting ideas from the students regarding which details to include in the contract. In a whole class discussion, collect ideas and engage students in ranking the relevancy and importance of the major suggestions. Then, invite a small group of interested students to create the class contract for individuals or to produce a class poster with an area for signatures from each class member.

Figure 2.2 provides one example of a contract for learning accountability. Introduce this contract by asking students to analyze

FIGURE 2.2:
**LEARNING ACCOUNTABILITY CONTRACT**

Three traits that describe me as a continuous learner:

1. _____
   _____
2. _____
   _____
3. _____
   _____

❑ I am accountable for my learning.
❑ I arrive on time; I am prepared and have my completed work with me.
❑ I show respect for everyone in the classroom.
❑ I demonstrate an effort to learn; I care enough to do my best.
❑ I think, I try, and I participate.
❑ I do everything I can to enable myself and others to learn.
❑ I endeavor to exceed expectations.
❑ I strive to become an autonomous citizen in this community of learners.
❑ _____
❑ _____
❑ _____

Student's signature _____
                                                    Date _____
Teacher's signature _____
                                                    Date _____

Kingore, B. (2013). *Rigor and Engagement for Growing Minds*. Austin, TX: PA Publishing.

their learning behaviors and identify three traits that describe themselves as productive learners. Rather than direct students toward preconceived correct answers, the intent of this activity is to focus students' thinking about the power they have and the role they can assume to continuously learn. Since students are curious about the ideas proposed by others, a grand conversation typically ensues regarding which learning traits classmates deem significant.

This contract continues by communicating concrete actions that affect learning success. It embellishes realistic expectations that students will learn at high levels and increases students' awareness that their behaviors in class substantiate their efforts to learn. A class accountability contract becomes a statement of the philosophy of the learning environment and clarifies to students and their families what is valued to expedite learning. Shared as either a learning poster or an accountability contract, this tool makes a important statement regarding realistic expectations for productive learning behaviors in a classroom learning community.

> ### *Realistic Expectations*
> •
> *The reality is, we cannot change students' backgrounds;*
> *we cannot influence what happened or did not happen*
> *before they came to us.*
> *Our power is in how we use this next step—this current learning opportunity.*
>
> *We affect students' future learning by our decisions and expectations.*

## RELEVANCE

Relevance is critical to rigor, long-term learning, and student ownership. Students constantly expect to know what the curriculum has to do with them. When learning is relevant, it makes more sense to students, enabling them to connect the unknown to what is known and retain information (Sousa, 2005; Willis, 2007a). When learning is relevant, students assume more ownership in learning because they understand the ways in which this current topic of study or skill applies to their lives. With relevance, students discover how they learn and experience different ways to learn as well as acquire specific skills and content. Relevant learning opportunities foster students' active problem solving and the development of their own processes. Less relevant applications primarily focus on memorizing and reporting facts.

Compare examples of skill and concept applications from traditional core-curriculum assignments to alternatives that focus on relevancy (Figure 2.3). These traditional tasks are effective, appropriate applications of targeted skills that are often quite student-centered. However, the advantage of efforts toward more relevant, authentic applications of skills and concepts is the increased potential for student ownership and engagement. Relevant applications integrating skills and concepts across disciplines enable students to understand how ideas are connected and relate to real-world situations. Some of the relevant applications in Figure 2.3, for example, connect parts of an integrated study for planning and developing a school vegetable garden involving several content areas. When learning tasks are relevant to students' point of view and interests, students arrive at deeper meaning with more authentic understanding.

Relevant learning experiences can range from simple to quite complex and apply to any grade level or discipline. A powerful by-product of relevant expectations is students' development of self-management skills as they actively engage in problem solving and develop learning processes.

Beginning in the primary grades and continuing with increasing sophistication through high school, students progress from tasks and processes directed by teachers to increasingly determining methodology for

**Recognizing Expectations**

FIGURE 2.3:

# TRADITIONAL VERSUS RELEVANT APPLICATIONS OF SKILLS AND CONCEPTS

## LANGUAGE ARTS

### TRADITIONAL ASSIGNMENT

- Hold one letter of the alphabet and move into place with others holding letters to complete the alphabet in sequence.
- Read nonfiction sources to learn about fruits and vegetables. Then, write an alphabet book that includes information about a fruit or vegetable for every letter.
- After reading several fables, use a graphic organizer to compare fables from different cultures.
- Write a critique comparing novels with the theme of social justice.

### RELEVANT APPLICATION

- Use the alphabet to organize the classroom bookshelves or teach others to find books in the school library.
- Access resources to learn about vegetable gardens. Write a sequenced plan for how to make a roof-top or in-ground garden at school.
- Write a fable to respond to a worldwide issue, such as bullying, from the perspective of different cultures.
- Blog about related novels on a classroom social network.
- Produce podcasts and other digital media comparing social issues of personal interest relevant to an issue in a novel.

## MATH

### TRADITIONAL ASSIGNMENT

- Use play money to show combinations of coins that demonstrate the requested total.
- Write and illustrate original math problems using area and perimeter.
- Draw and label a flow chart that explains how to apply this geometric proof.
- Explain the math concepts imbedded in this test question.

### RELEVANT APPLICATION

- Research current costs of grocery items in ads and stores and collect empty food cans and boxes to organize a class store. Research needed jobs and employees to run a grocery store, and organize employment opportunities for children in the classroom store.
- Plan and create a school garden with the maximum growing capacity in the smallest space. Prepare a budget for purchasing needed supplies.
- Use geometry and physics concepts to explain and diagram actions in a favorite sport.
- Write test items for classmates to complete to substantiate their mastery of relevant math concepts.

Kingore, B. (2013). *Rigor and Engagement for Growing Minds*. Austin, TX: PA Publishing.

## SCIENCE

### TRADITIONAL ASSIGNMENT

- Write and illustrate a fact book about crustaceans.
- Complete a three-way Venn diagram comparing the biome of your home with two other biomes.
- In pairs, create riddle statements about elements in the periodic table for others to solve: "I am a halogen with an atomic number higher than fluorine but lower than bromine."
- Create an informative brochure about the viruses and germs related to common illnesses students experience.

### RELEVANT APPLICATION

- Create a structure from recycled materials that the class hermit crab will choose to inhabit. Observe and record the results.
- Research flora for this area of your biome; plant a school garden with vegetables matched to ground conditions and area weather.
- Identify how many examples of specific periodic elements can be found in this school environment, and rank the frequency of the top ten elements found at school.
- Organize a Socratic seminar leading a group of peers to develop a plan that limits the spread of viruses and bacteria of greatest concern to people in this locale.

## SOCIAL SCIENCES

### TRADITIONAL ASSIGNMENT

- Create a class collage of people and places in the community.
- Read about and discuss civil rights, and role-play opposing view points.
- Develop a flow chart correlating the people, issues, and events leading to the First Amendment.
- Debate the pros and cons of the United States' electoral college system.

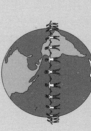

### RELEVANT APPLICATION

- Research and organize where and how school-grown vegetables can be donated for the betterment of the community.
- Interview community people regarding their perspectives and experiences during civil rights movements. Form conclusions regarding the human impact of the movement to present in each person's voice through monologues that share information from multiple perspectives .
- Propose a policy of students' rights and responsibilities in school settings according to the First Amendment.
- Organize and conduct a class or school election based upon the United States' electoral college system instead of a simple majority vote.

Kingore, B. (2013). *Rigor and Engagement for Growing Minds.* Austin, TX: PA Publishing.

Recognizing Expectations

themselves as they use realistic applications to build upon acquired knowledge and skills.

**4ME**

While students must ultimately determine what is relevant to them, teachers can facilitate students making those connections to specific content or skills. Hold up a small sign or a craft stick with a stapled message that reads *4Me* as a novelty to guide students' discussions of which aspects of this lesson are pertinent to them or how they will actually use this information or skill. When students see personal value in the lesson, they are more likely to respond positively to high-level expectations. If they perceive something as personally applicable and useful, they are more inclined to give their full attention, creating the conditions for maximum achievement. Demonstrating relevance is particularly significant with adolescents who are in the developmental stage of identity formation (Sullo, 2009).

It is imperative that education emphasizes the connection between instruction in school and the world outside (Crockett, Jukes, & Churches, 2011). When academic rigor includes relevance, authentic rather than synthetic learning experiences emerge, requiring students to connect core knowledge and skills to real-world applications. Synthetic learning experiences approach students as consumers who fill in skill sheets and complete learning tasks provided by adults. Authentic learning experiences approach students as producers who use known concepts and skills to discover relevant connections that are new to them. Students are more likely to perceive relevant expectations as significant rather than seemingly meaningless school assignments.

Relevance is transdisciplinary and connects content to real-world contexts and students' interests through:
- Authentic learning applications,
- Simulations,
- Teaching others in classroom or in virtual learning environments,
- Incorporating current issues,
- Problem-based learning,
- Concepts connected to national and global events,
- Interest-driven inquiry, and
- Service learning.

Rigor without relevance can result in students who do well academically but seem dysfunctional in the real world (Daggert, 2007).

With today's digital landscape, students not only think differently but also learn differently from the ways people learned in the past (Crockett, Jukes, & Churches, 2011). Digital kids are connected to the world through technology and operate in a multimedia, online, random-access, audio-visual world. Digital skills are less acknowledged and perhaps less valued in traditional definitions of education. Yet, digital access to information implies that it is less relevant or realistic to expect today's students to know every accumulated detail. It is possibly more relevant that they understand the big ideas of the content, the overarching concepts, and how to access, comprehend, and scrutinize needed data.

Kingore, B. (2013). *Rigor and Engagement for Growing Minds.* Austin, TX: PA Publishing.

## PROMOTING HIGH-LEVEL EXPECTATIONS

Rigor is associated with high expectations for students, but teachers provide the tools and environment that enable students to meet those expectations (Willis, 2011; Stronge, 2012). Expectations are directly related to our beliefs about students and our perceptions of their learning potential. We endanger high expectations if we think that we taught a great lesson but "these kids just can't or won't learn." Shift to a different instructional approach or network with another educator to discuss productive ideas for change. Educators' and students' mindsets, attitudes, and skills dictate whether high expectations are attainable. Figures 2.4 lists the roles of educators and students in environments fostering high expectations.

Mastering basic learning standards and covering core curriculum are not the ultimate goals of academic rigor. Rigor invites educators to use current concepts and standards as foundational skills that enable students to develop higher applications and aspirations for career and college success as they become productive citizens.

To facilitate students' willingness to risk participating and trying out ideas, educators

### FIGURE 2.4:
# ROLES IN HIGH EXPECTATIONS

### Educators' Role

High-level expectations are attainable when educators:

- Demonstrate respect for students, parents, and colleagues;
- Believe that all students can learn and will succeed in this learning environment;
- Provide positive feedback to students regarding their efforts to learn;
- Ensure that all students experience continuous learning; and
- Use core curriculum and learning standards as the foundation to build upon while eliciting students' unique, high-level applications to real-world situations.

### Students' Role

High-level expectations are attainable when students:

- Experience personal respect and exhibit respect for others in their learning community;
- Believe that they can learn and will succeed in this learning environment;
- Demonstrate an effort to learn and continue beyond minimum competencies;
- Strive to continuously learn; and
- Apply core curriculum skills and concepts to age-appropriate unpredictable, novel, real-world problems.

Recognizing Expectations

Kingore, B. (2013). *Rigor and Engagement for Growing Minds*. Austin, TX: PA Publishing.

model mutual respect and a conviction that everyone will learn. Mistakes and misconceptions are recognized as a step in the learning process and used to set new goals or analyzed for changes that will correct or overcome the error. Effort on the part of the learner is important and recognized by peers and educators. Educators' reflective feedback has a direct and powerful effect, influencing students' expectations for achievement and guiding their continuous learning goals. Rather than just practiced for mastery, concepts and skills are applied to interesting, real-world situations. Brain research confirms that information must be applied or acted upon to be retained and retrieved (Sousa & Tomlinson, 2010; Willis, 2011; Wolfe, 2010).

As one example of promoting high expectations in a rigorous learning environment, one primary teacher had each student switch to a grading pencil after completing a pre-assessment in spelling. As the teacher carefully spelled each word on the test, students reviewed their own papers and put a check by each letter they had written correctly in each word. Then, they circled any words with errors, and those words were used for their spelling work that week. For relevancy, students completed their spelling list with additional words they were interested in spelling. With this spelling technique, this insightful teacher provided students immediate positive feedback about correct approximations to spelling. Then, she used that pre-assessment information and students' interests to develop individualized spelling lists that ensured spelling was relevant to each learner. As the next step, students made brief entries in their journal each day noting the spelling words they had actually used in some personal context.

## ATTRIBUTES OF HIGH EXPECTATIONS

### CHALLENGE STUDENTS TO REACH HIGHER EXPECTATIONS

---

**HIGH EXPECTATIONS
GB, XL, AND 4ME**

**GB—GO BEYOND**
How did you go beyond the assignment and initiate a personal application or connection important to you?

**XL—EXTEND LEARNING**
What did you do to extend the learning challenge and accomplish more than expected so you experienced continuous learning?

**4ME—FOR MYSELF**
What did you do to help yourself learn more or benefit more from the task? How did you make this relevant to you and your interests?

---

When discussing high expectations, middle school teachers voiced their belief that they are less likely to get higher effort from students if teachers do not communicate their expectations. We began prompting high expectations by asking students to use the acronyms GB, XL, and variations of the 4ME novelty discussed earlier. Teachers and students inject these acronyms into small group discussions; students also apply them to their reflections, rubrics, and other self-assessment tools. The intent is to increase the students' motivation to extend their effort to learn and reach beyond minimum competency.

## COMMUNICATE CLEAR EXPECTATIONS

Develop laminated posters listing significant skills in each content area, such as the examples in Figure 2.5 for math and Figure 2.6 for history/social studies. Create each poster by reviewing school learning standards or referring to Common Core State Standards (2010). Before beginning class discussions or flexible group applications, place a check beside targeted skills so students see the learning expectations. As a conclusion, ask students to write or discuss how they incorporated the selected skills. The laminated poster allows you to wipe off checks and check different standards as the learning focus changes. A customizable template for listing learning standards is on the CD.

## CONNECT EXIT TICKETS TO RELEVANT OBJECTIVES

Posting or verbalizing an objective for a lesson is an effective teaching practice. However, it is more relevant to ask students to restate that objective in their own words to access insight into students' perceptions of the task and increase their understanding.

Exit tickets work well to scaffold students' restatements of objectives and increase relevance by inviting personal connections. At the conclusion of a lesson, allow a few minutes for students to complete an exit ticket, such as Figure 2.7 with one or more prompts emphasizing responses to learning objectives, and add a quick sketch illustrating how they feel.

- "In your own words, what was our learning objective?"
- "How is this relevant to you?"

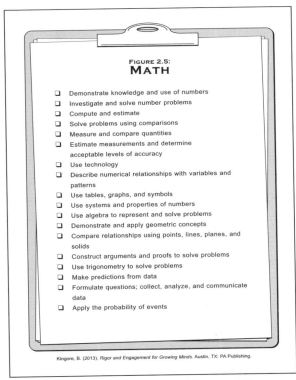

### FIGURE 2.5:
### MATH

- ❑ Demonstrate knowledge and use of numbers
- ❑ Investigate and solve number problems
- ❑ Compute and estimate
- ❑ Solve problems using comparisons
- ❑ Measure and compare quantities
- ❑ Estimate measurements and determine acceptable levels of accuracy
- ❑ Use technology
- ❑ Describe numerical relationships with variables and patterns
- ❑ Use tables, graphs, and symbols
- ❑ Use systems and properties of numbers
- ❑ Use algebra to represent and solve problems
- ❑ Demonstrate and apply geometric concepts
- ❑ Compare relationships using points, lines, planes, and solids
- ❑ Construct arguments and proofs to solve problems
- ❑ Use trigonometry to solve problems
- ❑ Make predictions from data
- ❑ Formulate questions; collect, analyze, and communicate data
- ❑ Apply the probability of events

Kingore, B. (2013). *Rigor and Engagement for Growing Minds.* Austin, TX: PA Publishing.

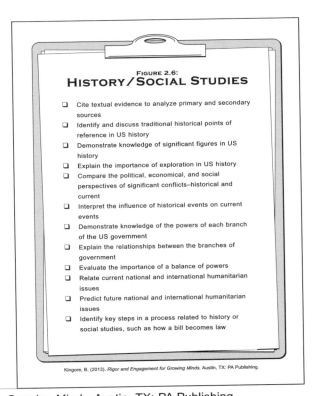

### FIGURE 2.6:
### HISTORY/SOCIAL STUDIES

- ❑ Cite textual evidence to analyze primary and secondary sources
- ❑ Identify and discuss traditional historical points of reference in US history
- ❑ Demonstrate knowledge of significant figures in US history
- ❑ Explain the importance of exploration in US history
- ❑ Compare the political, economical, and social perspectives of significant conflicts–historical and current
- ❑ Interpret the influence of historical events on current events
- ❑ Demonstrate knowledge of the powers of each branch of the US government
- ❑ Explain the relationships between the branches of government
- ❑ Evaluate the importance of a balance of powers
- ❑ Relate current national and international humanitarian issues
- ❑ Predict future national and international humanitarian issues
- ❑ Identify key steps in a process related to history or social studies, such as how a bill becomes law

Kingore, B. (2013). *Rigor and Engagement for Growing Minds.* Austin, TX: PA Publishing.

Kingore, B. (2013). *Rigor and Engagement for Growing Minds.* Austin, TX: PA Publishing.

- "What did you do to participate?"
- "What is a personal connection you can make to this lesson?"

Primary students are most successful when responding to one exit prompt. Older students can successfully respond to one or more prompts.

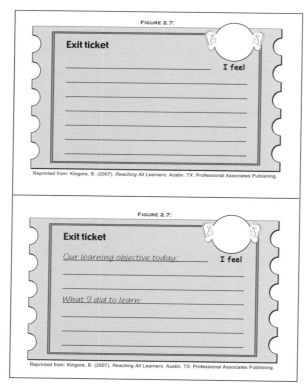

FIGURE 2.7:

Exit ticket
I feel

Reprinted from: Kingore, B. (2007). *Reaching All Learners*. Austin, TX: Professional Associates Publishing.

FIGURE 2.7:

Exit ticket
*Our learning objective today:*                I feel

*What I did to learn:*

Reprinted from: Kingore, B. (2007). *Reaching All Learners*. Austin, TX: Professional Associates Publishing.

### ELICIT GOAL SETTING

Goals establish higher expectations and give students a target to aim toward as they work. Before beginning learning assignments, ask students questions that focus their goal setting and guide them to plan actions to achieve their goals.

- "What do you intend to accomplish through your efforts on this learning opportunity?"
- "What are you planning to do to enable you to reach high expectations?"

- "On a scale of one to five, with five being the highest, how successful do you expect to be on this task?"
- "What different kinds of help or assistance might enable you to experience greater success?"

Involve students in writing and discussing their goals to nurture high expectations. If a student sets goals at a low level, intervene privately as others begin working to determine why that student has a low expectation and what action might be taken to increase the likelihood of success.

## INTEGRATE LEARNING STANDARDS

Effective teachers are very aware of core curriculum and learning standards, and they strive to promote the best ways to engage students in mastery and beyond. When using school-provided curriculum lessons, they include sets of learning tasks and graphic organizers to involve students in guided practice or application. Owing to the fact that teachers are in the best position to understand the needs of specific groups of students, teachers often have an idea for a different learning opportunity they want students to experience. Before substituting learning tasks, know the curriculum well and understand which skills and concepts can be applied in a productive manner that differs from the core curriculum. Initiate a method, such as a standards grid, to substantiate skill applications and ensure that standards are authentically integrated into instruction.

## A STANDARDS GRID: CORRELATING LEARNING EXPERIENCES TO STANDARDS.

A standards grid is a tool educators find useful to document which learning skills and concepts are applied through a particular learning experience (Figure 2.8). The grid emerged in response to teachers' concerns that, since the provided curriculum lesson directly focused on correct-answer tasks requiring learning standards and skills, substituting their ideas of engaging, open-ended learning experiences risked lowering learning outcomes. Teachers need a tool that enables them to confidently substitute relevant learning experiences without compromising targeted skill applications.

A standards grid relates to realistic expectations by visually substantiating which standards are practiced or extended as students complete learning tasks. It relates to relevance by allowing teachers to substitute learning opportunities that they conclude will highly engage specific students and more prominently require those learners to adapt and apply standards in profound ways.

Correlating standards to preferred learning experiences enables teachers to continue to use the best teaching practices, select the most appropriate activities and products, and integrate standards rather than isolate skills. (A customizable form for aligning standards to learning experiences is provided on the CD.)

To initiate a Standards Grid, use the left-hand column to list targeted skills in a discipline—the major initiatives over a significant portion of the school year. List your preferred

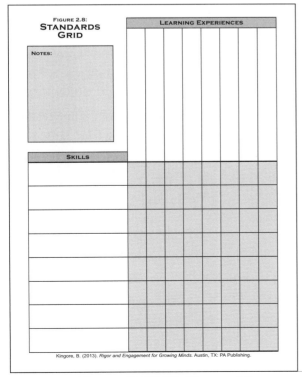

**FIGURE 2.8: STANDARDS GRID**

NOTES:
H = Highly applicable
S = Some application
NA = Not applicable

LEARNING EXPERIENCES

| SKILLS | Concept Map | Venn Diagram | KWL | Acrostic | Reader's Theater | Newspaper Article | Invitation | Digital Presentation |
|---|---|---|---|---|---|---|---|---|
| Sequencing events | S | S | NA | NA | H | H | NA | H |
| Organized for clarity | H | H | S | H | H | H | H | H |
| Complex, varied sentences | S | S | S | S | H | H | S | H |
| Academic vocabulary | H | H | H | H | H | H | S | H |
| Precise adjectives | H | H | H | H | H | H | S | H |
| Prepositional phrases | S | S | S | NA | H | H | S | H |
| Subject-verb agreement | H | H | H | H | H | H | H | H |
| Punctuation | S | S | H | S | H | H | H | H |

Kingore, B. (2013). *Rigor and Engagement for Growing Minds.* Austin, TX: PA Publishing.

Kingore, B. (2013). *Rigor and Engagement for Growing Minds.* Austin, TX: PA Publishing.

products or learning experiences along the top for column headings. Then, analyze and encode the degree that each standard can be woven into that learning task. You will not necessarily incorporate all of your encoded standards each time students complete a specific application; the intent is to identify the possibilities that can be incorporated. Add and analyze other products or activities when you select additional learning opportunities you plan to implement.

## STUDENT MOTIVATION

High-level expectations succeed when students are motivated to learn. There is a clear link between motivation and engagement. Students respond more positively to high-level expectations when they value the relevance of what they are doing and believe they can succeed. Unfortunate or not, it is true that high-ability students are motivated by *their* work; they may not be motivated by ours. Increase students' motivation to reach high-level expectations by incorporating students' interests, choice, authentic audiences, and authentic learning experiences.

### STUDENT INTERESTS

Egan (2009) poses a provocative question related to motivating high expectations: "What if every student were charged with becoming an expert on something?" Students are certainly more motivated and

*Motivating High-ability Students*

•

*Unfortunate or not, it is true that high-ability students are motivated by their work. They may not be motivated by ours.*

engaged when topics are relevant to their interests and needs.

High-ability students typically have learning passions—topics about which they want to learn everything. This is usually a short-list of specific interests that are often unique to them and not related to school content. This passion leads them to seek to know everything about a few topics rather than a little bit about most topics. These students are willing to spend considerable time in school and out of school learning and working on something that they care about. Consequently, survey students' interests and endeavor to integrate those interests into curriculum topics as often as feasible. Also, identify areas that students might want to pursue as advanced-levels studies and replacement tasks. As students demonstrate commitment to their projects, guide students to incorporate into their work the essential elements of rigor–complexity, depth, connections, adaptations, and transdisciplinary work (Washor & Mojkowski, 2007).

### A LIST OF INTERESTS

Ask students to write a list of ten personal interests to keep in a work folder. When appropriate, end a segment of learning by asking students: "Which one of your interests can you connect to this information?"

## INTEREST SURVEY

An interest survey can be as extensive as Renzulli's Interest-a-Lyzer (1997) or as simple as inviting students to draw symbols and multiple responses that illustrate what they most want to learn in school. In a graffiti style, students add words or phrases to their interest drawing to clarify those interests (Kingore, 2007a).

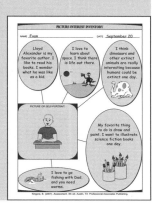

### CHOICE

Students are more inclined to exert the effort to reach higher expectations when teachers incorporate choice in assignments (Johnston, 2012). When appropriate, teachers offer more than one product option so students can select their best way to demonstrate learning or the option that is most relevant to them. Providing choices can increase students' ownership in the task and their motivation to excel beyond grade level as they perceive more application to their lives. It is another way to honor students' interests and modalities. The National Writing Project, for example, exemplifies how teachers nurture the development of writing skills by incorporating choice into writing tasks. There are considerable differences between the traditional teacher-assigned writing and writing assignments that promote choice (Figure 2.9.).

## FIGURE 2.9:
# CHOICE IN WRITING ASSIGNMENTS

| TRADITIONAL WRITING: TEACHER-ASSIGNED | WRITING ASSIGNED WITH CHOICE |
|---|---|
| Students write on the teacher-assigned topic. | Students are encouraged to develop relevant topics that interest them. |
| The teacher is the audience for the students' writing. | The audience and purpose for writing are as authentic as possible. |
| The teacher grades the students' writing. | Students are asked to reflect on their own growth before teacher evaluation. |
|  | —Adapted from the National Writing Project. |

Kingore, B. (2013). *Rigor and Engagement for Growing Minds.* Austin, TX: PA Publishing.

Recognizing Expectations

## GENERALIZABLE LEARNING TASKS

Foster student choices and still minimize preparation time by using more applicable product tasks that are generalizable. Generalizable products connect to multiple topics and have potential for multiple applications. Figure 2.10 compares topic-specific products with more general versions of a similar task. The generalizable Venn diagram is applicable to multiple content areas and topics. The math problem invites applications using different numbers and operations.

A task board of generalizable products is an effective tool to promote student choice.

*Student-Selected Projects*

•

*Self-selected, personally relevant projects engage high-ability students with an authentic purpose for learning and a motivation to excel.*

Task boards do not require students to complete a certain number or arrangement of products, as in three-in-a-row for a tic-tac-toe. Specifically avoid using a grading scale in which students get more points for the quantity of products they complete. Rather, a task board is intended to provide multiple options to stimulate student interest and choice through learning products with a high likelihood of eliciting content depth and complexity. With academic rigor, the criterion is quality. At a juncture of learning, students select one product to develop with the objective of creating a high-quality response demonstrating the depth of what they know, understand, and are able to do. At another time, with another topic, students can

### FIGURE 2.10:
## TOPIC-SPECIFIC VERSUS GENERALIZABLE PRODUCT OPTIONS

More generally applicable tasks save preparation time while providing a useful tool for student research and replacement tasks.

| TOPIC-SPECIFIC | GENERALIZABLE |
|---|---|
| **Venn Diagram** | **Venn Diagram** |
| Overlap three circles to create a three-way Venn that compares protons, neutrons, and electrons. | Overlap three circles to create a three-way Venn that compares the similarities and differences of _____. |
| **Word Problem** | **Word Problem** |
| Write and illustrate an addition word problem for 6 + 6 = 12. | Write and illustrate a word problem that results in the number _____. |

Kingore, B. (2013). *Rigor and Engagement for Growing Minds.* Austin, TX: PA Publishing.

revisit the same task board to select a different product to demonstrate learning.

The quantity of product options on a task board varies according to the age and interests of the class (Figure 2.11). While options can be added or changed, the intent is to minimize instructional preparation by including tasks that enable multiple applications over time for a variety of topics, concepts, and skills.

## FIGURE 2.11:
# PRODUCT OPTIONS

**PRODUCT OPTIONS DIRECTLY RELATE TO WHAT STUDENTS KNOW, UNDERSTAND, AND ARE ABLE TO DO (KUD).**

✓ Provide product options that document the learning objective and are appropriate to the class.

✓ Product options should demonstrate KUD rather than merely be some activity that students complete.

✓ Limit the number of options when the objective is to:
  • Introduce and model the process.
  • Nurture primary and special needs learners.

✓ Increase options as students demonstrate self-management and interest.

### PRODUCT OPTIONS

Product options can be analyzed for depth and complexity and aligned to tiered learning objectives. To facilitate tiering:

• Number the product options on a task board and analyze the potential complexity of each task.

• Write a list of the more complex tasks to refer to when a student needs options that promote a higher level of challenge.

### PRODUCT TASK BOARD

Task boards are quite effective when they include specific applications to a content area but are generalizable to multiple topics within that discipline. (Templates for generating tasks boards are included on the CD with options for both six and twelve generalizable products.) If a smaller number of options is more appropriate, simply leave some of the boxes blank and include additional options as students are ready for increased variety. Another alternative that piques children's curiosity is to supply options in all of the blanks, but cover some of them with cardstock squares to be revealed when students are able to proceed independently with that application.

Task boards for literature, math, and kindergarten through third-grade science products are included here as examples (Figures 2.12, 2.13, and 2.14 respectively). Many of the options feature authentic, relevant learning tasks to actively engage learners.

Kingore, B. (2013). *Rigor and Engagement for Growing Minds.* Austin, TX: PA Publishing.

## FIGURE 2.12:
# LITERATURE TASK BOARD

**1.** Create a study guide for a book club to use as they read and respond to this novel. Investigate how to post your study guide on the website for a library or book club.

**2.** Write an essay to the librarian or media specialist, persuading the school to include this book in the library. Incorporate supportive arguments explaining the book's literary merit and relevance to the student body.

**3.** Write a critique comparing an issue the protagonist faces with a similar issue confronting teens today.

**4.** Read Russell Freedman's *Lincoln: A Photobiography* and create a photobiography of the life of a significant community member. Share your photobiography at a local library.

**5.** Create a board game that others play to learn about this book. Sequentially incorporate the characters, plot, issues, assumptions, inferences, and problem resolution so players understand the content of the book as they finish playing the game.

**6.** Create analogies about the main characters and main ideas in the story comparing each to a current or historical person or event. Post your analogies online.

**7.** Summarize the novel by using the antagonist's name or the title as an acrostic and writing sentences for each letter organized in the sequence of the story. Post your acrostic summary on the class or school blog for discussion.

**8.** As a visual-spatial learner, draw a story board with captions or a comic strip with speech balloons to sequence the problem, major events, and resolution in the story to share in a literature circle or blog.

**9.** Create an artifact bag to present at a book talk. In a small paper sack, include eight to ten items with a log book explaining how each symbolically represents a character, problem, key event, resolution, or main idea in the story.

**10.** Complete a Venn diagram comparing yourself or a historical figure to the antagonist or protagonist physically, mentally, socially, and ethically. Write a summary of your comparison.

**11.** Organize a round-table discussion of books about the same topic or theme. Each participant prepares a summary of a book to present during the discussion.

**12.** Search online to access the Top 100 American Speeches of the 20th Century and select your favorite. Begin a class blog interpreting the impact that historical or current speeches have on teen's everyday lives.

Kingore, B. (2013). *Rigor and Engagement for Growing Minds.* Austin, TX: PA Publishing.

## FIGURE 2.13:
# MATH TASK BOARD

| | | |
|---|---|---|
| **1.** Survey twelve classmates and make a graph showing their favorite_____. Share your results with those classmates. | **2.** Show three different ways to complete this problem. Pair-share with a classmate. | **3.** Create a paper chain of equations that results in the number _____. Hang your paper chain in the math station for others to review. |
| **4.** Using _____ (operation/skill), write and illustrate a math word problem about a current sports event. Work with others to create a *Math in Sports* book. | **5.** Prepare a demonstration using graphics and manipulatives to teach peers about this math concept: _____. | **6.** Write a letter to someone of your choice explaining how to complete this problem: _____. |

## FIGURE 2.14:
# SCIENCE TASK BOARD

| | | |
|---|---|---|
| **1.** Write a summary of the science topic using rebus sentences to place in the science discovery station. | **2.** Create a collage of cut-out or drawn pictures illustrating the concept: _____. Plan a two or three minute oral presentation to explain your illustration to _____. | **3.** Take digital photographs and plan a presentation to explain stages in the growth or cycle of: _____. |
| **4.** Create a three-dimensional museum exhibit to teach others about: _____. Display your exhibit in the library or media center. | **5.** Graph an area's weather for one month and summarize what you learn about: _____. Compare your results with a classmate's graph of a different area. What do you conclude? | **6.** Develop and share a digital presentation demonstrating the sequence and conclusions of your scientific experiment for: _____. |

Kingore, B. (2013). *Rigor and Engagement for Growing Minds.* Austin, TX: PA Publishing.

## AUTHENTIC AUDIENCES

Students work more diligently when an authentic audience is involved, such as presenting a program for parents or delivering a plan for change to the school board. An authentic audience is real-world and often provides a more meaningful motivation to students than the audience provided by teachers' grading pens. Indeed, some high-ability learners are more motivated by an authentic audience than by a grade.

Levy (2010) refers to the *power of audience* and comments that students work so hard practicing for concerts, sports, and other performances because the audience is coming! Convey to students a sense that beyond the classroom, in the outside world, there is an authentic audience who is interested in their work. For example, students in a Spanish language class incorporated essential learning standards as they wrote primary-level books in Spanish. The finished books were sent to rural areas in a Spanish-speaking country where young children have limited quantities of books to read or use to learn to read. Authentic audiences are a catalyst for both teacher and student-developed projects. These projects are often long-term and can be as much process-directed as product-producing.

### AUTHENTIC LEARNING EXPERIENCES

Authentic learning experiences require students to connect core knowledge and skills to real-world applications. Students value the relevance and ownership of these learning opportunities that expect students to become producers using known concepts and skills to discover relevant connections that are new to them. Meaningful projects with appropriate support challenge students to use foundational skills in applications that exceed grade-level expectations.

Since authentic products have real-world applications, they are useful and should be actually used. Initially, students follow a teacher-prescribed task as they develop the independent work behaviors and learn the skills of individual inquiry. Then, progressively withdraw from designating the task or product as students increasingly assume responsibility for planning and completing the parameters of high-quality learning applications that are relevant to them. When authentic projects are designed and implemented by an individual or a flexible group, students confront ill-defined, ill-structured, real-world problems, particularly conducive to beyond core curriculum expectations. Levy asserts that when students' work culminates in a genuine product for an authentic audience, students' engagement, learning, and achievement dramatically increase (2008).

With students' input, compile lists of learning experiences and products that become choices for student projects and have potential for learning outcomes of interest to real-world audiences. The list of learning experiences in Figure 2.15 and the products listed in Figure 2.16 are shared to prompt thinking of applications that might best match your class. These products effectively serve as replacement tasks when students compact out of regular curriculum learning experiences. Products such as these could be organized on a task board as a continuous reference for student choice.

FIGURE 2.15:
# LEARNING EXPERIENCES WITH AUTHENTIC APPLICATIONS

✦ Student-developed computer program or application relevant to a current topic of study or student interest

✦ Infomercial for the school web site or school TV station

✦ Nonfiction picture book to teach a concept or topic to young children

✦ Original math proof

✦ Student-developed tiered learning station for in-class or other-class implementation

✦ Rubrics or other assessment tools students create for classroom use

✦ Informative skit to jigsaw information and bring complex information to life for peers

✦ Editorial response or policy statement related to an issue or current event that is submitted for publication in a school or local newspaper

✦ Bulletin board comparing topical information across disciplines to expand connections

✦ School board presentation relating to school or community-based problems

✦ Writing for the Community—service-learning compositions to address insights about community issues, such as homelessness

✦ Publish original writing or art

✦ Music created, arranged, and performed for a class or school production

✦ Landscape design or community garden incorporating botany, math concepts, and art for a community, school plot, or multi-generational project with a senior group

✦ Community displays to integrate the school and community, such as student art displayed in local businesses on a rotating schedule planned, organized, and implemented by students

✦ Program planning, including a student-planned PTA meeting or curriculum night

✦ Simulations creatively enacting historical or current events and processes, such as the Lewis and Clark Expedition or passing a bill in Congress

✦ Mock trial planned and enacted to present multiple perspectives of issues related to science, history, and literature

✦ Conclusions drawn from student interviews with people directly involved in an issue or current event relevant to the curriculum or student interests

✦ Computer generated or hand-drawn concept maps organizing complex information to teach others

✦ Peer tutoring with a remedial focus (more effective when sparingly used with a high-ability learner who wants to plan instruction and assist a peer in learning core curriculum)

✦ Mentor or buddy projects—two or three high-ability students working together within the same classroom, across classrooms, or participating long-distance through technology to pursue and extend understanding about a common interest beyond the core curriculum

✦ Writing a request to a foundation for a grant for the school

Recognizing Expectations

Kingore, B. (2013). *Rigor and Engagement for Growing Minds.* Austin, TX: PA Publishing.

## FIGURE 2.16:
# PRODUCTS WITH AUTHENTIC APPLICATIONS

| | | | |
|---|---|---|---|
| advertisement | economic forecast | math proof | readers theater |
| animation | editorial | memoir | rebus story |
| art gallery | epilogue | memorial | recital |
| audio recording | essay | menu | relief map |
| autobiography | evaluation | model | research report, |
| background music | exhibit/display | mosaic |   written or oral |
| banner | experiment | movie/movie script | resume |
| billboard | fable/fairy tale | multimedia | review |
| biography | family tree |   presentation | riddles |
| blog | fashion show script | mural | role-play |
| blueprint | festival | museum exhibit | rubric |
| board game | field guide | musical composition | rules |
| book/booklet | flannel board | mystery | satire |
| brochure |   presentation | myth | scale drawing/model |
| bulletin board | flip book or chart | newscast | scavenger hunt |
| business plan | flow chart | newspaper/ | scrapbook |
| campaign speech/ | folder game |   newspaper article | sculpture |
|   platform | gallery | observation log | self-portrait |
| cartoon | game/game show | oral history/report | sequel |
| chart | glossary | painting | simulation |
| children's story | graph | pamphlet | social action plan |
| choral reading | graphic organizer | parody | software application |
| class blog | infomercial | persuasive speech | storytelling |
| collage | illustration/icon | photo essay/journal | survey |
| collection | indexes | picture dictionary | symbols |
| comic strip | interview | play or skit | talent show |
| commentary | invention | podcast | taxonomy |
| computer animation | invitation | poem | test |
| computer game | jigsaw puzzle | political cartoon | textbook |
| community service | joke book | pop-up book | theory |
| critique | journal/log | portfolio | time line |
| crossword puzzle | judge an event | poster | travel folder/poster |
| dance | lab report | press conference | travelogue |
| debate | landscape design | proposal | trial |
| demonstration | learning station | public announcement | trivia game |
| diagram | lesson to teach | puppet /puppet show | TV commercial/ |
| dialogue | letter | puzzle |   program |
| digital montage/ | list | quiz/quiz show | video documentary |
|   presentation | machine | questionnaire | video game |
| diorama | magazine/magazine | questions | weather log/forecast |
| documentary |   article | quotation collection | webcast |
| dramatization | manual | radio show | website |
| drawing | map with legend | rap | wordless book |

Kingore, B. (2013). *Rigor and Engagement for Growing Minds.* Austin, TX: PA Publishing.

# THINKING REFLECTIVELY

### 1. IDEAS

Identify two or more ideas you intend to apply immediately.

### 2. RELEVANT APPLICATIONS

Review a current curriculum lesson and determine a more relevant, authentic application you can substitute for a core assignment to engage students in applying target concepts and skills to real-world situations.

### 3. BRAINSTORM

Brainstorm which topics of study might allow you to weave students' interests into the core curriculum to make it more relevant and foster higher expectations for students.

### 4. PRODUCTS

Create generalizable products with authentic learning experiences relevant to your students and content. Use Figure 2.18 to jot down your ideas. Later, use the templates on the CD to complete your task board with six or twelve product options.

Kingore, B. (2013). *Rigor and Engagement for Growing Minds.* Austin, TX: PA Publishing.

Recognizing Expectations

FIGURE 2.18:
# GENERALIZABLE PRODUCTS JOT DOWN

Content area _____ Grade _____

| | | |
|---|---|---|
| 1. | 2. | 3. |
| 4. | 5. | 6. |
| 7. | 8. | 9. |
| 10. | 11. | 12. |

Kingore, B. (2013). *Rigor and Engagement for Growing Minds.* Austin, TX: PA Publishing.

# CHAPTER 3
# INTEGRATING COMPLEXITY AND DEPTH IN CONTENT, PROCESS, AND PRODUCT

Complexity and depth entail more than high levels of thinking. Complexity denotes a focus on concepts that leads to intricate, interconnections of ideas, problems, and issues across disciplines. Depth denotes extensive and detailed study or understanding within the layers of a discipline from concrete to the abstract and from concepts to generalizations. Combined, they represent the comprehensive and thorough understanding expected in a rigorous learning environment.

Research has long confirmed that many students fail to make connections among the myriad of facts learned in classes and the big ideas and concepts reflected in understanding a discipline (Anderson & Krathwohl, 2001; Shepard, 1997). Students can know facts but fail to understand the related concepts that ensure deeper understanding and life-long learning. Educators recognize the importance of a conceptual level of understanding, and must help students apply factual content to increase their complexity and depth of content, process, and product. Consider the following two questions for students as an example. The first is a good question inviting high-level thinking. The second is a broader application requiring high-level thinking within the larger framework of conceptual structures and big ideas.

> **HIGH-LEVEL THINKING QUESTION:**
> "What can you conclude about the motivations of the antagonist?"
>
> **HIGH-LEVEL CONCEPT QUESTION:**
> "How is conflict a reoccurring theme in this novel compared to other novels we've read?"

Conceptual thinking is critical to complexity and depth as it provides a basis for deeper understanding (Erickson, 2007). For this reason, the frameworks created by researchers concerned with depth and complexity merge a taxonomy of thinking skills and a continuum of complex applications as two dimensions that complement rigor and foster complexity and depth. Erickson envisions hierarchical thinking skills as a vertical structure that needs to accompany a horizontal structure of processes and skills that progress from facts to concepts and then to principles and generalizations. Daggett proposes a horizontal, rigor-relevance hierarchy progressing from understanding one discipline, to transdisciplinary connections, to connections to real-world predictable situations, and finally to connections to real-world unpredictable situations (Daggett, 2007; Jones, 2010).

# DEPTH AND COMPLEXITY FRAMEWORK

The Depth and Complexity Framework shown in Figure 3.1 is a graphic summary adapting the revised Bloom's taxonomy, Erickson's concept-based learning, and Daggett's rigor-relevance applications to illustrate how multiple components activate depth and complexity. The rectangle in the top right-hand corner of the graphic–the Adaptation of Relevant Depth and Complexity–represents our ultimate target for relevant depth and complexity in instruction and in student responses.

When *analyze, evaluate,* or *create* intersect with *concepts, generalizations, principles,* relevant, high-end learning results. This

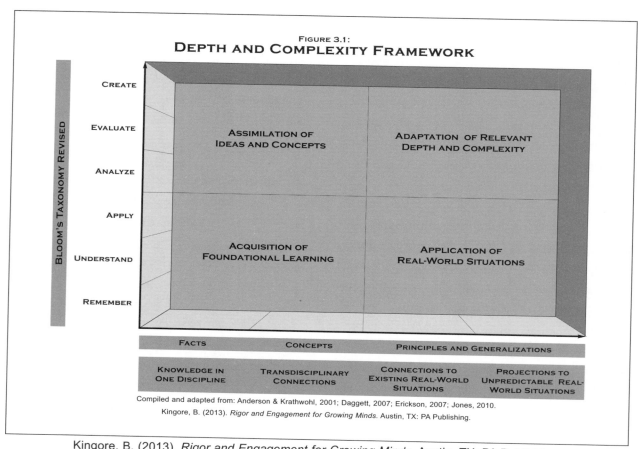

**FIGURE 3.1:**
## DEPTH AND COMPLEXITY FRAMEWORK

Compiled and adapted from: Anderson & Krathwohl, 2001; Daggett, 2007; Erickson, 2007; Jones, 2010.
Kingore, B. (2013). *Rigor and Engagement for Growing Minds.* Austin, TX: PA Publishing.

Kingore, B. (2013). *Rigor and Engagement for Growing Minds.* Austin, TX: PA Publishing.

intersection signifies students' active engagement in conceptual thinking, problem solving, and adapting solutions to real-world predictable and unpredictable situations. Successful engagement at this intersection documents that students have acquired the targeted background knowledge and skills of the core standards. The complexity and depth required from learners at these levels further broadens students' skills and is an optimum goal for high-ability learners.

Interpreting this framework, we affirm that high-ability students function at a higher level of depth and complexity when they know, understand, and are able to apply concept-based learning to other disciplines and to assimilate and adapt authentic problems that are predictable or unpredictable. Increased complexity and depth in content, process, and product are likely when teachers facilitate students' applications of concepts, principles, and generalizations by investigating fuzzy, real-world problems having transdisciplinary and multifaceted solutions.

To elicit maximum opportunity for rigor, the problem must be relevant to students, and students must be responsible for designing the process, content, and products rather than merely completing a learning task designed by the teacher. For example, students devise a procedure for testing consumer products, such as the flavor of peanut butter or the absorbency of paper towel brands. They collect and analyze data and then organize the results using graphing calculators and computer spreadsheets (Jones, 2010). As another example, students identify a school-related problem, such as a dangerous traffic crossing. They devise procedures using digital cameras to record data, edit and organize the data graphically, identify the person with the power to initiate change, and then write and present a substantiated, factual report to that person. This approach aligns with a key focus of the Common Core State Standards (CCSS) to change from students' personal opinions or connections with information to a concern for text-based, substantiated data.

Complexity and depth directly connect to core standards. Concept development lessons help reveal students' misconceptions and develop conceptions of significant ideas related to a discipline and connected to other disciplines. This background enables students to actively engage in problem solving and apply previously learned ideas to non-routine problems. High-ability students then progress to expert tasks that are rich, less structured, and require strategic problem-solving as well as high-level concepts and skills. Performance on expert-level tasks documents students' readiness for advanced content applications and adaptations outside of the classroom.

## CONCEPTUAL THINKING

Conceptual thinking is indicative of the level of complexity and depth in students' thinking and construction of meaning. Words that represent concepts can serve as a bridge connecting prior knowledge and new concepts, functioning as a useful tool to foster conceptual thinking.

Joseph Novak (1998), who developed the concept mapping technique, concluded that meaningful learning involves the assimilation of new concepts and propositions into existing cognitive structures. Concept words represent ideas that we can use to guide students' assimilation of new concepts into their existing cognitive structures for topics of study. Conceptual thinking empowers students to build upon factual understanding to derive or infer a new notion about the content that may be a more abstract idea or lead to a generalization. These words help us engage students' conceptual minds so they experience increased complexity and depth. Erickson noted that students with strong conceptual structures in the brain are better able to process the massive amounts of incoming information and better able to transfer and apply knowledge.

Figure 3.2 lists examples of the kinds of words that nurture conceptual thinking and lead to key concept questions. This list is but a sampling and is not an exclusive set of the concepts that are applicable. The process and products that ensue when applying these concepts are similar to ideas referred to as *enduring*

*understandings* (Wiggins & McTighe, 2005), *conceptual lenses* (Erickson, 2007), *key concepts* (International Baccalaureate, 2007), or *themes* and *elements of depth and complexity* (Kaplan & Cannon, 2000).

Conceptual thinking integrates high-level thinking with more complex applications that foster complexity and depth. High-level thinking is significant, but conceptual thinking at high levels is more likely to result in long-term memory as students bring their own thinking to the factual study and construct personal meaning. Students experience hundreds of specific occurrences they can access to provide a personal dimension to an abstract idea. With support, students use these personal experiences to exemplify abstract ideas and make content relevant through anecdotes, analogies, and nonlinguistic representations.

Children attain deeper understanding when their personal experiences or emotional responses connect to the learning experience (Sousa, 2009; Willis, 2010; Wolfe, 2010). For

## FIGURE 3.2:
# CONCEPTUAL THINKING WORDS

- Adaptation
- Beliefs/values
- Causation
- Change
- Choice/selection
- Conflict
- Connection
- Consequences
- Culture

- Cycles
- Emotions
- Ethics
- Force
- Function
- Human rights
- Innovation
- Issues
- Organization

- Patterns
- Perspective
- Power
- Relationship
- Responsibility
- Structure/form
- Survival
- Systems
- Time–past/present/ future trends

Kingore, B. (2013). *Rigor and Engagement for Growing Minds.* Austin, TX: PA Publishing.

example, when students experience or observe instances of bullying in their environment, conceptual thinking challenges them to enlarge on those experiences to consider ethical issues of human rights and explore applications in the wider world. As another example when studying ordinals, children search for connections in their personal experiences through multiple contents, disciplines, and processes. Some students continue at higher levels to conclude generalizations about organizational patterns in numbers, such as: "Numbers are useful to clarify sequences," and "Words can be used to signal numerical sequences." Older students, pursuing the perpetuation of a species, use their personal observations and prior experiences with videos and informational text to deduce conclusions about survival, structure, and change.

*Topic:* **BULLYING**
*Concepts:* Issue, power, ethics
*Questions:* "In what ways does power influence ethical standards affecting human rights? How is bullying similar to power issues relevant to world cultures and globalization?"

*Topic:* **ORDINALS**
*Concepts:* Organization, pattern
*Questions:* "What are all of the situations in which we can figure out different ways to use numbers to organize information? What patterns emerge?"

*Topic:* **UNDERGROUND RAILROAD**
*Concepts:* Belief, power, function
*Questions:* "Which had the greatest impact on the Underground Railroad: politics, power, or beliefs? In what ways did the Underground Railroad function like online social networks today?"

Try an application of this process using Figure 3.3 as a scaffold to organize your thinking. List a significant topic in your curriculum. Select one or more words from the list in Figure 3.2 that connect to this topic. Then, pose a question or two using a concept word to focus your thinking about the content in a different way, inviting increased complexity and depth from the concrete to the abstract within a discipline or transcending disciplinary boundaries. Reflect upon your results: "Is the question relevant, interesting, and an important vehicle for deepening understanding and extending learning?" Be patient as you explore this process. As with all learning, the first attempts are the most demanding.

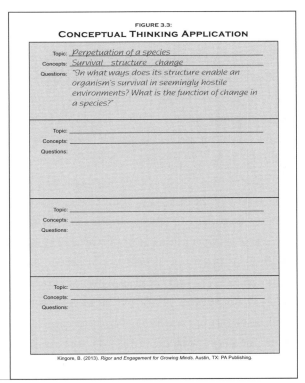

FIGURE 3.3:
**CONCEPTUAL THINKING APPLICATION**

Topic: *Perpetuation of a species*
Concepts: *Survival   structure   change*
Questions: *"In what ways does its structure enable an organism's survival in seemingly hostile environments? What is the function of change in a species?"*

Topic: _____
Concepts: _____
Questions:

Topic: _____
Concepts: _____
Questions:

Topic: _____
Concepts: _____
Questions:

Kingore, B. (2013). *Rigor and Engagement for Growing Minds.* Austin, TX: PA Publishing.

Kingore, B. (2013). *Rigor and Engagement for Growing Minds.* Austin, TX: PA Publishing.

Conceptual thinking words prompt thinking beyond facts to integrate information with students' personal connections and promote transfer to deeper understanding. The concept words change the focus for thinking about the topic so students intellectually process in more complex ways. Students express more interest in the topic when approached from this personal perspective and demonstrate an increased willingness to engage in intellectual risk taking. Responses or solutions evolving from this process are followed by students' reflection and examination of their process, reasoning, and conclusions. Frequently, the process triggers related concepts that springboard to further lines of inquiry, motivating students' continued research and study.

## MATERIALS AND RESOURCES

### ABOVE GRADE-LEVEL RESOURCES

The CCSS emphasizes text complexity as the most important factor in the development of skilled readers. Appropriate materials beyond grade level must be available if high-ability students are to be held to high expectations for complexity and depth. Further the development of advanced responses from high-ability students by increasing concept density and text difficulty. Increase students' access to a wide range of fiction and nonfiction beyond grade-level reading materials since some of today's anthologies water down original text and some textbooks limit elaboration and in-depth information in order to make room for alignment to standards and practice test questions. Facilitate high-ability students

as they access sophisticated text and websites that enable exploration of their interest-driven inquiry and foster greater complexity and depth in their responses to class topics.

### NONFICTION

The CCSS emphasizes that nonfiction is pivotal to comprehension of technical manuals or scientific and historical documents in higher academic settings and the workplace. The vision is to provide experiences enabling students to tackle simple to more complex informational text–speeches, technical documents, menus, brochures, catalogs, magazine articles, essays, websites, and graphic or digital displays–to construct the foundational knowledge, vocabulary, and literacy strategies required to comprehend nonfiction. This emphasis also aligns with the voracious appetite for nonfiction displayed at an early age by high-ability children, particularly when relevant to their areas of advanced interest (Duke, 2000).

In addition to providing appropriate nonfiction resources, one immediate challenge presented by the information text emphasis is the demand for training that helps teachers teach comprehension of nonfiction texts. Gerwertz (2012) cautions that most teachers, especially at the secondary level, are not taught how to teach reading and need help determining how they are going to pause long enough in their teaching to have students grapple with text describing the real world. Flexible group tasks and the flipped classroom technique might prove useful as authentic applications of nonfiction materials.

Use nonfiction for authentic purposes. Adults read nonfiction to obtain information we need to know or information that interests us–an authentic purpose for reading. To get students to read more strategically and with increased enthusiasm, ensure authentic purposes for reading informational text. Set up situations in which students are curious about an occurrence and need more information, such as observing ants in the classroom, hearing about a current event, or wondering what different reactions the observed catalyst might cause in other instances.

Use nonfiction to prime students for writing informative text. The CCSS stresses writing as a key component of literacy. Starting in kindergarten, include informative writing that emphasizes meaning rather than spelling and handwriting skills. Make it a priority that students engage in informative writing everyday in all grade levels and content areas. Depth and complexity build from comprehension of what is read and discussed.

### GRAPHIC TOOLS

Provide graphic organizers to structure active reading of expository text. For example, concept maps, KWL, and Venn diagrams prove engaging and effective to guide students' attention to key ideas. To increase depth, add a section across the bottom of an organizer and ask students to end with a conclusion or generalization to engage deeper thinking.

### READ ALOUD

In any grade level, incorporate informational text in your instruction by reading nonfiction aloud to students to help them develop background information that makes them want to know more. Research suggests that students are more likely to select nonfiction text for independent reading if their teacher has piqued interest by reading some of it aloud to them (Duke, 2004).

### READING-FOR-WRITING

For some students, reading-for-writing provides authentic purposes for reading informational text (Duke, 2004). Students are inclined to read nonfiction when they are interested in preparing written informative products for an audience, such as a history exposition, a class information book, a brochure explaining a local wildlife area, or problem-solving ideas about water resources in their community.

### *PRIMARY-TEXT SOURCES*

Primary-text sources are a specific application of nonfiction with high appeal to students. For example, students find famous speeches representing a time or event to be more personally interesting than solely reading

Kingore, B. (2013). *Rigor and Engagement for Growing Minds.* Austin, TX: PA Publishing.

about the topic. These primary sources challenge students to draw upon their own feelings and experiences to understand the emotions, backgrounds, and actions of the people who had both an impact on and were influenced by these real events. Primary sources make a topic of study personally relevant so increased complexity and depth are likely in students' work. Through online access, more primary sources are available than ever before.

### TOP AMERICAN SPEECHES

Accessing famous speeches and hearing the information presented in the author's own words rather than the interpretation of others motivates students. One resource that captures particular interest is the *Top 100 American Speeches of the 20th Century*, based upon the survey and ranking of Lucas & Medhurst (2008). Conduct an online search to access sites that include these transcripts and, in some cases, audio presentations of the original speeches.

### WEBSITES

Educators also need access to resources providing relevant information about instructional concepts and applications related to complexity and depth in content, process, and product. Two educational foundations merit particular consideration in this quest.

- *Edutopia* is sponsored by the George Lucas Educational Foundation. This site is dedicated to improving the K-12 learning process by documenting, disseminating, and advocating for innovative, replicable, and evidence-based strategies. Topics include comprehensive assessment, integrated studies, problem-based learning, social-emotional learning, teacher development, and technology integration.

  *(*http://www.edutopia.org*)*

- *My Group Genius* is a project of the Bill and Melinda Gates Foundation. The vision of this site is to improve education through collaboration. The Foundation invites teachers to explore best teaching practices and discuss specific examples of how to integrate the CCSS into math and literacy curriculum.

  *(*http://www.mygroupgenius.org*)*

### INTERNET SAFETY

Typically, students are well versed at online searches to access information. However, a literate person in today's world needs to cautiously consider ways the digital culture both improves and hinders our lives (Chiao, 2011). Teach students to navigate the internet in a responsible manner. Facilitate students as they access web sites that enable advanced exploration with greater complexity, breadth, and depth relating to their interests and topics of study.

Common Sense Media is a nonprofit organization whose top priority is Internet safety for children. Free classroom lessons and parent education resources, including a cyber bullying tool kit, guide children to safe, smart, and ethical decisions online.

(http://www.commonsensemedia.org)

# INQUIRY AND IN-DEPTH STUDY

## INQUIRY IS A DIFFERENTIATION STRATEGY

•

Inquiry, or in-depth study, is a productive differentiation strategy that empowers each student to extend personal learning at a level and pace uniquely suited to that person as a scholar.

The inquiry process begins with teacher-directed experiences to develop foundational skills and continues as students move toward increasing independence to develop and investigate authentic problems. In the process, students practice and refine self-management, research skills, and productive habits of mind as they apply, interpret, and adapt the ideas they discover. The complexity and depth of the inquiry process rests on the teacher's skill in planning and preparing foundation-level tasks and the availability of resources and technology for students.

The International Baccalaureate program (IB) is an excellent example using inquiry to generate cognitive skills and nurture the natural curiosity that leads students to solutions for complex problems. IB (2007) stresses that inquiry is not merely a novel way of repackaging subject-specific content. Rather, it is a way for students to use a range of subject-specific knowledge, concepts, and skills in order to develop a deeper understanding of transdisciplinary themes.

The implementation of productive inquiry and in-depth study is framed by KUD–what we want students to know, understand, and be able to do (Erickson, 2007). It starts with students' current understanding, proceeds with their research and active construction of meaning, and results in enduring skills and higher-level understanding of new concepts and ideas derived from the inquiry. Content becomes personally noteworthy when it is something to discover rather than memorize. Hence, inquiry or in-depth study is a productive differentiation strategy that empowers each student to extend personal learning at a level and pace uniquely suited to that person as a scholar.

A number of terms are used to identify this strategy. I generally avoid the terms *independent study* or *independent research.* While the terms intend to convey working more independently from the teacher, some adults infer that students must also work alone. Since professionals in a field often collaborate with a colleague when problem solving, students may also elect to work with a peer for in-depth study if all participants are equally committed to the topic. I want to clarify that this personally relevant process of inquiry and in-depth study fundamentally differs from cooperative projects in which students work in small groups but proceed in similar ways to complete the same teacher-designed task within the same schedule.

The terms *inquiry* and *in-depth study* more closely relate to how people pursue authentic problems in real life as they apply the steps and skills of research. To me, these terms connote what is most significant in this process–the formulation of key questions and

Kingore, B. (2013). *Rigor and Engagement for Growing Minds.* Austin, TX: PA Publishing.

the intellectual pursuit of lifelong, comprehensive understanding. Framing research as questions piques curiosity, fosters depth and complexity, and triggers the emergence of additional unanswered questions. Render guidance and support at the minimum level required to ensure student success. The intent is to enable students to develop the research and self-management skills that permit them to assume an increasingly active role in designing and managing their own learning through solving problems in a variety of ways. When we allow high-ability students to inquire and construct personal meaning, they typically experience joyful learning pursuing a topic relevant to them for extensive periods of time (Willis, 2007b).

Investigations look quite different within each age group and depend on the experience of the students. Inquiry is developmentally appropriate when it relates to students' first-hand experiences and fosters new connections evolving from that background. Young children experience inquiry through purposeful play in which they ponder, question, and explore possibilities as we act as facilitators. Older students, early in their development of research skills, experience teacher-structured inquiry in which we instruct, facilitate, and provide helpful feedback. Students with a more extensive background in inquiry experience focused, strategic study initiated by the individual to construct purposeful learning as we observe and coach. Beginning researchers may conclude their inquiry in a matter of days, while a more rigorous and sophisticated learning project could

*Inquiry*

•

*Content becomes personally noteworthy when it is something to discover rather than memorize.*

necessitate deep immersion and extensive time. The length of time required for students to achieve autonomy and become masters of their own investigations is as variable as the children involved.

Help our colleagues understand what you know: having students pursue in-depth studies is quite realistic in a mixed-ability classroom. Preassess before beginning each segment of learning and document which students already understand and can apply the targeted concepts and skills. Then, provide those students time for replacement tasks inviting inquiry and in-depth study. It is a win-win situation as teachers now have a reduced number of students who need direct teaching of core curriculum and all students are provided opportunities to experience continuous learning.

## THE CYCLICAL PROCESS OF INQUIRY AND IN-DEPTH STUDY

Inquiry, or in-depth study, is a differentiation strategy; research steps and skills are the means to acquire and process the information that leads to deeper understanding and new learning. As shown in Figure 3.4, the sequence of a study is cyclical when students are actively engaged in learning. It begins with a student's personal interests and identification of a relevant topic to pursue. Then, it circles back and forth among question formation, finding information, organizing information, and formative assessment. Additional information or insight from one step affects the others. Eventually, the student develops a solution or product resulting from the experience and reflects to evaluate the content, process, and product as a whole. The cyclical process might even begin again as one conclusion may prompt another quest.

## FIGURE 3.4:
# THE CYCLICAL PROCESS OF INQUIRY

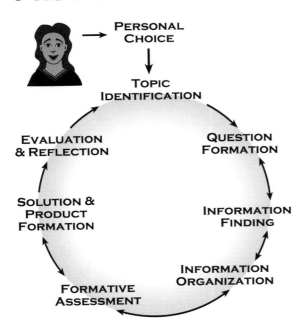

Recognizing that creative thinking and adaptation are highly valued in our fast-changing digital world, the creative problem-solving process interplays with the steps and skills of research as well as the personal attributes of students. We understand the decisive role of adaptation, and appreciate the value of students mentally playing with possibilities and questioning, "What if..." They must go beyond reporting or organizing information to constructing new knowledge and meaning through critically analyzing and drawing conclusions relative to content. Inquiry and in-depth study are intended to develop the intellectual skills that enable students to eventually produce high

quality work that sets a standard for scholarship and contributes to the community beyond the classroom. Figure 3.5 displays the interdependent relationship of the process, skills, and personal attributes required in the inquiry process.

Digital access switches *information finding* and *information organization* from an emphasis on accessing information to a concern for how to use accessed information in ways that demonstrate higher-level comprehension, relevant connections, and unique applications. Require students to change the form of accessed information from downloaded content to applied connections because inquiry and in-depth study require interpretation rather than mere reporting.

Multiple product formats promote original inferences and conclusions. Moline (2011) refers to this technique as *recomposing*–reading information in one format and summarizing it in another format. For example, students read a nonfiction article and summarize it as a concept map or read a flowchart and summarize it in a written paragraph. Recomposing is a powerful deterrent to copying and an aid to comprehension as it obligates students to internalize key facts and concepts in order to translate and organize them in a different format. As Moline comments, "Thinking has to occur" (12).

Conduct a class discussion about using Wikipedia for *information finding* and *information organization.* Survey how often students use Wikipedia, and lead small groups to address the merits and concerns about this resource. In each group, a recorder folds a paper into three rows and notes the group's ideas for the value, negative potential, and

Kingore, B. (2013). *Rigor and Engagement for Growing Minds.* Austin, TX: PA Publishing.

FIGURE 3.5:
# RESEARCH SKILLS AND STUDENT ATTRIBUTES RELATED TO INQUIRY

## TOPIC IDENTIFICATION

*Research skills:*  Determine an authentic, personally interesting topic

Refine or narrow the topic to a reasonable focus of inquiry

Question how this topic has value beyond the classroom

*Student attributes:*  Awareness of self-interests and skills

Alert to real-world problems

## QUESTION FORMATION

*Research skills:*  Pose compelling, relevant, concept-based questions

Apply the language of creative thinking: IWW... ("In what ways...")

*Student attributes:*  Curiosity and intellectual interest

A spirit of inquiry

## INFORMATION FINDING

*Research skills:*  Plan courses of action, set goals, and collect information

Selectively access varied, relevant, and reliable resources such as
text, nonlinguistic data, the Internet, interviews, and observation

Record and interpret information for relevance and authenticity

Seek diverse perspectives

Recognize when and how to seek help

*Student attributes:*  Self-management and self-direction

Intellectual openness

Perseverance

Independent judgment

Enthusiasm and enjoyment of learning

## INFORMATION ORGANIZATION

*Research skills:*  Interpret and construct meaning

Record/describe organized data nonlinguistically and linguistically

Problem solving

Resolve conflicting data

Examine evidence, methods, and conclusions

Compare, categorize, and summarize

*Student attributes:*  Intelligent risk taking

Integrity and independent judgment

Originality; innovation

Kingore, B. (2013). *Rigor and Engagement for Growing Minds.* Austin, TX: PA Publishing.

Appreciation for diversity

Tolerance for complex, messy problems

Enthusiasm and enjoyment of learning

## FORMATIVE ASSESSMENT AND ADAPTATION

*Research skills:* Metacognition and reflection

Reasonability of constructed meaning and interpretations

Reliability, validity, and importance of the evidence

Analyzing complexity and depth of information

*Student attributes:* Thoroughness

Reasoned judgment

Delay of immediate gratification

Self-monitoring (metacognitive skills)

Enthusiasm and enjoyment of learning

## SOLUTION AND PRODUCT FORMATION

*Research skills:* Draw conclusions from organized information

Determine the best-fit product format

Communicate in-depth understanding, results, and conclusions to
an audience

*Student attributes:* Imaginative, innovative, and adaptive thinking

Communication in a succinct, cogent manner

Productivity

Enthusiasm and enjoyment of learning

## EVALUATION AND REFLECTION

*Research skills:* Self-assessment of product and process

Ability to explain and support judgments

Critique the value of the constructed meaning

Seek peer and public scrutiny

Apply appropriate evaluation tools

*Student attributes:* Self-confidence as a learner

Self-regulation (metacognition and self-reflection)

Tolerance

Respect for self and others

Receptive to change: "What I will do differently next time?"

Kingore, B. (2013). *Rigor and Engagement for Growing Minds.* Austin, TX: PA Publishing.

cautions or dangers, such as the concern that anyone can edit Wikipedia so how does the information retain credibility?

### EVALUATING INFORMATION

*Information finding* and *information organization* challenge students to rigorously examine evidence for potential bias or other inaccuracy and evaluate the reliability, validity, and quality of a source. Invite interested students to:

* Create an infographic or checklist others can use to evaluate resources.
* Investigate how major news organizations validate their information and sources.

During the inquiry process, *solution and product formation* is most significant when students perceive that there is an authentic audience who is interested in their work, motivating students to proceed more diligently to communicate ideas that have an impact on others through verbal, written, symbolic, visual, or graphic formats. The ubiquitous research paper remains a possible form, but variations that promote students' interpretations and construction of new meaning, such as nonlinguistic formats, a math proof, music score, or computer program, are also viable possibilities. The intent is always for children to use accessed information in new ways, forming new connections or conclusions, not just reporting or paraphrasing information.

### A TIERED LEARNING STATION FOR CELEBRATING INQUIRY

Designate a corner of the classroom as the location for Expert Quests–student-developed learning stations where students display the results of their research for peer scrutiny and enjoyment (Kingore, 2011). The stations should emphasize in-depth content and interpretation rather than flashy production. Each inquiry should include:

* One or more essential questions of the project,
* A visual aid or graphic,
* Interactive elements for classmates to experience as they explore the information, and
* A conclusion or generalization as well as a reflection of the work by the researcher.

Challenge students to develop a rubric for peers to use to assess the inquiry and provide feedback to the researcher.

### BREADTH

Complexity and depth are a priority for all students and crucial for high-ability students in advanced learning pursuits. Yet, breadth is also significantly related to high expectations. Breadth, denoting a wider range and scope of content knowledge, emerges as particularly pertinent to students' interests and areas of specializations. Scholars do not become experts when they have a superficial awareness of information; creative problem solvers cannot create or adapt content and products at high levels if they do not extensively know and understand.

High-ability students characteristically endeavor to become an expert in one or more topics or disciplines. That objective requires a long-term, impassioned immersion in a topic with access to sophisticated text, field-based terminology, and peer or public scrutiny. Breadth enables students-as-experts to conclude transdisciplinary connections and realize their work is never finished–there is always more to learn!

## RELATING INQUIRY TO CURRICULUM STANDARDS

An inquiry or in-depth study requires students to enlarge prior understanding by investigating real-world questions and discovering new concepts in the process. The CCSS emphasizes student research throughout the standards but most prominently in the writing strand, connecting the critical nature of written analysis and the presentation of findings that result from inquiry in any content area.

• Design inquiry and in-depth study to overtly document mastery of required concepts and skills, thus freeing high-ability students to explore more complex concepts that exceed core standards and ensure that they experience continuous learning.

• Use preassessment data of a current set of concepts and skills to substantiate each student's capabilities or prior mastery. Determine which students should extend those core-curriculum learning objectives through personally relevant inquiry and in-depth study instead of continuing with the regular curriculum learning tasks.

• With older students, specify the targeted concepts and skills they must apply in their inquiry. As they proceed, students must substantiate in writing how they apply those concepts and skills, such as on the Proposal for Inquiry and In-Depth Study in Figure 3.6. In this manner, any student-selected topic or concept of interest to the student can be used to meet the expectation of mastery of required concepts and skills.

• Ask young, high-ability students to inform you when they have learned a targeted skill. Tell them: "Come to me when you know this or think you have learned it, and we will assess it together."

• When necessary for classrooms fervently concerned with achievement targets, limit inquiry to directly related concepts and topics that spring from class work and standards. While more restrictive of personal relevancy, selecting inquiry from a narrower standards-related focus honors individual learning needs better than redundant work on previously mastered concepts and skills.

## STUDENT PROPOSAL FOR INQUIRY AND IN-DEPTH STUDY

Teachers scaffold procedures to support students' initial development of plans for inquiry and in-depth study. Provide simple templates, such as Figures 3.6 and 3.7 that guide students through the process of initiating a personal replacement task customized to their learning interests yet applicable to learning objectives. Inquiry tasks personalized to a student's area of profound interest can still substantiate that core curriculum skills and concepts are integrated.

With students inexperienced in the research process, these plans or proposals provide an important opportunity to discern their perspectives about inquiry and readiness to conduct a study. Build on those insights to facilitate the organization and management of the how-to-learn skills students need to use throughout their lives.

### TECHNOLOGY

Technology is a productive accompaniment to inquiry and in-depth study. Use technology to access mentors and advanced digital resources.

## INQUIRY PRODUCTS

As a timesaving technique to stimulate student decisions regarding *solution and product formation*, post a list of potential products that relate to any inquiry process. This technique is most useful to students with less experience with inquiry and in-depth study. It supplies them with potential ideas and empowers them with choice and decision-making opportunities regarding possibilities that might be more interesting and productive ways to finalize their learning experience. Figure 3.8 is a task board of generalizable research products that uses a simple reading vocabulary to enable younger children to refer to the products for consideration as they plan and then complete their inquiry. Figure 3.9 shows a task board for older students. It models how teachers enlarge on a list of products to develop generalizable learning tasks inasmuch as this task

---

**FIGURE 3.6:**
**PROPOSAL FOR INQUIRY AND IN-DEPTH STUDY**

Topic _____

1. What are you interested in studying?

2. What are your inquiry questions?

3. Who is your audience?

4. What will be your final product?

5. List the resources you plan to access and what you might need.

6. How may I or others help you?

7. How does your plan apply these skills?

❑ _____    Applications    _____

❑ _____                    _____

❑ _____                    _____

8. Plan for Success: On the back, sketch a time line or flow chart showing the dates and steps for your inquiry from the beginning to the completion of your work.

---

**FIGURE 3.7:**
**INQUIRY PLAN**

Topic _____

I want to learn:

I wonder:

My finished product will be:

I want to share this with:

**This my plan.**
First:

Second:

Third:

Fourth:

Fifth:

Sixth:

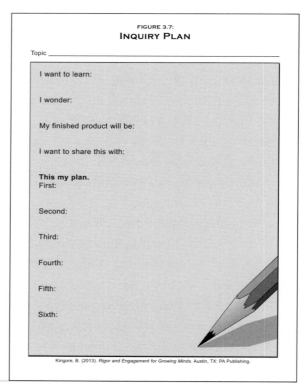

---

## FIGURE 3.8:
# INQUIRY PRODUCTS FOR PRIMARY CHILDREN

| | | |
|---|---|---|
| **1.** Make a recording for a reading center or library.  | **2.** Write and illustrate an ABC book for another class.  | **3.** Make a flipbook with questions and answers. 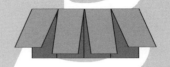 |
| **4.** Make a poster with words and pictures.  | **5.** Write a rebus report.  | **6.** Perform a puppet show to teach others.  |

board adapts many of the suggestions for authentic applications of learning experiences shared in Chapter 2, Figure 2.12. Product lists or task boards should not be used to limit students to the posted options as that would undermine the individual nature of inquiry and in-depth study. Rather, use task boards as a stimulus to students' planning.

A task board supports children needing guidance with *solution and product formation.* The following applications support other stages in the inquiry process through efficient and effective learning opportunities.

### CONCEPTUAL THINKING WORDS FOR INVESTIGATIVE QUESTIONS

When appropriate, invite students to use the conceptual thinking words in Figure 3.2 to promote concept-based question formation with deeper connections to their interests and topical investigations. After modeling the concepts to guide thinking with the class or groups, provide a short list of concept words that are applicable to a student's inquiry. Challenge that student to use one or more of the words to think about the topic in a new way and formulate investigative questions.

Kingore, B. (2013). *Rigor and Engagement for Growing Minds.* Austin, TX: PA Publishing.

## FIGURE 3.9:
# INQUIRY PRODUCTS

| | | |
|---|---|---|
| **1.** Create an online *Room for Debate* organizing your perspective and the viewpoints of three additional stakeholders in a topic. Present logical arguments based on substantive claims, sound reasoning, and relevant evidence. | **2.** Conduct interviews with people who have first-hand experiences; then summarize your results and draw conclusions that impact prior understandings. | **3.** Create a digital presentation that uses precise vocabulary to relate conclusions from your case study or historical research. |
| **4.** Design an original Venn diagram using a symbol for your topic and contrasting two perspectives while including at least five similarities. Conclude with your personal connections and newly constructed understandings. | **5.** Create a complex concept map that establishes connections among the most significant points of a topic. Create symbols in different sizes to represent the relative importance of each idea. End with your conclusions from your inquiry. | **6.** Compose an article for *Wikipedia* explaining your topic and concluding with implications for the future and areas for continued research. |
| **7.** Design a bulletin board comparing topical information across three or more disciplines to expand applications and connections for others. | **8.** Using original symbols representing the key ideas and significant people influencing outcomes, organize a flow chart of relationships and conclusions. | **9.** Develop an infomercial explaining significant information, summarizing content, and drawing conclusions to post online. |
| **10.** Create a board game to teach a family member or peer about your research. The game must teach your key concepts, use appropriate academic vocabulary, have visual appeal, and be fun to play. | **11.** Construct a learning station including an inquiry question and interactive ways for others to gain a more complex understanding of information. | **12.** Organize a Write-for-the-Community project. Set up a blog or website where students can post service-learning compositions that share insights and construct more meaningful connections between school and society regarding a community need or issue. |

Kingore, B. (2013). *Rigor and Engagement for Growing Minds.* Austin, TX: PA Publishing.

## NARROWING A TOPIC

When students need assistance narrowing a topic to a reasonable size for research, have them complete the first two columns of a KWL–Ogle's (1986) strategy of listing *what I know, what I want to know,* and *what I learned.* Ask students to circle one or two items in the *W* column. These items identify students' initial research focus and investigative questions, such as: "In what ways and for what reasons do reindeer communicate?" Later, students may elect to return to their list and expand their research with further breadth or depth. Meet with them briefly to facilitate planning.

## RECORD KEEPING

Ensure that high-ability students maintain records of progress, evaluating their intellectual accomplishments and their personal changes as learners rather than gauging their results through comparisons with grade-level peers.

# DEVELOPMENTALLY APPROPRIATE INQUIRY FOR YOUNG CHILDREN

Facilitate children's interests, curiosity, and enthusiasm for learning at an early age.

Young, high-ability learners are among the most curious and driven to solve problems. They are interested in knowing *now*, not waiting until they are old enough to read and write more independently. Inquiry should begin the first day of preschool and never stop. But, it needs to be approached with and proceed from developmentally appropriate practices. Whenever feasible, respond to the children's interests and emphasize their original thinking and conclusions rather than having them only collect and report existing information. Ask: "What do you think about this now?" or "Tell us what you decided after learning about this."

Maintain a realistic perspective. Expect students to acquire new understanding through their inquiries, but appreciate that a young child's creation of new information through inquiry must be considered within the context of the learner's age and experience. Something that is known information for an older student may be a newly researched insight for a primary child. Most primary children can demonstrate abstract thinking when building from their prior concrete experiences, but concrete first-hand experiences are preferred for explorations and discoveries. They greatly enjoy pretending and acting out their newly acquired insights and information.

## FACILITATE QUESTIONING AND INQUIRY

Model a respect for children's questions and respond with new questions that facilitate their thinking and guide their active pursuit of information.
- "Why do you think that is so?"
- "Why did you assume that?"

Integrating Complexity & Depth

- "What do you observe?"
- "What do you wonder?"
- "What else might it be?"
- "Have you considered...?"
- "How could you investigate that?"

## CONNECT INQUIRY WITH ACTION

With younger children, define research as "finding out anything you are interested in knowing more about." With that definition, inquiry becomes a daily, active priority rather than a special situation. Be enthusiastic and respond to children's curiosity.

- When children ask about a word, respond: "We need a word researcher. Who would like to research that word?"
- Any object children ask about is a motivation for research. "Who is interested in researching that for us?"
- As an exit question, ask children to answer the question: "What have you researched today?" Invite family members to ask that same question to spur personal interest and more specific conversations with a child about school-day experiences.

Scaffold children's research with graphic organizers. Structure individual inquiry with simple formats that emphasize their head more than their hand and promote original thinking. Plant the idea that research is interesting and personally rewarding by pursuing applications in the topics and content areas that most fascinate children.

✓ Learning with My Senses (Figure 3.10) invites children to do what comes naturally and explore through their senses. While learning information from books is possible at this age, learning through first-hand experiences is more childlike as they rely on sensory experiences to acquire and reflect on new information.

FIGURE 3.10:
**LEARNING WITH MY SENSES**

Topic: _____

My question: _____
_____

| | |
|---|---|
| 👀 See | |
| 👂 Hear | |
| ✋ Touch or Feel | |
| 👄 Taste | |
| 👃 Smell | |

Now I know: _____
_____

Kingore, B. (2013). *Rigor and Engagement for Growing Minds*. Austin, TX: PA Publishing.

✓ A Research Riddle (Figure 3.11) provides an appealing tool for sharing research information with an audience. Copy back-to-back the two-page format. Children analyze and organize their topical information on the riddle and record their personal connections on the back. They fold the page in half so information shows on the front and then lift the half-page to reveal conclusions to the audience before sharing more about what they have learned.

Kingore, B. (2013). *Rigor and Engagement for Growing Minds.* Austin, TX: PA Publishing.

**What I liked about my research:**

I think these are the four most important words about my research:

1. _____   2. _____

3. _____   4. _____

**MY RESEARCH CONCLUSION**

"Before my research, I did not know: _____."

---- (STUDENTS FOLD THE PAPER HERE) ----

**FIGURE 3.11:**
**A RESEARCH RIDDLE BY** _____

I am _____ and _____

I am not _____

I like _____

I need _____

_____

Who or what am I?

A B C D E F G H I J K L M N O P Q R S T U V W X Y Z

---

**FIGURE 3.12:**
**RESEARCHING NUMBERS ABOUT ME**

My favorite number is _____ because _____
_____

The number of family members I have: _____

The number of pets in my home: _____

My age: _____   My height: _____

The number of teeth I have: _____

The number of freckles I have on my face: _____

My birthday: _____

The time I wake up: _____

My bed time: _____

The time I really want to go to bed: _____

I think the most important number is _____

because _____

The largest number I know is _____
_____

I think the most confusing number is _____

because _____

In our classroom, I see numbers _____
_____

0 1 2 3 4 5 6 7 8 9

Kingore, B. (2013). *Rigor and Engagement for Growing Minds.* Austin, TX: PA Publishing.

---

✓ Researching Numbers About Me (Figure 3.12) prompts children who love math to research numbers in their lives and inject their personal thinking about numbers. For example, one first grader responded to the prompt about the most confusing number with: "Eight because that *numeral* is so hard to write." Another said: "Infinity because nobody can count that one. It looks like an eight lying down" [the student draws: ∞].

Some students who would benefit from more in-depth or complex content may be too immature to proceed independently. They may lack the reading or writing skills, research skills, or independent work habits to complete individual inquiry. Arrange for assistants to provide needed support.

• Allow a child to record ideas and insights rather than write them.

• Provide a corner of the classroom, hallway, or school library where the child can work with adult facilitation.

• Use parent aides, volunteers, and older students to scribe and model research skills and work habits to support inquiry

When families ask how they can help a high-ability child, share ideas for research at home. Clearly communicate to families your expectations for learning. Some family members will assume an assisted, grand project is expected unless you clearly share your intentions. Specify that you expect the task to be child-like and completed by the learner. Consider sharing a letter with families, such as the example in Figure 3.13, to encourage developmentally appropriate research at home. If helpful, supply simple graphic organizers for families to use to interact with their child's inquiry.

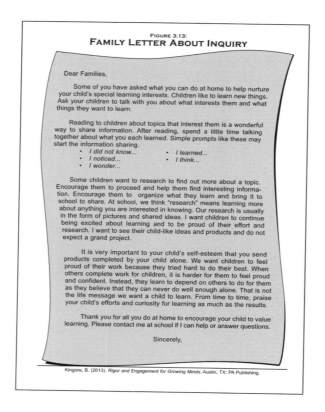

**FIGURE 3.13:**
**FAMILY LETTER ABOUT INQUIRY**

Dear Families,

Some of you have asked what you can do at home to help nurture your child's special learning interests. Children like to learn new things. Ask your children to talk with you about what interests them and what things they want to learn.

Reading to children about topics that interest them is a wonderful way to share information. After reading, spend a little time talking together about what you each learned. Simple prompts like these may start the information sharing.

- *I did not know...*          - *I learned...*
- *I noticed...*               - *I think...*
- *I wonder...*

Some children want to research to find out more about a topic. Encourage them to proceed and help them find interesting information. Encourage them to organize what they learn and bring it to school to share. At school, we think "research" means learning more about anything you are interested in knowing. Our research is usually in the form of pictures and shared ideas. I want children to continue being excited about learning and to be proud of their effort and research. I want to see their child-like ideas and products and do not expect a grand project.

It is very important to your child's self-esteem that you send products completed by your child alone. We want children to feel proud of their work because they tried hard to do their best. When others complete work for children, it is harder for them to feel proud and confident. Instead, they learn to depend on others to do for them as they believe that they can never do well enough alone. That is not the life message we want a child to learn. From time to time, praise your child's efforts and curiosity for learning as much as the results.

Thank you for all you do at home to encourage your child to value learning. Please contact me at school if I can help or answer questions.

Sincerely,

Kingore, B. (2013). *Rigor and Engagement for Growing Minds.* Austin, TX: PA Publishing.

## VOCABULARY DEVELOPMENT

Vocabulary development also relates to complexity and depth; it is a major element connecting comprehension and achievement across the curriculum. The focus of academic vocabulary is beyond uplifting vocabulary for its own sake to applying content-based vocabulary for deeper understanding of a single content area or transdisciplinary connections. There is a direct relationship between the development of academic vocabulary and achievement gains in content areas. Research shows that academic vocabulary is one of the strongest indicators of how well students learn subject-area content. Gifford and Gore (2008), for example, found that immersing middle school students in specific math vocabulary resulted in higher levels of achievement and an increased pace of learning for all students.

Furthermore, higher cognitive processing requires a high-level academic vocabulary specific to content fields (Marzano, 2006; Sousa, 2009).

The important role of vocabulary is further supported through requirements by the CCSS that students' vocabulary experiences enable them to gain, evaluate, and communicate increasingly complex information, ideas, and evidence. Thus, effective teachers use increasingly complex and specific academic vocabulary in meaningful contexts with all ages of advanced students, encouraging them to apply, explore, and expand academic vocabulary. In particular, recognize and honor a child's idea by restating and embellishing it with more academic terms. Then, continue using the higher-level term consistently in context. As one example during a math lesson, one teacher added: "A mathematician would say: _____." Another teacher used the technique of elegant words to stimulate students' more academic oral and written applications: "I know an elegant word for that," or "Who can find an elegant word to use instead of _____?"

A teacher's personal vocabulary and knowledge of how to teach language is of key importance in vocabulary development. Stronge (2012) reports that students taught by teachers with greater verbal ability and more authentic contextual applications of language learn more than those taught by teachers with lower verbal ability.

Consistent contextual applications are paramount to purposeful instruction for vocabulary development. Engage students in discussing and using key terms in their own words during instruction and group applications. Marzano and Pickering (2005) propose a six-step process for vocabulary instruction that is highly effective and research-based. Figure 3.14 summarizes an adaptation of that process. The first three steps are applications of direct instruction, and the last three steps are the parts of the process that promote practice and reinforcement for learners.

While proposed as steps, practical application of this vocabulary development process allows some variation in the sequence. Specifically, steps three through six could be implemented in a different order and repeated as appropriate, as long as we ensure that students understand the targeted words thoroughly enough to apply them in varied ways.

## VOCABULARY DEVELOPMENT APPLICATIONS

Implement applications for each of the steps of vocabulary development to immerse students in acquiring an extensive, relevant vocabulary to strengthen content learning and heighten deeper cognitive processing. Since the development of academic vocabulary is so significant and directly related to student achievement, develop a repertoire of easy-to-implement applications to frequently integrate in current learning contexts. Several of the following vocabulary learning experiences may prove useful.

## FIGURE 3.14:
# STEPS TO VOCABULARY DEVELOPMENT

1. **INTRODUCE VOCABULARY.**
   Provide a description, explanation, example, or nonexample of a new word.

2. **RESTATE MEANINGS.**
   Ask students to use their own words to provide a description, explanation, example, or nonexample of the new word.

3. **INCORPORATE VISUAL TOOLS.**
   Invite students to draw and explain a picture, symbol, or graphic to represent the new word.

4. **INTEGRATE ACTIVITIES.**
   Provide activities designed to provide more knowledge and deeper understanding of the word in multiple contexts.

5. **FOSTER VOCABULARY IN DISCUSSIONS.**
   Specifically, invite students to discuss academic terms and purposefully use significant vocabulary with peers.

6. **INITIATE WORD PLAY.**
   Ask students to play word games that provide more reinforcement of their new developing vocabulary.

Kingore, B. (2013). *Rigor and Engagement for Growing Minds.* Austin, TX: PA Publishing.

Integrating Complexity & Depth

## VOCABULARY ANALOGIES

The comparisons imbedded in direct analogies afford a simple-to-implement tool for vocabulary connections. Provide analogies that omit a key term, requiring students to understand the concept and the relationship among the items in order to supply the missing content-related terminology. Working in pairs encourages students to engage in academic conversations about the content.

- A minute is to an hour as _____ is to a yard.
- Slippery slope is to alliteration as gurgle and meow are to _____.
- Calcium is to bone as _____ are to DNA.

## ROOTS AND AFFIXES

Sixty percent of all English words have Greek or Latin roots and affixes. Hence, understanding word stems targets the academic language of professional life. Understanding and applying roots and affixes results in an exponentially more powerful vocabulary development than learning one word at a time allows (CIERA, 2001; Thompson, 2001). Have students collect interesting sets of words with a common root particularly relevant to a current skill or concept and then post them for others to discuss, such as *biomes, biographer, biohazard,* and *biofeedback* or *thermostat, thermal imaging, thermodynamics,* and *thermos.*

## ABC FORMAT

Ask students to use an ABC format applying targeted vocabulary to retell a story, science experiment, math process, or historical event. The activity simply requires them to construct their writing so the first sentence begins with a word that starts with *A*, the second sentence must begin with a word starting with *B*, and so forth. This format requires thinking about vocabulary in a more direct manner, typically resulting in students researching word choices to construct meaningful connections.

## WHAT'S THE DIFFERENCE?

State two related words, such as *imagery* and *description* or *information* and *data*. In pairs, students explain the differences and draw an illustration or cite an example of each.

## VOCABULARY CHARADES

In small teams, a student randomly selects a word card from content-related vocabulary to pantomime for others to decipher, such as the math-related terms *circumference or hexagon.*

Kingore, B. (2013). *Rigor and Engagement for Growing Minds.* Austin, TX: PA Publishing.

### INDIVIDUAL WORD LISTS

As students read, ask them to make a list of any complex, academic words they think might be important. Later, students come together in small groups to compare and discuss their selected words and perhaps reach a consensus ranking the significance of the words. Alternately, a teacher or peer assistant uses those words to respond directly to the student's vocabulary interests, enhancing comprehension and cognitive processing.

### VOCABULARY OF CLASSIC CHILDREN'S LITERATURE

For one of the most rewarding (and simplest) ways to develop a strong vocabulary, invite children to read outstanding books from an earlier time, before the vocabulary was simplified and literature was dumbed-down for anthologies. Rudyard Kipling's *Just So Stories,* J. M. Barrie's *Peter Pan,* Frances Hodgson Burnett's *The Secret Garden*, and so many others will amaze you with their sophisticated vocabulary. It is a most engaging and rewarding way to learn wonderful words.

# PROMOTING COMPLEXITY AND DEPTH

### TIERED INSTRUCTION

Tiered instruction is well researched and developed with clarity by leaders in our field, particularly the work of Carol Tomlinson. Since multiple, extensive discussions of tiered instruction already exist, it is not within the focus of this book to expand on tiered instruction applications. However, I remain committed to the need for tiered instruction, and it would be an oversight not at least mentioning it in this context as a facilitator of complexity and depth. It is important that we tier the complexity of learning experiences so every child is involved in the appropriate level of challenge that elicits high-level thinking and allows effort to result in achievement.

Tiered instruction remains a decisive differentiation strategy. It is significantly connected to promoting complexity and depth by layering lessons that foster above-grade-level as well as at-or-below-grade-level mastery of concepts and skills. Tiered learning experiences are relevant to high-ability learners when lessons maintain the learning objective but provide routes of access at varying degrees of complexity and depth.

In keeping with the CCSS emphasis on text complexity, tiering requires a range of text complexity, enabling high-ability students to access nonfiction and fiction at higher levels of readability and concept density. Tiered lessons foster continuous learning for all students through learning experiences that explore ideas building on prior knowledge, not limiting instruction to core curriculum. As Tomlinson

Kingore, B. (2013). *Rigor and Engagement for Growing Minds.* Austin, TX: PA Publishing.

Integrating Complexity & Depth

(2001, 5) cautions, "Only when students work at appropriate challenge levels do they develop the essential habits of persistence, curiosity, and willingness to take intellectual risks. To ask less of advanced learners is to predict less productive and engaged adult lives".

### QUICK STARTS TO COMPLEXITY AND DEPTH

Figure 3.15 lists several quick starts to enhance complexity and depth. When your plate seems too full, try a small step toward increased complexity and depth and then build on your results.

## FIGURE 3.15:
# QUICK STARTS TO COMPLEXITY AND DEPTH

✦ **ALWAYS IN WRITING**

Always in writing = more thinking! Require students to jot down ideas before sharing or raising their hands to volunteer a response. Preplanning with quick notes results in more complex, developed ideas.

✦ **ONE OR MORE LETTERS**

If students cannot spell complete words, teach them to write one or more letters they know are in the word and then draw a line to indicate that they know the word is incomplete. This technique aids children's memory so they don't have to respond: "I had an idea but I forgot." It also encourages more complex vocabulary as children can correctly apply a word they do not yet know how to spell.

✦ **LIST RESOURCES**

Requiring students to list their resources on their work substantially increases content depth for many learners. Instead of a glib response, they must cite sources and examples from the text.

✦ **GIVE ME FIVE**

Hold up your hand with fingers stretched apart. Challenge students to come up with five different examples or non-examples or attributes relating to your topic or skill. Close each finger as an idea is offered until your hand is closed. This technique provides a visual stimulus for students to keep thinking beyond a single answer.

✦ **MULTIPLE RESPONSES**

Students write sentences producing as many ideas or solutions as possible and then mark their best idea. Seldom do students mark their first response as their best. Discuss how thinking longer and building on initial ideas leads to more complex or higher thoughts.

✦ **CLARIFY YOUR BEST**

Ask students to explain what they think makes one of their ideas or responses their best. Have them write a sentence clarifying their criterion for *best*. One primary child wrote, "It's my best idea because when I showed it to my friend, he went, 'WOW!'"

Kingore, B. (2013). *Rigor and Engagement for Growing Minds*. Austin, TX: PA Publishing.

FIGURE 3.16:

# THINKING REFLECTIVELY

**1. IDEAS**

Identify two or more ideas you intend to apply immediately.

**2. A ROUND OF APPLAUSE TO VALIDATE AND CELEBRATE YOUR CURRENT PRACTICES**

*An effective technique or learning experience I incorporate*

*for complexity and depth in my instruction is:*

**3. ACADEMIC VOCABULARY**

For an academic content area and grade level of interest to you, create a brief list of the specific key terms you believe that students must personally understand and use in appropriate contexts in order to be proficient in that content. Rank-order your list to prioritize implementation.

**4. PLANNING FOR CHANGE**

Use Figure 3.17 as a planning task for action.

Kingore, B. (2013). *Rigor and Engagement for Growing Minds.* Austin, TX: PA Publishing.

FIGURE 3.17:
# PLANNING FOR CHANGE

List a current curriculum learning task by each numeral on the left. Beside the lightbulb underneath each task, jot down your ideas for potentially increasing the depth and complexity of student responses when implementing that task. At the bottom of the graphic, formulate one or more generalizations for increasing complexity and depth; clarify your insights to further your continued professional growth and actions for change.

**#. CURRENT CURRICULUM TASK**

    • **APPLICATIONS TO INCREASE DEPTH AND COMPLEXITY**

1. _____

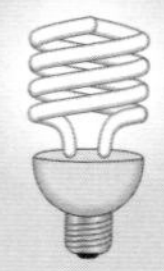

    • _____
    • _____
    • _____

2. _____

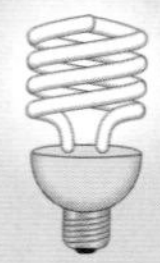

    • _____
    • _____
    • _____

3. _____

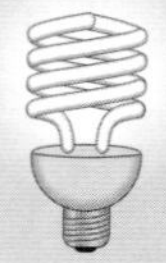

    • _____
    • _____
    • _____

4. _____

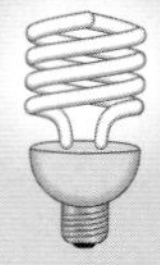

    • _____
    • _____
    • _____

*"I get it!"*
**GENERALIZATIONS:**

# Chapter 4
# Generating
# Cognitive Skills

> *"We've taught you that*
> *the earth is round,*
> *That red and white make pink,*
> *And something else*
> *that matters more—*
> *We've taught you how to think."*
>
> –Dr. Seuss and Jack Prelutsky, 1998

The phenomenal Dr. Seuss and Jack Prelutsky charmingly remind us in *Hooray for Diffendoofer Day* that thinking is an ultimate objective of education. However, without strategic rethinking and redefining of what makes excellent instruction, instructional priorities may fail to generate cognitive skills. After observing hundreds of classes, Wagner (2010) concluded that core classes and even AP courses drilled on specific content and standards at the expense of open-ended inquiry, reasoning, innovation, collaboration, and presentation. The latest Gates Foundation report found teachers implementing few high-level thinking applications. They observed teachers performing well with procedural tasks but experiencing difficulty with tasks involving high-order skills, such as reason, logic, problem solving, conceptual development, and investigation-based approaches (MET, 2012). If schools do not provide opportunities for students to develop their higher-order, cognitive skill sets, our graduates will lack the skills best suited for life's complexities and the professional jobs of their future. Students fail life skills if schools drill for the test at the expense of teaching students to think (Wagner, 2010).

Neurology refers to the highest cognitive processes as *executive functions* while education uses *higher-order thinking* or *critical thinking* to refer to the same functions. These human skill sets exceed what computers can do since they allow for flexible, interpretive, creative, abstracting, and multidimensional thinking (Willis, 2011).

Kingore, B. (2013). *Rigor and Engagement for Growing Minds.* Austin, TX: PA Publishing.

## COGNITIVE SKILLS

While learning standards often distinguish among critical thinking, creative thinking, and reflective thinking, Nodding (2009, 91-92) surmises that what most teachers have in mind when they talk about cognitive skills or thinking is "the sort of mental activity that uses facts to plan, order, and work toward an end; seeks meaning or an explanation; is self-reflective; and uses reason to question claims and make judgments." I would add cognitive flexibility and adaptability to this list of skills to emphasize the creative mental activity that explores new relationships and connections. The Common Core State Standards (CCSS) emphasizes that adaptation of current ideas is needed to prepare for future academic and the workplace cultures. Creative thinkers use cognitive skills to question the known, inject new possibilities, and tackle problems in a diverse fashion.

*Effective teachers realize that they do not teach information and meaning; they facilitate so students develop meaning in the information they learn.*
–Sousa & Tomlinson, 2010

A key point is that any topic or content area can foster cognitive skills when approached in intellectually challenging ways. High-level cognitive skills activate when students apply basic knowledge to novel or unique situations, particularly when the task involves complex, unpredictable problems. Higher cognitive applications result when students use knowledge as a springboard to expand possibilities rather than as an end in itself. This construction of new understanding is best developed through purposeful, engaging applications requiring cognitive work, rather than through explicitly teaching cognitive skills. Promote cognitive applications

that evidence the dispositions of curiosity and open-mindedness across disciplines for all age levels and throughout learning experiences. Students should exhibit a range of cognitive skills in problem-solving tasks, such as those included in Figure 4.1.

Effective cognitive strategies enable students to move toward the executive functions of higher-order thinking. With executive functions, the higher brain is at work with skills such as risk-assessment, judgments, critical analysis, problem solving, and evaluating ideas and data (Willis, 2007a). We must ensure students' opportunities to exercise those skills so they enter the future armed with information and cognitive tools to apply higher-order thinking to real-world concerns.

Authentic applications of cognitive skills require students to resolve problems and evaluate their work. As students reflect on the quality of their reasoning, they form intellectual standards, including relevance, significance, accuracy, depth, logic, and fairness (Paul & Elder, 2004). In future applications requiring cognitive skills, students learn to self-impose those intellectual standards and elevate the quality of their thinking. Over time, students' demonstration of critical and creative thinking becomes self-directed, self-disciplined, self-monitored, and self-corrective (Paul & Elder, 2004).

Nodding admonishes, however, that today's standards-driven instruction poses a serious danger if it reduces content to CliffsNotes

Kingore, B. (2013). *Rigor and Engagement for Growing Minds.* Austin, TX: PA Publishing.

## FIGURE 4.1:
# COGNITIVE SKILLS

- **CRITICAL THINKING SKILLS** include: Interpret, determine ambiguity and bias, persuade, discern multiple perspectives, use judgment, strategically plan, prioritize, substantiate, use logic, reach decisions, and evaluate.

- **CREATIVE THINKING SKILLS** include: Question the known, generate ideas, maintain open-mindedness, adapt, substitute, apply in a unique way, think flexibly, identify new relationships, create analogies, combine, and redesign.

- **LITERACY SKILLS** include: Compare and contrast, question meaning, predict, identify patterns, note similarities and differences, establish cause and effect, infer, summarize, and communicate through oral, written, graphic, or technological means.

for everything and forecloses learning to think. If too much of the thinking required to wrestle out new knowledge is done for students, the result could be students who pass tests but have not learned to think and will quickly forget much of the memorized material (Nodding, 2009). To generate cognitive skills, educators need to understand the implications of brain-based instruction and emphasize cognitive strategies, such as high-level thinking, questioning, analogous and comparative thinking, summarization, and inference.

## BRAIN-BASED INSTRUCTION

Brain-based instruction draws from neurology, psychology, technology, and pedagogy to equip educators to engage students in deeper understanding. In a nurturing learning environment, instructional decisions that stem from brain-based research help students

understand more about their own brainpower—thinking more critically about their own thinking. While cautiously waiting to determine which brain-based discoveries stand the test to time, many current conclusions deserve attention. Consider the following brief summary of brain-based information that provides promising insights for classroom practice (Figure 4.2).

### MODEL THINKING ALOUD

Model your applications of comprehension and reasoning strategies by thinking aloud as you read or problem solve. Express contextual comments such as: "That did not work out the way I wanted, so I have to change...," or "I do not understand that idea, so I need to read it again." Students benefit when you model cognitive strategies in process.

Kingore, B. (2013). *Rigor and Engagement for Growing Minds*. Austin, TX: PA Publishing.

FIGURE 4.2:
# BRAIN-BASED LEARNING

✦ *WE HAVE THE ABILITY TO LEARN NEW THINGS OUR ENTIRE LIFE.* Medina (2009), a molecular biologist, states that researchers did not know this until five or six years ago. Today, the prevailing notion is that some parts of the brain can grow new connections and strengthen existing connections throughout our lives.

✦ *THE GROWTH OF THE PREFRONTAL CORTEX (PFC) IS GREATEST BETWEEN THE AGES OF 8 AND 16.* High-order thinking functions develop in the PFC. Stimulating these higher-brain networks during this stage of rapid development strongly influences students' lifelong executive functions of judgment, critical analysis, relational thinking, and prediction. Growth continues through age 25 before slowing, but we never totally lose our ability to change our brains (Sousa, 2010; Willis, 2011).

✦ *INTELLIGENCE IS NOT FIXED.* The brain is a muscle that improves with use, building brain-power through the very act of learning (Dweck, 2006). Challenging learning experiences with appropriate support stretch thinking muscles. To experience challenge, however, students must encounter a task or situation beyond current capability, suggesting that high-ability students may not build brainpower when limited to core curriculum experiences.

✦ *THE BRAIN ACTIVELY ATTENDS TO CONCENTRATED INFORMATION FOR EIGHT TO FIFTEEN MINUTES.* After fifteen minutes or less, the brain becomes distracted with daydreaming or attending to external stimuli (Medina, 2009; Sousa, 2010; Willis, 2011). Hence, factual lectures should be broken into shorter segments and interspersed with student application or interaction.

✦ *THE BRAIN CAN ONLY FOCUS ON ONE THING AT A TIME.* When it seems as if we are focusing on more than one thing, we are actually quickly switching between tasks. This rebuts the popular idea of multi-tasking (Medina, 2009; Tokuhama-Espinosa, 2010).

✦ *HEALTHY SOCIAL AND EMOTIONAL LEARNING IS PARAMOUNT TO ACHIEVEMENT.* When students feel anxious, the amygdala blocks learning by scrambling learning circuits and switching information to the lower 80 percent of brain used by animals for survival, instead of using the 20 percent of the PFC where higher learning occurs (Willis 2011). When teachers use strategies providing emotional comfort and pleasure as well as knowledge, students gain emotional resilience and learn more efficiently at higher cognitive levels (Willis, 2007a).

✦ *FEEDBACK IS A MAINSPRING OF LEARNING.* Effective feedback guides student learning. Use formative assessment to check for advanced insights or misconceptions early and often in a segment of learning, and offer effort-based encouragement rather than discouragement (Dweck, 2010).

Kingore, B. (2013). *Rigor and Engagement for Growing Minds.* Austin, TX: PA Publishing.

◆ **PHYSICAL EXERCISE BOOSTS BRAINPOWER.** More cardio-vascular activity during the day increases the flow of oxygen-rich blood to the brain, heightening students' ability to concentrate. (Early childhood and kindergarten teachers have always seemed to know this!). Medina (2009) urges schools to combine fitness with academics to boost brainpower.

◆ **NOVELTY SHIFTS THE BRAIN TO FULL ATTENTION.** Willis (2010; 2011) explains that the reticular activating system (RAS) filters incoming stimuli, deciding if information deserves autopilot (daydreaming or off-task) or full attention. Changes in the learning environment and instruction can pique children's curiosity and reactivate the brain. Novelty is an attention-grabber for the brain. Bring new energy to a lesson with art, movement, music, students' interests, color, and surprise, such as walking backwards while discussing negative numbers (Willis, 2011).

◆ **SENSE AND MEANING ARM UNDERSTANDING.** Students exhibit significantly more brain activity and a dramatic improvement in retention when learning makes sense and is relevant to the individual. Effective teachers realize that they do not teach information and meaning; they facilitate so students develop meaning in the information they learn (Sousa & Tomlinson, 2010). Superior learning occurs when classroom experiences are relevant to students' lives, interests, and experiences (Willis, 2007a).

◆ **INFORMATION IS RETAINED AND RETRIEVED ONLY WHEN APPLIED OR ACTED UPON.** Memorized information will not build long-term neural networks in the PFC, where higher order thinking occurs, unless students have the opportunity to construct relationships to their prior knowledge and/or apply new learning to new situations (Sousa & Tomlinson, 2010; Willis, 2011; Wolfe, 2010). Through a variety of active mental manipulations with prior knowledge, new information becomes incorporated into the established neural network of previously acquired related memory and leads to better retention (Sousa & Tomlinson, 2010).

◆ **JOYFUL LEARNING PROMOTES ATTENTION AND RETENTION.** When classroom activities have pleasurable associations linked with learning, the brain releases dopamine—a neurotransmitter that stimulates the memory centers and promotes increased, focused attention (Willis, 2007b).

> *For students to be best prepared for the opportunities and challenges awaiting them, they need to develop their highest thinking skills—the brain's executive functions. These higher-order neural networks are undergoing their most rapid development during the school years, and teachers are in the best position to promote the activation of these circuits.*
>
> *—Willis, 2011*

Kingore, B. (2013). *Rigor and Engagement for Growing Minds.* Austin, TX: PA Publishing.

## HIGH-LEVEL THINKING

The CCSS calls for teachers to incorporate rigorous content in which all students apply knowledge through higher-order thinking skills. High-level thinking (using the taxonomy of thinking developed by Benjamin Bloom) is widely incorporated. Yet, two specific problems emerge. The first problem concerns the terminology typically used to describe the thinking levels during informal discussions. Many educators refer to low-level versus high-level thinking to contrast curriculum applications. In multiple contexts, however, the term *low-level* is associated as something less desirable or unacceptable, so the implication is that low-level thinking is inappropriate. Of course, the reality is that no level of thinking should be avoided. Beginning levels of thinking are foundational; even high-ability people cannot process content at a high level when they know nothing about the subject.

A second problem results from educational resources that use Bloom's taxonomy to differentiate the instruction by suggesting that teachers implement *remember, understand,* and *apply* for struggling to grade-level students while requiring *analyze, evaluate,* and *create* for grade-level to high-ability students. Reconsider this interpretation. Wiggins and McTighe (2005) remind us that knowledge and comprehension are necessary but not sufficient elements of understanding for long-term retention and achievement. All students can and should be involved in high-level thinking as often as possible to

promote lifelong learning. Hence, I consider three points crucial when we intend to generate cognitive skills.

### GENERATE COGNITIVE SKILLS: KEY POINTS

✓ Filter our terminology. Refer to Bloom's taxonomy as eliciting *beginning*-to-high levels of thinking rather than *low*-to-high levels.
✓ Engage all students in the process of high-level thinking as frequently as feasible.
✓ Raise the complexity and depth of high-level thinking for advanced students. For example, analytical thinking can concern a concrete or more complex and abstract concept.

*Promote High-level Thinking*

•

*High-level thinking is more engaging as it invites students to interpret, relate, and apply the content rather than only know the content.*

Levels of thinking are classified in a hierarchy, but should also be tiered to apply complexity and depth at conceptual levels of thinking. Specifically, all students need to operate at high-levels of thinking with some addressing higher thinking in concrete and scaffolded ways while others engage in higher-thinking processes with greater complexity and depth in an abstract, multidimensional, undefined situation.

Kingore, B. (2013). *Rigor and Engagement for Growing Minds.* Austin, TX: PA Publishing.

## SUGGESTIONS TO GENERATE COGNITIVE SKILLS

✓ Avoid the use of any curricula or commercial materials that limit struggling learners to beginning-level thinking instead of higher thinking opportunities.

✓ Tier thinking levels to promote an appropriate complexity level for high-ability students as well as on-or-below grade-level students in mixed-ability classrooms.

✓ Differentiate instruction by tiering applications of *analyze, evaluate,* and *create* to ensure simpler, concrete applications as needed as well as more complex, conceptually-abstract adaptations when feasible.

Examples pertaining to social studies and math, Figures 4.3 and 4.4 respectfully, compare analytical tasks at two tiers of complexity. Both tiers require students to analyze; however, Tier I incorporates somewhat simpler and more concrete analytical tasks when compared to the analytical challenges prompted by Tier II. Tier I provides relevant high-level thinking opportunities for all students. These are valuable prompts to engage students in analytical responses to content. Simultaneously, Tier II invites adaptations with greater complexity through more sophisticated information and processing of content. Tier II increases the likelihood that high-ability students are processing more complex content with more complex thinking to construct new meanings. When tiering high-level thinking, promote complex and in-depth responses from high-ability students as you generate cognitive skills for all learners.

### FIGURE 4.3:
### TIERED THINKING IN SOCIAL STUDIES

| *Tier 1* ANALYSIS TIER 1 | *Tier 2* ANALYSIS TIER 2 |
|---|---|
| • What aspects of the topography encouraged _____ to settle in _____? | • Discuss the historical event from the perspectives of _____ and _____. |
| • Explain three similarities and differences about the needs of different cultures for _____. | • Using past and present conditions, predict future cultural trends for _____. |
| • Use a Venn diagram to compare _____ and _____. | • Use a three-way Venn to compare the concepts of _____, _____, and _____. |
| • What do the artifacts of _____ imply about their civilization? | • Construct complex generalizations with analogies comparing two concepts with related items in different locations. |
| • Explain how the _____ of the past influence today's _____. | • Does history repeat itself? Compare this event to another time this happened and forecast future probabilities. |

Kingore, B. (2013). *Rigor and Engagement for Growing Minds.* Austin, TX: PA Publishing.

### FIGURE 4.4:
### TIERED THINKING IN MATH

| *Tier 1* ANALYSIS TIER 1 | *Tier 2* ANALYSIS TIER 2 |
|---|---|
| • Explain addition to someone who does not understand. | • Create analogies comparing the concepts of addition, subtraction, and multiplication. |
| • Add one to each number in this problem. Tell me three things you notice. | • Explain three patterns you notice about even or odd numbers in addition problems. |
| • Use math terminology to write a description of this polygon. | • Use a three-way Venn to compare polygons. Conclude with the concept of a polygon. |
| • Identify the flaw in this problem and explain how to correct it. | • Explain three conclusions you can make from this problem. |
| • Make a graph comparing _____ to _____. | • Collect 10 examples of how graphs are used outside of school and then generalize the function and application of graphs. |

Kingore, B. (2013). *Rigor and Engagement for Growing Minds.* Austin, TX: PA Publishing.

Kingore, B. (2013). *Rigor and Engagement for Growing Minds.* Austin, TX: PA Publishing.

### WAIT TIME

Remember the importance of wait time to promote high-level thinking. When asking questions requiring high-level thinking, pause appropriately to allow time for reflection and analysis. Model that reasoning takes time and that it is an intelligent behavior to think and plan responses before speaking.

### WHAT'S THE FLAW?

Students work in pairs to analyze each incorrect answer in a multiple-choice question to identify and discuss the flawed reasoning that makes each wrong.

### UNDERSTANDING TERMINOLOGY

Challenge students to use the language of high-level thinking and logical reasoning in their communication and class discussions. Purposefully using terminology such as *analyze, prioritize, use logic to, identify a new relationship,* and *interpret* in contextual conversations reinforces vocabulary development and the process of their reasoning.

# CREATIVE THINKING

Anderson & Krathwohl (2001) adapted Benjamin Bloom's taxonomy by changing the term of *synthesis* to the active verb *create* and elevating it to the highest level of intellectual functioning. Consequently, creative thinking and creative problem solving are the ultimate manifestation of critical thinking and personal connections. This elevation of creativity in problem solving is supported by future-oriented observations of learning demands and highlights the important role of creative thinking in solving society's increasingly complex problems to uplift the quality of life. In today's business or college setting, people confront broad objectives and are expected to conceive the best way to achieve. There are no predefined answers, only profitable or unprofitable strategies (Wagner, 2010). A respect for the critical function of creative thinking parallels the emphasis of the CCSS for adaptation of current ideas to prepare for future academic and workplace cultures. This focus moves educational standards from a major concern for testing content toward understanding how instruction influences students' life after high school.

### CREATIVE THINKING PROMPTS

#### • VERBS FOR CREATIVE THINKING

Specific verbs trigger creativity and promote personal adaptations of prior knowledge. Incorporate words from the list of verbs in Figure 4.5 to foster students' intellectual play with alternative perspectives, patterns, and connections among elements and ideas. The verbs can switch-on creative problem solving, inviting students to consider prior information in new ways, and thus promote originality, adaptation, and unique solutions or decisions.

• THINK STRIPS

Think strips are ready-to-use sentence stems children use to prime their creative thinking. To stimulate high-level thinking and *out-of-the-box* problem solving, provide one or more of the strips to students who are engaged in problem solving, flexible group tasks, or reading silently. Students can choose to use either side of a strip to promote written or oral responses as they think about the content at higher levels and in more diverse ways.

On cardstock or colored paper, write sentence stems using critical and creative thinking prompts, such as those shown in Figure 4.6. Duplicate the stems back-to-back and cut them into individual strips in such a way that a different sentence stem is on the front and the back of each strip. (Refer to the CD for full-page reproducible figures.)

In classes with children who speak more than one language, vary the Think Strips by duplicating a critical or creative thinking stem in English on the front of the strip and the same thinking prompt in a second language on the back of the strip, as Figures 4.6 and 4.7 illustrate for English and Spanish.

## FIGURE 4.5:
# VERBS THAT PROMOTE CREATIVE THINKING

| | | | |
|---|---|---|---|
| Abstract | Edit | Mold | Substitute |
| Adapt | Elaborate | Multiply | Subtract |
| Add/adjust | Eliminate | Observe | Switch |
| Arrange | Extend | Organize | Symbolize |
| Balance | Extrude | Originate | Transfigure |
| Bend | Formulate | Predict | Transform |
| Breakdown | Frame | Rearrange | Translate |
| Combine | Illustrate | Recast | Transpose |
| Complement | Imagine | Reconsider | Turn |
| Construct | Increase | Redefine | Unify |
| Convert | Integrate | Refine | Vary |
| Decrease | Interchange | Relate | Visualize |
| Design | Invert | Reorder | |
| Devise | Magnify | Reverse | |
| Diagram | Maximize | Rotate | |
| Disguise | Minimize | Separate | |
| Dissect | Modulate | Shift | |
| Distort | Morph | Stretch | |

Kingore, B. (2013). *Rigor and Engagement for Growing Minds.* Austin, TX: PA Publishing.

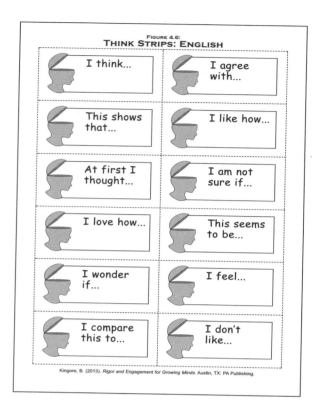

**FIGURE 4.6:**
**THINK STRIPS: ENGLISH**

| I think... | I agree with... |
| This shows that... | I like how... |
| At first I thought... | I am not sure if... |
| I love how... | This seems to be... |
| I wonder if... | I feel... |
| I compare this to... | I don't like... |

Kingore, B. (2013). *Rigor and Engagement for Growing Minds.* Austin, TX: PA Publishing.

**FIGURE 4.7:**
**THINK STRIPS: SPANISH**

| Yo pienso... | Yo concuerdo con... |
| Esto muestra que... | Me gusta como... |
| Al principio yo pensé que... | No estoy seguro si... |
| Yo amo como... | Esto parece ser... |
| Me pregunto si... | Yo siento... |
| Yo compare esto a... | No me gusta... |

Kingore, B. (2013). *Rigor and Engagement for Growing Minds.* Austin, TX: PA Publishing.

This variation respects both languages and enables all students to explore learning in more than one language. As one English-speaking student exclaimed: "I can read English and Spanish!"

**Get going!**

**RANKING**

Ranking content is a higher cognitive task. Follow-up brainstorming or the development of multiple solutions by asking students to rank the responses. Extensive high-level thinking results as students must establish ranking criteria and engage in academic conversations to reach decisions.

**Get going!**

**EVERY STUDENT ENGAGED**

When problem solving as a class, engage everyone in the reasoning process, adaptations, and active listening. Randomly select name cards to determine who to call on to either paraphrase classmates' responses or build on previously shared ideas.

## QUESTIONING

A generation ago, classroom questioning involved the teacher asking students questions to determine who knew or who did not know predetermined answers. Today, the greater purpose

Generating
Cognitive Skills

of questioning is to gather information that guides our instruction and furthers students' high-level thinking. Asking: "How did you accomplish that?" or "How did you figure that out?" requires students to bring their thinking to a conscience level and discuss a current strategy or action that they can then invoke at a different time for refining or application.

During direct instruction, guided applications, and student-inquiry projects, our questions help students refine their thinking as we assess their perceptions, misconceptions, and depth of information. Thus, questioning provides formative assessment information that enables us to productively adjust the pace and level of instruction. Figure 4.8 illustrates the kind of questions asked in rigorous learning environments to ratchet up students' thinking before, during, and after instruction. These questions also recognize that students have information and insights to share if only we ask. In many learning situations, students are the experts who know what they are doing, and we ask questions to understand their process.

Effective questioning requires us to know our students well. Limit questioning to content you believe students should understand. This is not intended to imply that we ask simple questions; rather, we ask questions most relevant to the content for which students are responsible. Questioning is too stressful when students feel they risk looking foolish in front of others.

We invite students to ask questions, but students' willingness to do so is less related to our encouraging them to pose questions than it is to our response when they ask ques-

tions. Our well-intended responses can actually stifle initiatives. For example, praising a student for a great question can deter others from posing questions because their questions may not be as great, and not allowing enough time for students' responses communicates that questions are not welcomed. Figure 4.9 provides strategies to upgrade our level of questioning.

## TEACHING QUESTION FORMATION

Several instructional strategies promote questioning and teach question formation to students. Question That and Question the Number are two strategies that productively engage students in question formation.

### • QUESTION THAT

Question That is an interactive technique proven quite effective in numerous classrooms to blend student question formation with applications of skills and content. Post a different content-related answer each day, such as *14%* to signal a math question or *Nelson Mandela* to signal a social sciences question. Students write an appropriate, meaningful question requiring that answer, and post their responses for peer scrutiny.

To organize the process, place posters around the room with a place at the top for the answer of the day. The poster is sized to accommodate a standard sticky note so students can write their question on the note and place it directly on a poster. Position the posters so students leave their seats to post questions. Encourage comparative thinking as students are quite interested in reading classmates' responses. Academic conversations about the topic often ensue regarding any

Kingore, B. (2013). *Rigor and Engagement for Growing Minds.* Austin, TX: PA Publishing.

FIGURE 4.8:

# QUESTIONING FOR HIGH-LEVEL THINKING

Engaged students should elaborate, clarify, and support ideas with examples, paraphrase as they build on and question input from others, and synthesize and reach decisions as group work concludes. Provide time for academic conversations so students use key vocabulary in context, learn from one another, benefit from multiple points of view, and extend meaning beyond prior knowledge. To facilitate critical and creative thinking, ask these questions as you interact with students or provide a selection of these questions as guides to small groups applying respectful questioning.

- "Tell me about your work."
- "What do you already know and understand about this?"
- "How would you _____?"
- "Why did you _____?"
- "How do you know _____?"
- "How did you decide whether _____?"
- "Describe what you did."

### AS STUDENTS WORK, ASK...

- "Elaborate what you mean."
- "How did you figure that out?"
- "Why do you think that?"
- "Is that a reasonable answer?  Why?"
- "What if _____?"
- "How is this like _____?"
- "How could you do this another way? "
- "What is a significant question you would ask? "
- "Identify a potential problem or issue."

### AFTER STUDENTS FINISH, ASK...

- "How did you arrive at your answer?"
- "What evidence do you have to support that?"
- "Who might have a different perspective? Why?"
- "How might someone get the same answer but by a different way of reasoning?"
- "How would you explain this to someone else?"
- "What question is essential to this topic?"
- "How could you use this to _____?"
- "What is the most important thing you learned?"
- "What do you not understand?"
- "What is something you are doing to help yourself learn?"
- "Does this lead you to another question or problem? Explain."

Kingore, B. (2013). *Rigor and Engagement for Growing Minds.* Austin, TX: PA Publishing.

## FIGURE 4.9:
# STRATEGIES FOR HIGH-LEVEL THINKING

◆ **RESPOND TO STUDENTS' QUESTIONS WITH A PROBING QUESTION.** This strategy compels students to process their own reasoning: "Why do you think that is so?" "Why not?" "What is another way?" "What is a question you have not answered yet?"

◆ **ASK HYPOTHETICAL QUESTIONS.** "What might happen if we do not resolve fossil fuel issues?" "What if all money was coins and no paper money was allowed?" "What if school buses were black?" Hypothetical questions are not meant to be humorous; they are intended to incorporate content in a new way and challenge students to use logical reasoning and abstract thinking.

◆ **ENCOURAGE REASONING IN REVERSE.** Propose that this kind of questioning and reasoning is what forensic investigators do to solve crimes and forensic anthropologists use to analyze ancient cultures. "How might it help our thinking if we started with this solution (or result) and then worked backwards?"

◆ **INVOKE DIFFERENT POINTS OF VIEW.** Ask questions that invite students to ponder information from more than one perspective or purposely switch from the typical point of view.

◆ **MODEL THAT YOU VALUE INPUT.** Students are more inclined to risk asking a question when they perceive that we value their input more than evaluate it. For this reason, our most productive response to a student's question is to recognize the act of questioning. "Thank you for making us think about that," "I'm glad you are thinking about that." Then, guide the response to meaningful levels by asking students to support their ideas and open-up the question for others to build on.

◆ **PROVIDE A RESCUE.** Students need to know that support is available if they risk failure or deadlock. Preplan your reactions when students cannot answer a question or when the answer is wrong. For example, honor the student for thinking and recognize any part of the response that is correct. Ask the student to signal you when prepared with a response, and then absolutely return to that student to consider the thought-out comeback.

◆ **AVOID ASKING: "DOES ANYONE HAVE A QUESTION?"** Teachers are often met with blank stares when we ask that. Wolfe (2012) reminds us that brains must be primed to pay attention and decipher what is meaningful. Therefore, we waste time asking for questions without priming the brain. A more productive strategy is to engage students' background understanding before asking for questions. Specifically, invite students to discuss possible questions with a shoulder partner for a minute. Then, ask the group: "What possible questions emerged from your thinking?" Being diplomatic in word choices and tone encourages students to participate.

Kingore, B. (2013). *Rigor and Engagement for Growing Minds.* Austin, TX: PA Publishing.

unexpected questions or more thoughtful questions that extend beyond the obvious. This learning experience fosters high-level thinking, as students must understand the content and process information before reasoning in reverse to form a question.

Teachers are sometimes surprised to realize that students have difficulty posing appropriate questions in this format. Initially, some students ask questions that contain the answer while others pose a statement instead of a question. Question That provides an opportunity to practice question formation in a manner that is interesting and relevant to many children. Increase the complexity of the task by requiring students to demonstrate specific skills in their question. For example, in Figure 4.10: "The answer is *Cinderella*. Apply the skills of inference, cause-effect, or sequence in your question."

### • QUESTION THAT NUMBER

Present a math word problem that has the task question omitted from the end, as in the example shown below. Based on the information presented in the word problem, students work in pairs to write a possible question to respond to each of the provided multiple-choice answers. For each provided answer, students have to collaborate to determine: "If this choice is the correct answer, what is the mathematical question?" In many cases, there is more than one possible question, promoting students' thinking beyond a predetermined answer.

When using this technique, students read critically, apply mathematical skills and vocabulary in their discussions, analyze the information in the problem more carefully, and apply multiple math principles and concepts to

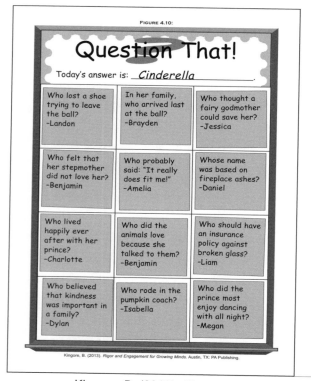

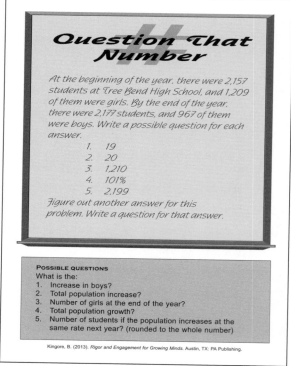

form their questions. Students also conclude a relevant test-taking generalization: rather than only projecting random numbers, test-makers design multiple-choice responses based on the most common errors students make.

## STUDENT-GENERATED QUESTIONS

Questioning is central to intellectual pursuits, so the focus in a rigorous learning environment switches from students answering questions to students posing questions that activate their curiosity. While many resources address different types of questions, such as convergent, divergent, factual, and evaluative, it is possibly more important to address the issue of the competency and skill by which students pose quality questions. Rigorous instruction should challenge students to pose essential questions relevant to the real world more than basic questions with simple answers.

The technique of student-generated questions improves comprehension (Duke, 2004). Rather than answer a question from the teacher or text, a higher-level of thinking may be required when students pose relevant questions for peers to answer. Indeed, many students are motivated to put forth more effort when they are developing questions peers must answer. Working in groups of two or three, students review the text, compare class notes, and discuss possible questions before being able to formulate their questions.

Ensure an authentic purpose for these questions by having students generate questions for class discussions, to post for peer scrutiny online or in the classroom, and even for use on tests and quizzes. At best, the questions should incorporate relevant academic vocabulary and be concept-based instead of more simple detail questions. Caution students to avoid asking questions that can be answered with a single word since elaboration reveals more thinking. Alert students to focus on generating questions that call for a deeper level of understanding, avoiding questions that be answered by others not focusing on the content.

Increase applications of high-level thinking by requiring students to prepare a list of the components of the strongest answer they expect from classmates in response to their generated question. During a class discussion, students use their planned-response components to facilitate their interactions with peers. For example, in response to a proposed answer, the group could respond, "Absolutely, that is part of the answer. What else can you add?"

Socratic seminars—a method of intellectual engagement founded upon questioning skills—is another technique providing rich opportunities to model and apply the art of questioning. Implement Socratic seminars in which students take the leadership roles in preparing and conducting the seminars. In today's classrooms, the intent is for students to think critically, address ambiguity of content and thinking, analyze multiple possibilities, and communicate among themselves with clarity, confidence, and respect. Socratic seminars activate those skills. On the internet, you can locate multiple resources and applications using Socratic seminars in a variety of content areas and grade levels.

Kingore, B. (2013). *Rigor and Engagement for Growing Minds.* Austin, TX: PA Publishing.

## APPLICATIONS THAT PROMOTE COGNITIVE SKILLS

### ANALOGIES AND COMPARATIVE THINKING

While no instructional strategy works equally effectively in all situations and with all populations, research results continue to support that identifying similarities and differences is one of the most significant strategies for increasing students' achievement (Dean, Hubbell, Pitler, & Stone, 2012). Since analogies are the most complex format for comparative thinking, they merit particular attention for application by high-ability students.

Analogous thinking is a cognitive process transferring and relating meaning from one subject to another. It fosters students' abstract thinking, requiring the ability to go beyond literal interpretations and employ problem-solving skills. It is complex because it involves the recognition of abstract relationships and extends beyond the establishment of the more literal similarities and differences expected on graphic organizers, such as concept maps and Venn diagrams. When presented with an analogy, students must interpret the abstract connection between two items. Analogies, then, are a test of understanding for both items as students must wrestle with how these seemingly dissimilar items are related or similar. As a result of that process, students deepen personal understanding and construct new meaning. Analogous thinking plays a significant role in problem solving, decision-making, perception, memory, creativity, emotional connections, and communication.

*Analogies Promote Cognitive Skills*

•

*Analogies facilitate long-term memory as they enable students to make meaningful connections instead of focus on memorizing facts.*

### • ORAL ANALOGIES

While formal analogy formats (A:B::C:D) may be too complex for young children, oral analogies are proven to work well with young high-ability learners. Oral analogies emphasize high-level thinking through the verbal communication of reasoning. They employ the problem-solving approach of synectics that some teachers refer to as *linking thinking* because it prompts students' to make new connections to content.

An oral analogy is a comparative thinking device that invites students to verbally compare a concrete item with current content and is usually expressed as a simile or metaphor. For example, hold up a picture or object the children clearly recognize and then request which connections they can make to their present topic of study.
- "How is this water bottle like our bodies?"
- "How is a mammal like a plant?"
- "How is this calendar like mathematics?"
- "How is the space station like a planet?"

Encouraging multiple responses increases the likelihood of in-depth thinking and models that there is often more than one potentially correct idea to share. With young children, initial responses are typically simple and concrete but may prompt others to build on those ideas with more complex, abstract answers.

It is rewarding as new and surprising solutions emerge. For example, in a kindergarten class where children were fascinated with dinosaurs, I asked the children how my paper coffee cup was like anything they knew about dinosaurs. After a thoughtful pause, the responses ranged from children comparing a cup and dinosaurs through colors and round shapes to a child using the term *non-biodegradable* to compare how the styrofoam cup was like dinosaur fossils.

## • DIRECT ANALOGIES

Direct analogies are thought-provoking tools to tease out inferences. For example, ask students to pose and explain an analogy expressing how the historical explorer being studied is like different parts of a house or how a scientist is like an item in the laboratory. Analogies facilitate long-term memory as they enable students to create meaningful connections instead of focus on memorizing facts.

Direct analogies are an effective technique to use for review and closure when concluding a lesson because they require students to demonstrate their understanding of the information and apply it in a new context. In this manner, direct analogies provide formative assessment information to guide instructional decisions regarding students' readiness for extensions or the need for clarifications.

Direct analogies are normally presented in a written format with ample time allowed for processing the relationship, inasmuch as the intent is to foster abstract thinking more than

to determine a correct answer. The following examples illustrate potential instructional applications of analogies.

- Provide content-related analogies pertinent to your topic, and facilitate a group discussion reasoning the relationship(s) among the elements.
  - "Blue is to purple as yellow is to green."
  - "Johnson is to Kennedy as Truman is to Roosevelt."

- As students gain experience, provide incomplete analogies that either require students to determine the relationship and select the best word to complete the content analogy or require students to supply missing words. Purposely vary the position of the omitted word(s) to foster students' processing information in different ways.
  - "Judge is to (a. jury; b. robe; c. impartial; d. law) as author is to literate.
  - "Stem is to flower as (a. bark; b. trunk; c. leaf; d. deciduous) is to tree."
  - "John Steinbeck's _____ is a time capsule of the Great Depression just as Harriet Beecher Stowe's _____ is of _____."

- When students write original, direct analogies, teachers often suggest that students include *because* or *when* to explain their thinking and reveal the relationship so others understand. Analogy templates scaffold students' applications.
  - "_____ is like _____ because _____."
  - "_____ _____ is like _____ when _____."
  - "Martin Luther King is like a broken clock because both ran out of time before their work was finished."

Kingore, B. (2013). *Rigor and Engagement for Growing Minds.* Austin, TX: PA Publishing.

## KINDS OF ANALOGY RELATIONSHIPS

When applicable, involve students in concluding some of the kinds of relationships most often used in analogies, such as synonyms, antonyms, opposites, members of a category, part to whole, or function. Discuss with students why it might be useful to understand analogy patterns.

### • PERSONAL ANALOGIES

Personal analogies are a variation of direct analogies in which students connect themselves to a content-related object or topic. This form promotes a social, emotional response to content that increases relevancy.

- "I am like the antagonist when _____."
- "I am like an anthropologist because _____."
- "If I were a graph, I would be _____ because _____."
- "If I were an element of physical science, I would not want to be a _____ because _____."

Challenge students to develop original versions of direct or personal analogies to demonstrate their understanding of content. The following similes and metaphors were posed by a primary, elementary, middle school and high school student, respectively.

- "Addition is like compound words and subtraction is like contractions."
- "I am like a raccoon because I'm curious, busy, and not judged by appearance."

- "Gifted kids are a square light bulb. They are bright, unique, but need a regular bulb base as eventually they have to fit into the real world."
- "Students with different backgrounds and capabilities are like an algebraic equation—both sides look very different, but in reality, they are equal in value."

## SUMMARIZATION

Summarization is a cognitive process that requires students to synthesize information for long-term memory. The mental engagement when identifying textual main ideas and connecting to prior knowledge consolidates any new information into existing memory circuits (Willis, 2011). As students determine the essence of the text in a succinct manner, the brain chunks concepts into long-term memory. Wormeli (2005, 2) suggests that summarization is an underused instructional technique yet shown by research to yield "some of the greatest leaps in comprehension and long-term retention of information." Indeed, extensive research substantiates that summarizing is one of the most significant strategies for increasing students' achievement (Dean, Hubbell, Pitler, & Stone, 2012; Marzano, 2004). Since summarization has such a powerful effect on memory and since high-ability students prefer minimum repetition in learning situations, they benefit when they acquire extensive skill in summarization.

While a summarization is intended to be brief, it must retain the essence of the whole. More than a main idea or key point, a summary must extract the substance of the entire information. In Konigsburg's *Silent to the Bone,* two characters express experiences with a technique that they refer to as *SIAS*–Summary In A Sentence. In reality, this technique only works as a summarization if the sentence elicits explanation and elaboration, such as writing the SIAS and then supporting it through written or verbal explanation. The two characters actually construct summary sentences that stem from their extensive discussions and generalizations of their shared experiences.

Summarization is a cognitive strategy pertinent to most lessons. It remains most relevant when it is implemented with widely varied instructional applications for novelty. Remember that factual lectures should be broken into shorter segments for maximum student attention (Medina, 2009; Sousa, 2010; Willis, 2011). Hence, after eight to fifteen minutes, facilitate a summarization task to guide students' formation of long-term memory before returning to the lecture format. While this process may seem to require more class time, teachers save repetitive instruction later because students retain more of the information. Summarizing at the conclusion of a lesson is a support for all students as everyone's mind lapses from time to time.

It is surprising to many teachers that summarization is quite difficult for numerous students. However, when we analyze the kinds of thinking essential to composing a summary, we can appreciate that it is indeed a cognitively challenging task.

Once students comprehend the written material, they must categorize ideas and sequences to conclude which

relate to a certain concept or character, which are superordinate versus subordinate, and in which part of the text an idea occurs. In so doing, students evaluate what content is most important and what can be deleted while still retaining the essence of the author's message. At that point, students are prepared to compose the summary in a shorter form.

**THINKING SKILLS REQUIRED IN SUMMARIZATION**

Summarization requires students to:

*   Comprehend the written text,
*   Classify data,
*   Evaluate the relative importance of the information,
*   Delete less pertinent content, and
*   Synthesize results into a form considerably shorter than the original.

**COMPREHEND**
**CATEGORIZE**
**EVALUATE**
**DELETE**
**COMPOSE**

• **TEACHING SUMMARIZATION**

The sequence detailed in Figure 4.11 supports students as they learn to construct relevant summaries. Summarization strategies are not intuitive, and students benefit from explicit instruction (Dean et al., 2012). Teachers also need to scaffold summarization for students experiencing difficulty.

*Summary*

•

*Summarization has a significant effect on memory and achievement.*

Kingore, B. (2013). *Rigor and Engagement for Growing Minds.* Austin, TX: PA Publishing.

FIGURE 4.11:
# TEACHING SUMMARIZATION

### 1. BEGINNING—MIDDLE—END

#### Beginning—Middle—End

To ensure that a summary represents the essence of the whole, emphasize the simplest structure of text: the beginning, middle, and end. For each of those three parts, students write two or three sentences to represent the salient information from the beginning, then from the middle, and finally from the end of the text. Stress that every sentence stems from their individual thinking and synthesis; it is not a sentence they copy from the original text. Discuss and compare results to clarify the process and celebrate success.

### 2. TOPIC SENTENCE

#### Beginning—Middle—End + Topic Sentence

A topic sentence is a key to unlock the meaning of the content and explain the author's claim or main idea that the rest of the summary supports and describes further. Since students experience difficulty and waste valuable time trying to determine a topic sentence, have them continue with what they now know well: how to write a beginning, middle, and end. Begin this step by having students summarize the three stages. Then, students revisit their ideas and add a topic sentence at the top. More students are successful composing topic sentences after determining the beginning, middle, and end.

### 3. TRANSITION WORDS

#### Beginning—Middle—End + Topic Sentence + Transition Words

Transition words are the bridges that keep ideas together. They increase fluency by segueing between ideas for continuity. Initially, have students use one of their previously composed summaries to practice inserting a transition word as the first word in each section of their writing. Later, explore different placements of transition words for increased effect.

Work together to organize a collective list of transition words that are highly applicable to summaries. With the class, continue to expand the list over time. Eventually, ask students to determine overused transitions to omit from the list and substitute more sophisticated choices.

#### TRANSITION WORDS

| | | | |
|---|---|---|---|
| • Additionally | • Consequently | • First, next, finally | • On the other hand |
| • As a result | • Conversely | • Furthermore | • Therefore |
| • Before/after | • Even though | • However | • While |

### 4. SUMMARIZATION OF A PROCESS

When students are proficient at writing text summaries, progress to constructing summaries for an academic process that is not text-based, such as a science experiment or math problem-solving task. This leads students to develop the ability to summarize any learning event, hence fostering long-term memory.

Kingore, B. (2013). *Rigor and Engagement for Growing Minds.* Austin, TX: PA Publishing.

### • ASSESSING EFFECTIVE SUMMARIZATION

Identify and discuss which criteria are most significant when evaluating the quality of summarizations, such as the criteria elaborated in Figure 4.12. Guide students to analyze both effective and less-effective examples of summarization to expand their understanding of how to construct better summaries. Use a reverse thinking technique by providing completed summaries that students evaluate in small groups. For example, use the summaries written by students for MacLachlan's *Sarah, Plain and Tall* (Figure 4.13) and challenge the class to conclude which summary is the strongest. Discuss the evaluative criteria that influenced their thinking about each summary.

### CAUTIONS CONCERNING SUMMARIZATION INSTRUCTION

✓ Begin with a shorter length of text so the process can be taught in a more reasonable amount of class time. Progress to longer discourse when appropriate.

✓ Model and repeatedly practice one step at a time, continuing over time. When students feel comfortable and are proficient at one step, add the next.

✓ Learning to summarize is a skill that progresses with time and multiple applications. It is not a skill that most student master easily.

## FIGURE 4.12:
# ASSESSING SUMMARIZATION

| | |
|---|---|
| *Accuracy* | "Is the information accurate and complete?" |
| *Originality* | "Are these my own words? Is my paraphrasing appropriate?" |
| *Value* | "Could someone gain a basic understanding and valid overview of the subject from this summary? Does it relate what is most important to the author?" |
| *Organization* | "Is the information sequenced correctly to communicate the original information?" |
| *Length* | "Are all of the key elements included? Is it too narrow or broad? Is it too long?" |
| *Opinion free* | "Do I report the essence of the content without distortion, opinion, or bias?" |

Summarize

## FIGURE 4.13:
# STUDENT SUMMARIES

### *SARAH, PLAIN AND TALL*
#### BY PATRICIA MACLACHLAN

1. Caleb and Anna live with their father in their prairie home. When their father invites a mail order bride to live with them, Caleb and Anna are worried and then fascinated by her. She is nice to them and I believe they learn to care about her. They hope that she will stay, and they want to make her happy too.

2. A lonely man with two children places an ad in the newspaper for a mail-order bride. Sarah Elizabeth Wheaton describes herself as plain and tall. She arrives from Maine to stay with the father and his children in their prairie home. Sarah misses her home and her life by the sea. The children miss their mother and their life before she died.

3. The children of a widower miss their mother and the happiness of a complete family. Their father shares the news that a mail-order bride from Maine is coming to live with them in their home on the prairie. Sarah is plain and tall and misses her home by the sea. Over time, the family learns to love her, and they find ways to help meet each others' needs.

### FLAWED SUMMARIES

Randomly assign each group a different summary criterion, such as those in Figure 4.12. Each group collaborates to write a summary of the current topic, purposely incorporating errors based on that criterion. Later, all groups share and compare the summaries to identify the flawed criterion in each. Using eight or more groups allows some criteria to be used more than once and decreases students' attempts to guess by eliminating previously used criteria. This application elicits multiple perspectives for summarization and fosters the transfer to long-term memory.

### SIAS

Summary in a sentence, described earlier, could be an appealing and quick summary tool. Students will enjoy having to write only a one-sentence summary instead of a longer discourse. However, the cognitive process they use to derive that sentence will most likely require the high-level thinking intended with summarization. Then, the students compare and discuss their summaries in small groups, during which elaboration and clarification occur naturally.

Kingore, B. (2013). *Rigor and Engagement for Growing Minds.* Austin, TX: PA Publishing.

## FIVE WORDS

Five words is a technique proven effective in numerous class applications. Working in pairs, students ponder, discuss, and then write on sticky-notes the five words they think are most significant to the topic or concept. Post the notes on a wall or board for student comparison. The technique always piques curiosity and evaluative discussions as students explain and defend choices. Extend the concentrated attention to this content by facilitating a group discussion. Record all selected words to establish how frequently each was chosen; perhaps, reach consensus to rank the words most significant to understand this topic. This learning experience:

- Results in comparative and summative thinking.
- Promotes academic conversations and consensus building among students.
- Encourages academic vocabulary and applications of the terminology of a field in context.

## *INFERENCE*

Inference enables students to derive a logical conclusion on the basis of partial evidence and reasoning. It integrates high-level thinking skills such as synthesis, interpretation, logic, and abstract thinking but must be based on evidence collected and carefully analyzed. The analysis required in the process of inference not only reveals the parts within a complex topic but also simultaneously increases the understanding of the whole as we infer additional meaning. Thus, similar to summarization, inference is an example of the mental manipulation that promotes consolidation of new input into existing memory circuits (Willis, 2011).

Inference is a cognitive process skill essential to the conduct of multiple disciplines, such as in science where inference skills allow students to interpret and project conclusions based on the results of their scientific investigations. It plays a significant role in transdisciplinary discussions involving ethics and issues as students infer perspectives, purpose, bias, prejudice and motives. Some may view inferences as guesses, but inferences are actually educated projections accompanied with supporting evidence.

Particularly in science and the social sciences, it is critical to distinguish between observations and inferences. For example, David Macauley's *The Motel of Mysteries* humorously parodies an amateur anthropologist making erroneous inferences about his *observations* regarding an ancient 1985 motel he uncovers in the year 4022. He falls into a shaft, finds a Do Not Disturb sign hanging from the archaic doorknob, and concludes that it is clearly the entrance to a still-sealed burial tomb, thus beginning a series of flawed inferences. Use this book to initiate a lively discussion of the differences and dangers of interchanging inferences and observations.

## • PICTURE PAIRS

Increase students' awareness of their use of inference by implementing a learning experience I call Picture Pairs, described in

Kingore, B. (2013). *Rigor and Engagement for Growing Minds.* Austin, TX: PA Publishing.

Figure 4.14. The task involves students reading descriptions of pictures and inferring what the picture is without viewing it. This task requires a bit of preparation, but the novelty and effect on students' thinking makes it worth the effort.

### • POPCORN RIDDLES

Popcorn is an instant attraction in a classroom. Provide popped kernels for an energized lesson with inference, description, and simile.

Allow each child the option to eat a small sample of popcorn as you brainstorm together ideas to describe popcorn with a variety of words for each of our senses. Organize students' ideas on a five-column senses chart, such as Figure 4.15, encouraging numerous, unique responses. Some students may even choose to consult a thesaurus for more varied word choices.

Provide three kernels to each child and ask them not to eat this popcorn. Students are to secretly select one of their kernels, put a dot on the bottom of it with a colored marker, and then write a popcorn riddle for that chosen popped kernel using Figure 4.16. Challenge them to review the senses chart and select words that allow more creative, unusual connections. They end their riddle with a simile.

Later, students walk about the classroom, read others' riddles, infer which kernel it describes, and then peek under the popcorn piece to see if they are correct. Conclude the learning experience by discussing which words guided their inferences, and sharing favorite similes.

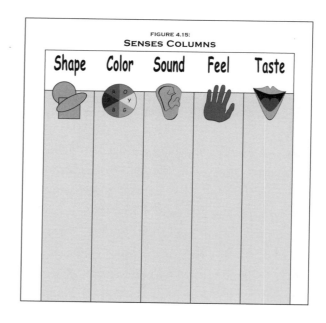

FIGURE 4.15:
SENSES COLUMNS

| Shape | Color | Sound | Feel | Taste |

FIGURE 4.16:
POPCORN RIDDLES

I am _____ and _____ .
I am not _____ or _____ .
I look like _____ .

Which one am I?

*Get going!*

### CONTRASTING OBSERVATION AND INFERENCE

Students fold a paper in half, writing *observations* on one half and *inferences* on the other. Then, they record sentences explaining their observations and inferences about an event or process, such as watching the life in an aquarium or viewing a brief content-related video. After opportunities for discussion and comparison, facilitate students' clarification of the differences between the terms *observation* and *inference*.

Kingore, B. (2013). *Rigor and Engagement for Growing Minds.* Austin, TX: PA Publishing.

FIGURE 4.14:
# PICTURE PAIRS

1. Collect matching pairs of pictures relevant to your content. Place one picture in each envelope and number the envelopes in sequence in such a way that one set of pictures has even numbers and the matching pictures are odd numbers. This numbering system enables you to keep track of the matching pairs.

2. Students work in groups of two or three, and each group receives one envelope. Tell students that the name of the activity is *Pictures Worth Less-Than-1000 Words* so you don't reveal the punch line.

3. Caution the groups to keep their pictures hidden from others so no one sees what your group is describing. Since pictures may have content on both sides, tell the groups: "If your picture is folded, you are to describe the picture on the inside as you open the picture."

4. Ask students to write a paragraph describing the picture without specifically naming it. Post the following sequence or provide a copy to each group to scaffold their process and produce stronger paragraphs. (The CD includes a page of the following directions for students.)

### PICTURES WORTH LESS-THAN-1000 WORDS

a. List two prominent nouns in this picture. Rename them to be accurate but not obvious.

b. List two or three verbs. Add an adverb or adverbial phrase to each.

c. List three to five adjectives. Elaborate each into a descriptive phrase.

d. On a separate page, combine these ideas into a written paragraph about the picture that causes readers to infer the exact subject or scene.

5. Tell the groups: "When you finish, write the envelope's number at the top of your paragraph. Later, we will walk around, read each others' descriptions, and try to figure out each picture without looking at it."

6. Later, each group moves about, reading a description, recording the number of the paragraph, and writing beside each numeral their inference of what the picture shows. Students are intrigued to read and infer a picture's content without viewing it.

### CONCLUSION

Determine one of the numbers for which several groups completed the inference activity. Ask the group who wrote that numbered description to read their paragraph. Then, ask each responding group to tell what they inferred and compare the results. Continue sharing other numbered paragraphs as interest and time permits or until someone begins to question if their group had the same picture.

Reveal that each group has a picture that matches another. Combine the groups with matching pictures to compare and contrast their written responses. Suggest that the groups find one thing similar and one thing different on their written responses. As a class, identify clues that guided their inferences. Also, discuss perspective as an influence in writing style.

Kingore, B. (2013). *Rigor and Engagement for Growing Minds.* Austin, TX: PA Publishing.

FIGURE 4.17:
# THINKING REFLECTIVELY

## 1. IDEAS

Identify two or more ideas you intend to apply immediately.

## 2. A ROUND OF APPLAUSE TO VALIDATE AND CELEBRATE YOUR CURRENT PRACTICES

*An effective technique or learning experience I incorporate
in my instruction to generate cognitive skills is:*

## 3. SHOP TALK

*It is engaging and often exciting to talk shop with a valued colleague. Putting
your heads together produces ideas that may not have developed alone.*

Talk with a colleague about any learning experiences involving analogies, summarization, or inference that interest you and have a high likelihood to enhance opportunities for your students to construct deeper meaning.

✓ List those that have immediate appeal to engage students in your classes.

✓ Pick one for each of you to implement. Later, meet again to mutually enjoy your students' responses, share results, and brainstorm more effective or additional applications.

Kingore, B. (2013). *Rigor and Engagement for Growing Minds.* Austin, TX: PA Publishing.

# Chapter 5
# Orchestrating Support Systems and Scaffolding Success

Academic rigor is driven by high expectations for students, but it requires educators to build scaffolding and provide feedback to enable students to fulfill those expectations. Students benefit from support for their efforts to learn as well as alternatives for assistance, feedback, and encouragement when you are not available. Support systems respond to students' efforts to learn by bridging the gap between what is known and what needs to be learned. Effective support systems involve adults, peers, and differentiated strategies responding to all students, as there are occasions when even the most resilient students need support.

While all students need support in learning environments, the degree and kind of support varies in response to individual students and the academic opportunities they have

*Orchestrate Support*

•

*Support systems bridge the gap between what is known and what needs to be learned.*

experienced. Many students need support to master basic competencies while high-ability students need support to extend learning beyond core curriculum. The instructional pace for some students is most productive when they experience more examples and opportunities for guided practice; high-ability learners frequently require an accelerated pace of instruction because they previously mastered instructional targets or reached mastery with minimum repetitions. Thus, while all students benefit from some similar support-system strategies, high-ability students require certain strategies that significantly differ from the needs of other students. Figure 5.1 compares several examples of the kinds of support strategies teachers employ to benefit struggling students compared to the support teachers offer to enhance the achievement of high-ability students.

FIGURE 5.1:

# Instructional Support Strategies in Mixed-Ability Classrooms

| Strategies for *Struggling Students* | Strategies for *All Students* | Strategies for *Highly Capable Students* |
|---|---|---|
| ◆ Organize peer tutors and aides for more individualized support. | ◆ Develop academic vocabulary to enhance comprehension and cognitive processing. | ◆ When feasible, accelerate instructional pace and level to avoid intellectual stagnation. |
| ◆ Provide additional time and opportunities for incubation and guided practice. | ◆ Foster critical thinking and explanation to promote deeper understanding. | ◆ Allow self-nomination and student choice for replacement tasks. |
| ◆ Scaffold core curriculum lessons. | ◆ Facilitate the summarization of content and processes to enhance understanding and long-term memory. | ◆ Solicit mentors either on-site or long-distance through technology. |
| ◆ Record directions and explanations of the process or product that students can reference and re-read as needed. | ◆ Form interest groups so students mutually engage each other in personally relevant content. | ◆ Ensure access to intellectual peers in class or across classrooms. |
| ◆ Highlight key sentences and vocabulary in significant text to designate the most important information. | ◆ Use flexible groups for discussions, problem solving, and hands-on applications to maintain a dynamic learning environment. | ◆ Prompt students to transcend core curriculum through investigations of issues related to current topics or concepts. |
| ◆ Post a copy of lecture notes online or in the classroom for students to review. | ◆ Provide online or classroom videos of lecture information so students can learn at their own pace. | ◆ Provide websites and resources that promote complexity, depth, and abstract thinking while enabling access to content that exceeds grade-level. |

Kingore, B. (2013). *Rigor and Engagement for Growing Minds*. Austin, TX: PA Publishing.

Advanced learners flourish in a supportive environment that enables them to access beyond grade-level information while pursuing the unique critical and creative thinking characteristic of the construction of deeper meaning and advanced levels of achievement. Without support to continue learning beyond core curriculum, many high-ability students step onto a school treadmill where they continue to work and complete many tasks but do not advance academically.

## SCRUTINIZE ENRICHMENT ACTIVITIES

Review the enrichment experiences included in current curriculum materials to guide your decisions regarding the quantity or quality of enrichment activities. Are the suggestions predominantly a quantity of tasks at the same level of mastery, or are they qualitatively different in learning content, processes, and products? Students as well as educators are discouraged by completing and grading assignments that are simply *more of the same.*

# A SUPPORTIVE ENVIRONMENT

With academic rigor, set high expectations and endeavor to maintain high standards. All children have more potential than we understood how to maximize in the past. The goal today is not to push children faster and harder, but rather to establish an encouraging and stimulating environment that is nurturing in tone and rich in challenges and expectations.

A significant goal in academic rigor is to facilitate students becoming autonomous learners. Along the pathway toward that goal, students require support from adults and peers in the learning environment. Students do not exist in a learning vacuum; a supportive environment must provide the tools and encouragement that activate student success through multiple opportunities and multiple ways to learn. This environment must ensure emotional and intellectual safety as most children will not risk engaging with others or attempting challenging learning tasks when they feel emotionally unsafe.

A supportive learning environment provides a safe, nurturing place empowering all children to experience academic progress. This environment fosters achievement by employing differentiated classroom practices, encouraging respectful interactions, promoting students' sense of belonging, and honoring the diversity of background and thought. Implementing proactive support strategies facilitates students' success in reaching high standards.

Educators and families want high-ability students to be responsible and autonomous learners, but an interesting conundrum emerges: children's experiences with responsibility are unintentionally restricted in school. In response to standards and high-stakes testing, there obviously is need for curricula that designates what students will learn and when they learn it. However, for management reasons, educators may drastically limit many learning-related decisions students are allowed to make

Orchestrating Support Systems

including with whom students may work, when they can talk, and what products they complete to demonstrate understanding.

Insightful teachers share classroom power whenever it is realistic to do so. Provide students with choices that promote decision-making and responsibility, such as allowing them to select different ways to demonstrate their learning, where they sit, and with whom they may work some of the time. Without ownership and personal responsibility, students have little motivation to succeed. Conversely, when students feel empowered, they tend to exhibit greater responsibility, prefer more challenging academic tasks, set higher goals, and persist when confronted with difficulties (Guskey & Anderman, 2009). Daniels and Bizar (2005) assert that if we want to raise the kind of responsible students we claim to treasure, we have to invite them to make meaningful decisions, and then live with all of the consequences those choices entail.

### POSTED SCHEDULE

Post a schedule of daily learning activities that enables students to predict what happens next and allows them to proceed more independently. Plan the schedule so students engage in meaningful learning options and experience learning in a variety of ways throughout the day. Change the options and groupings as frequently as needed to match students' capabilities and current learning objectives.

### SIGN-UPS

Sign-Ups uniquely invite students' decision-making and ownership in learning. Organize opportunities for a variety of small group sessions involving reteaching, silent reading, skill practice, and extensions. To participate, students self-nominate by signing-up for one of the options (Kingore, 2007c).

### CONTRACTS

Contracts increase student responsible for meaningful decisions. Completing a learning contract requires students to plan, set goals, and engage in record keeping to expedite their achievement. Contracts differentiate instruction by empowering students to determine the sequence and pacing of learning experiences as they manage their replacement tasks.

To support classroom learning, Sullo (2009) asserts that teachers must create a needs-satisfying environment that responds to students' five basic needs: survival/safety, belonging/connecting, power/competence, freedom, and fun. When these basic needs are being met, all students are more likely to be engaged in learning and less likely to demonstrate behavior problems. Every classroom activity does not need to address every need, but during a block of time, ensure a reasonable chance that those needs are met.

While educators continuously assure survival/safety for all students, several of these basic needs have specific implications when differentiating instruction for high-ability students. For the high-ability student:

- Belonging and connecting require students' respectful interactions with intellectual peers as well as age peers in class and in virtual teams through technology.

- Power and competence require an environment that promotes responsibility and autonomy through continuous learning, opportunities for decision-making, and intellectually demanding work.

- Freedom requires choice and the right to be passionate about personal interests and talent areas without apology (Siegle, 2011).

- Fun activates retention and results from interacting in engaging learning tasks with supportive, respectful peers who flourish when cognitive complexity is increased. After awhile, simple learning tasks are just not much fun for high-ability learners.

### RISK TAKING

School cultures do not value and acknowledge risk taking enough (Dweck, 2010). To risk a high-level or unique idea, students must feel safe to mentally stretch and take intelligent risks. It is important to ensure a learning environment in which students feel safe socially and emotionally as well as safe to participate academically. It is evident that the students who are thinking and participating are also the ones who are learning (Wills, 2011). If students do not actively participate, the brain is not engaged. Hence, every person in class needs to be mentally responding to every question that is asked and predicting content. Yet, students fear making a mistake in front of others; they hesitate to participate if they think they may be viewed as foolish or less able.

*Empowered to Learn*

•

*When students feel empowered, they exhibit greater responsibility, engage in more intellectual tasks, and persist when confronted with difficulties.*

One solution is to remove the barrier to risk taking (Wills, 2011). The barrier is that students do not want to appear *stupid* in front of others. So, provide a means that allows all students to simultaneously and privately demonstrate individual responses.

The *every-student-responds* technique is simple to use and encourages all students to remain actively engaged instead of mentally disconnecting, such as when only one student responds to a question. Technological devices, simple wipe-off boards, or laminated four-by-six-inch index cards ensure a way for all students to indicate their level of understanding by writing and revealing their responses for your review. You can non-verbally acknowledge responses or offer verbal feedback with comments that summarize or contrast responses without naming individual learners. When every student responds, they feel it is safe to try an idea instead of protecting themselves with silent withdrawal.

Kingore, B. (2013). *Rigor and Engagement for Growing Minds.* Austin, TX: PA Publishing.

In addition to encouraging risk taking, individual responses provide a significant formative assessment tool as you instantly ascertain the students' understanding or misconceptions for a specific skill or concept. (See Formative Assessment techniques in Chapter 6.)

Intelligent risk taking is significantly important for high levels of learning, and classroom environments must protect students so they feel safe to try. A supportive environment with mutual respect among peers and adults leads students to be less afraid of making errors in front of others and more willing to take intelligent risks.

## THE FLIPPED CLASSROOM

Inasmuch as skilled teachers actively seek both time and techniques to provide more support for individual learners, the flipped classroom emerges as a viable application in a supportive learning environment. A flipped classroom inverts traditional instruction so that *lectures* are completed at home through online videos and *homework* applications are completed at school, allowing students more hands-on work, problem solving, and face-to-face interaction among the teacher and peers. Teachers Jon Bergmann and Aaron Sams (2011, 2012) developed and articulated the flipped classroom concept, but the success of Khan Academy and its proliferation of free educational videos increased interest in the practicality of the instructional approach.

When a classroom is flipped, relatively brief and usually teacher-created online videos deliver the lecture information at home so class time can be used for labs or group interactive tasks that illustrate and apply concepts. Teachers move to higher rungs of the instruction ladder as they are freed from being the sage and are available to interact with students for inquiry, insights, mini-workshops, and opportunities to expand on higher-order thinking skills. The videos are actually a tool blending direct instruction with constructivist learning by providing a means to increase class-time interaction and personalized contact time as you foster student responsibility.

The video lectures provide a differentiated learning experience as they permit all students to process and review the information at their own pace, recording questions and communicating through online discussions with peers and teachers. Videos enable students to repeat sections of the lecture when preparing for summative assessments and also ensure ready access to the information if they miss a day of school. When extended beyond teacher-prepared lectures to wider online resources, videos allow students to access specialized, more complex resources and function as global citizens interacting with people from around the world.

Educational technology is both a positive and negative component of flipped instruction. Technology is most certainly an engaging influence on students yet adversely affects students who lack Internet access and equipment at home. For students without home access to technology, flipped classrooms must provide alternative access at school and address appropriate scheduling of that access to benefit all students. Furthermore, while the availability of online video is increasing, teachers in flipped classrooms must become skilled at using software to record some or most of their lectures for online viewing.

The face-to-face interactions and meaningful learning experiences that occur during class time are the most significant aspects of the flipped classroom concept and outweigh potential disadvantages. Class time can be more academically rich and productive as it is devoted to concept engagement and active learning with peer and instructional support. Flipped classrooms provide time for the collaboration, discussion, problem solving, and support so desired by educators and students alike. However, enduring problems can roadblock success. In particular, Carter and Doyle warned in 1987 that the kinds of tasks required for problem solving are more difficult to manage than the routine tasks associated with rote learning. A lack of knowledge about how to manage an inquiry-oriented classroom can lead teachers to revert to passive tactics that dumb down content. Educators who are only secure with didactic lecturing need a framework to assist them in implementing flipped classroom interactions. Networking with other educators helps teachers understand how to integrate strategies such as inquiry-based activities, problem-based learning, and project-based experiences during class time to transform students from passive listeners to active participants in learning.

## ROLES IN A SUPPORTIVE ENVIRONMENT

The support systems in both rigorous learning environments and flipped classrooms change the traditional roles of the people with vested interests in learning outcomes. Support systems invite more collaboration among educators, students, and families as they engage in an ongoing information exchange. Teachers experience a shift toward becoming a guide on the side and move away from being what Betts (1999) refers to as a DOK (Dispenser of Knowledge). Simultaneously, students increase their active participation and ownership in learning processes. A collaborative communication forum between schools and families replaces the traditional approach in which professionals assume they know what is best and need to educate parents. Instead, families and students are viewed as a valued source of information as well as an audience for achievement results. Family members, students, and educators benefit from a collaborative attitude of mutual respect, cooperation, and shared responsibility as they collaboratively form a support system for learning success in rigorous learning environments.

## ADULTS IN THE SUPPORT SYSTEM

### FAMILIES

An effective student support system actively involves families and extends to community members as integral partners with school personnel. Families participate as collaborators with educators, encouragers of their child and teachers, and co-learners seeking information as they also provide valuable information and family perspectives.

Family life is a significant factor in students' success. While educators continue to

Kingore, B. (2013). *Rigor and Engagement for Growing Minds.* Austin, TX: PA Publishing.

recognize parental influence, today's family units have diverse structures, often markedly different from that of prior generations. A child's home influence might involve two parents, a single parent, an extended family member, an older sibling, or another adult. The family influence on a child's learning may result in quite positive or adverse effects depending on factors such as economic survival, emotional stability, and attitudes about the school or academic learning in general.

Educators who make an effort to understand the conditions and perspectives of families are better prepared to initiate mutual respect, trust, and a three-way sharing of information involving students, families, and school personnel. Experienced educators know that family engagement leads to student achievement. When both students and families are engaged, students perform better. Thus, educators must respect all family structures and collaborate to support a shared vision for the child's success. In an attitude of shared partnership, effective communications with families involve many of the objectives shown in Figure 5.2.

### THREE-WAY COMMUNICATION

Encourage three-way, in-person communications and conferences among students, families, and teachers as the student's perspective may differ considerably from the teacher or family representative. The intent is for the three groups most vested in the student to learn and share together.

## FIGURE 5.2:
# SCHOOL AND FAMILY COMMUNICATION

These are some effective ways to facilitate productive communication between schools and families to benefit and support students. Interact with students and families to determine additional productive ideas.

✓ Establish an active information exchange.

✓ Foster mutual respect and trust.

✓ Reach families in their dominant language.

✓ Communicate through multiple means, understanding that some families respond better to letters or phone calls while others may be more responsive to texts, emails, or in-person conversations.

✓ Make communication timely and focused on the child's education and academic progress rather than any characteristics or behaviors of the family.

✓ Promote understanding of the culture of the family and what is academically important to them.

✓ Promote understanding of the culture of the school so families understand your perspective and instructional priorities.

Kingore, B. (2013). *Rigor and Engagement for Growing Minds.* Austin, TX: PA Publishing.

### FAMILY RESPONSES TO EFFORT

Encourage families to actively respond to children's efforts to learn as well as their achievements. Rather than only focus on the grade received on a learning task, recommend that a family representative discuss with the child: "What did you learn doing this?" "What is something you are pleased with about your work?" "What skills were you working on for this task? (In standards-based instruction, learning objectives are openly discussed with students.) The intent is to address effort as a precursor of achievement and encourage a child's continued efforts to advance through new learning accomplishments.

Integrate informative writing as a means for children to directly correspond with families through written reflections about learning. The frequency of this communication depends on the teacher's objectives as well as the needs, interests, and capabilities of students. Informative writing is authentic and in keeping with standards emphasized in the Common Core State Standards. Figure 5.3 includes several examples of informative writing applications between the student and family representatives.

### ALL EDUCATORS

An effective support system promotes high levels of achievement and strives to increase personalized relationships among adults and students. All educators have a stake in students' learning success. Of course, the classroom teacher is the educator with the largest quantity of time invested in supporting students' success. However, administrators are responsible for several aspects in a support system (Figure 5.4).

Take an active role in expanding school-wide support systems. The following ideas suggest ways you can facilitate the assistance of other educators in a supportive learning environment.

◆ **ACCESS NONFICTION**
Access nonfiction resources to support and supplement students' acquisition of information. Network with media specialists or librarians for their guidance and suggested resources at a wide range of levels to match students' reading readiness.

◆ **SUPPORT ELL**
Seek specialists or competent volunteers resourceful in providing materials and recordings in students' first languages to support students' development of background knowledge before they proceed to work extensively in English text.

◆ **IDENTIFY ADULT RESOURCES**
Identify staff members and central office coordinators who can offer assistance by providing resources, training, or strategies. Resource specialists may be available to assist, co-teach, or peer coach in the classroom.

◆ **ACCESS AND TRAIN AIDES**
Train instructional aides and parent volunteers to support students' success as they complete challenging academic tasks and

Orchestrating Support Systems

## FIGURE 5.3:
# STUDENTS' INFORMATIVE WRITING TO FAMILIES

✦ **SUMMARIES**

Students produce periodic summaries of their learning experiences and outcomes. In the summary, students address open-ended prompts such as:

• "When I look at my work, I notice _____."

• "These are things I am doing well: _____."

• "My next academic goal is _____."

• "I am changing as a learner by _____."

• "I feel _____."

• "This learning is important to me _____."

✦ **FAMILY LETTERS**

Students write a letter to their family from your perspective. It is interesting and often entertaining for families to see the student's interpretations of the teacher's point of view. This written version of role-playing requires multiple perspectives and high-level thinking.

Dear Mr. Lewis,

Jayden is working to learn a lot. He works well in groups and is a very productive thinker when problem solving with others. He is trying to be more collaborative, actively listen to others, and not dominate conversations.

Science continues to be his favorite subject. He prefers to do writing tasks about scientific topics instead of just practicing the writing skills we must learn. I arranged with his other teachers for him to use science information to practice most of our required reading and writing skills.

He loves the digital readers now available in class. He is reading important information about geophysics and continues his inquiry of the global effects of seismic activity in the Ring of Fire.

He has to work the hardest in math right now. Quadratic equations are hard for him. His math partners, Hannah and Cesar, work with him to complete the applications. I provided three videos about solving quadratic equations that they are watching and analyzing to learn.

Jayden is keeping a portfolio of representative work. He is ready to share it with you.

Sincerely,
Ms. Jan Scott

✦ **TWITTER**

At scheduled times, students twitter messages to families about what they are learning or experiencing in class. Twitter is an appealing and appropriate choice for young learners because the responses are so brief.

✦ **EXIT TICKETS**

Students complete exit tickets as a family communication tool. Exit tickets, discussed in Chapter 2, are typically used to provide relevant information to teachers. However, after teachers quickly review exit tickets for information, students take the ticket home. Families learn to ask children to show them the exit ticket for the day. This simple application provides a framework for families to discuss school-related topics with their child and eliminates the counterproductive exchange of the past: "What did you learn at school today?" followed by "Nothing," or "I don't remember."

Kingore, B. (2013). *Rigor and Engagement for Growing Minds.* Austin, TX: PA Publishing.

## FIGURE 5.4:
# ADMINISTRATORS' ROLES IN A SUPPORT SYSTEM

Administrators:

✓ Fervently reinforce the value of rigor and engagement.

✓ Support complex curriculum and students' development of deeper meaning.

✓ Ensure professional development opportunities in strategies appropriate for rigor and engagement.

✓ Are crucial in providing the time and materials teachers require to create a rigorous and supportive learning environment.

✓ Facilitate different school-wide support systems.

✓ Ensure that schools schedule time for teachers to network and function on active collaborative teams.

✓ Organize time for school personnel to be available as appropriate for facilitating, reflecting, and communicating formally or informally with students and families.

✓ Advocate for specialized services as needed for academically advanced as well as special needs students.

✓ Support high-ability students through a differentiated curriculum with accelerated pace and level of instruction.

✓ Endeavor to be in classrooms to mentor and interact with students as well as evaluate instruction.

facilitate students' problem solving in flexible groups.

✦ **HIGHLIGHT TOPIC SENTENCES**
Find a high school student or adult who understands the class content and summarizes well. This person can highlight the topic sentences and key passages in the text to guide twice exceptional or ELL high-potential learners to focus on a shorter amount of print to assimilate the major ideas.

✦ **COLLABORATE AND NETWORK**
Network with teachers experienced with your student population to share ideas.

### TEACHERS

A critical requirement in a support system effective for high-ability learners, as with all learners, is a teacher who is a master of differentiation and respectful of diverse learning levels on a continuum from below to beyond grade level (Brulles, 2010; Tomlinson, 2003). Research results continue to document the vital role teachers play in promoting student success, proving time and again that the teacher is the most influential school-related force in student achievement (Stronge, 2012). Research in teacher effectiveness substantiates that a supportive and challenging teacher creates a positive effect on student achievement and a lasting effect on students' lives.

Teacher's support is crucial for high expectations when students interact in small, flexible groups for independent applications. Let students know that, while you do not participate in their groups, you observe and are available to support their progress. Your

Kingore, B. (2013). *Rigor and Engagement for Growing Minds.* Austin, TX: PA Publishing.

observation also reassures individual members that you are aware of individual contributions. There are several roles teachers assume when flexible groups interact to complete a learning task (Figure 5.5).

Ensure that students have opportunities to share their perceptions with you and to reflect their feelings or opinions about whole-class and flexible group learning experiences. Students must clearly understand that these reflections serve to inform you and guide instruction; they do not influence grades. Review students' reflections to guide future task selections and instructional pacing as well as form flexible groups.

- Provide a suggestion box on your desk where young children can insert notes with their suggestions and ideas.
- Invite students to complete one of these two-word sentence stems at the bottom of any assignment: "I think...," "I notice...," or "I wonder..." The stems are intentionally ill-defined to elicit students' perspectives.

## FIGURE 5.5:
# TEACHERS SUPPORTING FLEXIBLE GROUPS

| ROLE | ACTION |
|---|---|
| **Observe** | Observe to non-verbally recognize collaborative progress. Observe and jot down: <br> a. Assessment data to guide later instruction and group formation. <br> b. Key points or problems to discuss at the conclusion of the task so you do not interrupt the flow of the group at this time. |
| **Interject questions** | Interject questions to: <br> a. Redirect a group in a more productive direction. <br> b. Activate non-participating members. Ask: "What is your role in your group right now?" <br> c. Elicit students' perspectives and problem-solving ideas. |
| **Intervene** | Intervene in one group when you notice: <br> a. A group is so significantly off-task with their discussion or direction that success is in jeopardy. <br> b. A personality clash severe enough to cause bad feelings and counterproductive behaviors. <br> Intervene and address the whole class when you notice that more than one group is experiencing a similar difficulty. |
| **Facilitate** | Facilitate a concluding discussion after the groups reconvene as a whole class. |

Kingore, B. (2013). *Rigor and Engagement for Growing Minds.* Austin, TX: PA Publishing.

### PROJECT EMAILS

For long-term group projects, ask students to copy to you any emails among group members so you stay informed of what is going on.

Sagor (2009, 53) believes that students need continuous encouragement and guidance from schools if they are to invest positive energy in learning. He challenges us to ask ourselves two questions every day as students exit class:

- "As a result of today's experience, will these students be more or less confident that their futures are bright?"
- "Will students walk out of the classroom feeling more capable than when they walked in?"

In biographies and autobiographies, eminent people often recognize one person who served as their encourager by believing in and nurturing them; that encourager is typically a parent or an educator. Advanced students often acknowledge the lifelong effect of a teacher who served as their mentor. It follows that high-ability students need someone to encourage their unique potential even when it seems a bit weird because it differs so substantially from the norm. Teachers must be skilled in planning learning experiences that stretch students just beyond their comfort zone of mastery to continue learning at a level that is challenging but attainable (Sousa, 2009; Vygotsky, 1962). Fostering continuous learning for high-ability students necessitates

that differentiation exceeds core curriculum expectations.

### CHALLENGE

Provide meaningful in-class problems or learning tasks that require high-ability students to stretch beyond mastered material. Initially, remain in close proximity to support their progress until they are confident of their success.

Elicit students' perspectives regarding which characteristics of supportive teachers are most relevant to them. Teacher roles are changing in contemporary classrooms promoting academic rigor. Propose a list of characteristics to prompt their thinking; as the discussion continues, add or omit characteristics from the list. Then, make a commitment to the class that you will try to live up to their selected characteristics. Later, revisit their list and challenge the class to determine student characteristics that parallel each teaching quality. Request a commitment from students to try to live up to those qualities. The following is a sample of the teacher characteristics students might propose: cheerleader, knowledgeable, coaching, motivational, encourager, inquirer/ questioner, open-minded, and mentor.

I am a teacher by choice. I have had the honor of teaching for a long time. Throughout my teaching career, most of my high-ability students, from preschool to graduate school, have loved the classes I teach. I like to flatter myself, but I know that their appreciation isn't really about me. Rather, it is a response to what I see in them and the encouragement and feedback regarding their effort that I wholeheartedly offer when I view their potential and passion. Teacher support matters!

### • TEACHERS SUPPORTING EFFORT

Many educators today are familiar with Carol Dweck's (2006) research regarding an individual's mindset of a fixed or growth model of intelligence. Specifically, some adults and children perceive intelligence as a fixed, static entity—you either have it or you don't. This fixed-intelligence perception suggests that you are less smart if you make mistakes or don't instantly know the answer, thus leading students to avoid challenge in order to look smarter. With fixed mindsets, mistakes become crippling when students encounter difficulties (Johnston, 2012). If high-ability children have fixed mindsets and only receive feedback about how intelligent or correct they are, they develop patterns of underachievement and avoid tasks they perceive might be difficult to protect themselves from being wrong.

A growth model leads children and educators to a very different perspective regarding intelligence. A growth model proposes that intelligence can develop substantially in response to a learner's actions. This belief leads students to understand that they have potential and their effort has a direct and profound effect on their learning. When students

*Teacher Support Is Vital*

•

*The key to success for many advanced students is a teacher who respects high-ability learners and substantially differentiates instruction.*

believe ability can be developed, they feel they have some control over achievement and are motivated to work harder. After all, even geniuses have to work hard to make their contributions (Dweck, 2010). Students with growth mindsets understand that hard work gets them somewhere and effort is the pathway to mastery, so they are more resilient, try harder, persist longer, and accomplish more. This perception results in high-ability students exhibiting a willingness to take on more intellectually challenging work.

Educators cannot hand students confidence on a silver platter. Instead, we help them gain the tools they need to develop their confidence in learning (Dweck, 2007). Students' perception of what they are capable of doing is different than students responding to extrinsic motivation. For example, in preparation for an upcoming high-stakes test, adults can excite kids by talking about how great they are and that they can accomplish anything, but that is not a complete truth (Johnston, 2012). Without accompanying effort, struggle, and commitment to persist, enthusiasm becomes short-lived. Dweck's research equips us to understand the role of student effort and its influence on achievement. The next step is to translate that research into instructional practices.

### • PROCESS FEEDBACK

Create a growth-mindset culture in your classroom by ensuring the kinds of feedback and encouragement that move learners forward. Providing feedback for the process students engage in—the effort they apply, their strategies, their choices, their persistence—yields more long-term benefits than praising them for being smart and having a perfect paper (Dweck, 2006).

Your feedback to students has a direct and quite powerful effect on students' interpretations of what is actually valued in learning environments. Teachers of high-ability students need to further student's high expectations for achievement by focusing on student effort and process as well as their products and grades. Focused and productive feedback develops with modeling and practice. We know to avoid person-oriented criticism, such as: "You're just not good at this," or "How could you not know that?" However, we must also avoid simple, correct-answer, product-dominated comments such as: "Great job; a perfect paper again," or "You get an *A+* on this!" These comments risk students' interpreting that *accurate* is more valued than *effort* to grow.

Incorporate feedback that promotes personal growth and high achievement while simultaneously modeling to students more productive ways to support each other in peer interactions. Focus on feedback that generates a clear sense that effort leads to achievement, as in Figure 5.6. Acknowledge the learning process rather than predominantly emphasizing perceived ability.

Process feedback recognizes students' strategies and resilience. In a supportive environment, it may sound like these examples.
- "You adapted the assignment to make a personal metaphor to your life. That is a very productive strategy and enabled you to go beyond the task."

## FIGURE 5.6:
# TEACHERS' FEEDBACK TO STUDENTS

Students need to believe that their effort produces results. Guide them to understand that academic work is about confronting a challenge and making progress, not immediate perfection or being able to work fast. As students work, provide supportive feedback on these behaviors to encourage a growth mindset.

Acknowledge these learning behaviors as you observe them.
- Effort and struggle
- Strategy choices
- Selection of difficult tasks
- Constructing new and/or deeper meaning
- Learning something perceived to be difficult
- Constructive ideas to help improve or correct something
- Inquiry
- Incubation
- Adaptability
- Reflection and self-assessment
- Resilience in the face of obstacles
- Goal setting initiatives to expand current knowledge and skills
- Growth and change as a learner

Kingore, B. (2013). *Rigor and Engagement for Growing Minds.* Austin, TX: PA Publishing.

- "Your effort is obvious. Together, let's figure out what to do differently or another way to approach this."
- "I think the reason you are not finished yet is because you selected a difficult task that takes time. Let's consider the progress you are making and what to do next."
- "You studied for this and your improvement shows it. Your decision to outline the key points was a great strategy for you."
- "All of you figured this out together by making a plan, graphically organizing information, and listening to each other. Look how well that effort worked for you."

I used to tell students: "When you are learning something more difficult, there is a feeling only you can give yourself. It is the feeling you get when you work on something and you get it!" Brain research enables us to understand that this productive feeling is because pleasurable associations linked with learning are more likely to release dopamine and result in joyful learning (Wills, 2007b). Figure 5.7 supplies several strategies that encourage both students' effort and their development of a growth model of intelligence.

Teachers are a major influence on the learning success of students. Students differ in their degree of independence and skill but all learners benefit from a teacher's instruction, modeling, interaction, guidance, support, encouragement, coaching, and feedback—even high-ability students whom some educators traditionally perceived as always making it on their own. While teachers feel overwhelmed at times by the pressure and time required to enable struggling students to succeed, no teacher intentionally wants to ignore any members of the class. Yet, teachers typically participate in

more professional training geared toward strategies and accommodations to raise achievement for struggling learners than to advance learning for students above grade level. As a faculty or instructional team, network and develop realistic ways to support high-ability students in all classrooms. The ideas in Figure 5.8 are included to prompt decisions regarding support that is practicable for busy teachers to provide.

We have worked for several years to become skilled at supporting struggling learners—and that support is needed and appropriate. Now, it is time to increase our skills at also supporting high-ability learners.

## PEER SUPPORT

Johnston (2012) advises us to take seriously the fact that the adult is not the only teacher in the room. Productive collaboration among students should activate students as instructional resources for one another to a degree that is significantly beyond peer tutoring.

### FLEXIBLE GROUPS

Flexible grouping is a foundational strategy in a support system and crucial to core standards, ensuring that students have opportunities to interact with and learn from students like themselves and students dissimilar in backgrounds and interest. College and work force cultures expect people to interact

## FIGURE 5.7:
# STRATEGIES TO ENCOURAGE GROWTH MINDSETS

◆ **OBSERVE, LISTEN, AND OFFER FEEDBACK ABOUT EFFORT AND PROCESS.**
Listen to students to denote their perception of their ability or intelligence. What are they saying about their success or lack of accomplishment? Respond positively to their efforts. Model and implement change if a fixed mindset emerges.

◆ **EXPLORE EXAMPLES OF FAMOUS PEOPLE EXHIBITING EFFORT.**
Help students access anecdotes about famous people who were not always regarded as able learners and had to struggle at something before they mastered it. Einstein, for example, swore he was slow to learn and had to ponder the same questions for years. That proved to be an excellent strategy.

◆ **SHARE BRAIN-BASED LEARNING.**
Some students are quite fascinated by brain and learning development. Help them access interviews and information about a growth mindset to develop applications for themselves and peers.

◆ **ADVOCATE THAT EASY IS BORING.**
Portray easy tasks as boring and useless to the brain. For example, a student proudly announced: "That was easy!" Her teacher responded: "Oh, I am sorry I didn't plan better for you. Something is easy once you know how! So *easy* is cheating yourself out of opportunities to continue to grow and learn. Let's plan something interesting that is more challenging for you."

◆ **COMPARE PREASSESSMENTS AND SUMMATIVE ASSESSMENTS.**
Use preassessments so students can compare those results with their improved performance on post assessments and prove to themselves that it was their effort that produced achievement and growth. As a student compares a preassessment with final results, ask: "How are you changing as a learner?"

◆ **INCORPORATE *NOT YET* WHEN WORKING WITH STUDENTS.**
Frequently use the language of *Not Yet* (Johnston, 2012). Whenever students say, "I'm not good at this," or they say they don't understand a concept, add: "Not yet." This simple verbal change has powerful consequences and conveys the idea that ability is fluid and depends upon the situation. *Not yet* switches children's thinking from negative ability to positive action, emphasizing that learning is in-progress. *Not yet* promotes a growth mindset.

Kingore, B. (2013). *Rigor and Engagement for Growing Minds.* Austin, TX: PA Publishing.

## FIGURE 5.8:
# SUPPORTING HIGH-ABILITY IN ALL CLASSROOMS

➤ Encourage English Language Learners and young high-ability learners with only beginning literacy skills to conduct research, pursue projects, and share complex ideas with the support of a mentor, an older student, or through verbal recordings rather than be limited to written responses.

➤ Regularly employ preassessments to document exempting high-ability students from work they have already mastered. Implement replacement tasks instead of redundant work.

➤ Encourage student autonomy by posting a list of generalizable products and authentic learning experiences from which students can select when pursuing replacement tasks.

➤ Work with high-ability students to generate criteria that promote complexity and depth so students can document their approximations to personal excellence when pursuing replacement tasks.

➤ Daily, require high-ability students to self-assess learning behaviors, effort, and results when working on replacement tasks or projects. Review these self-reflections and debrief with students when feasible.

➤ Ensure that high-ability students maintain records of progress and reflect on personal changes as learners rather than gauge their results through comparisons with grade-level peers.

➤ In a mixed-readiness class, periodically place high-ability students in similar-readiness flexible groups to promote applications beyond grade level.

➤ Form interest-based groups across grade levels to ensure intellectual peers for high-ability students and nurture more in-depth information and problem solving. These students should regularly work together when teachers place others in small groups for re-teaching or to practice and apply grade-level skills previously mastered by high-ability learners.

➤ As flexible groups, implement text clubs or literature circles with a diverse range of materials that allow all students opportunities to appropriately select text at, below, and beyond grade-level.

➤ Jigsaw using more complex materials for advanced students during cooperative learning.

➤ Implement Socratic Seminars in which students take leadership roles in preparing and conducting the seminars.

➤ When practicing grade-level learning standards, allow high-ability students to use higher-level materials for applications. For example, all students can be practicing mathematical operations using a range of materials instead of only the grade-level textbook.

➤ Implement cluster-grouping classrooms so high-ability students have consistent access to an intellectual-peer group as well as an age-peer group. The key to success in cluster grouping is a teacher who has esteem for high-ability students and is quite accomplished at differentiating instruction.

Kingore, B. (2013). *Rigor and Engagement for Growing Minds.* Austin, TX: PA Publishing.

and communicate effectively, and school cultures believe that learning is advanced through small group applications (Crockett, Jukes, & Churches, 2011; Sousa & Tomlinson, 2010; Wagner, 2010). Hence, schools provide opportunities for students to develop the social and communication skills that facilitate group interactions and ensure that students learn to work cooperatively and collaboratively as well as independently. An important focus of the CCSS is that students should gain, evaluate, and present complex information, ideas, and evidence through listening and speaking as well as through technology. Students develop and use these skills when they collaborate to refine understanding and problem solve in flexible groups. As they accomplish tasks and simulate real-life collaborative situations, flexible groups challenge students to learn academic subject matter while practicing team building, conflict resolution, management, group decision-making, and leadership skills.

Academic rigor requires a clearly articulated plan that provides structure for the class when students work in flexible groups without direct teacher instruction. Flexible grouping is much more than students sitting together to help each other if needed as they independently complete similar work. Willis (2009) concludes that cooperative learning activities are most likely to succeed when the tasks assigned to students truly require them to work together to meet the objective. Relevant group tasks demand positive interdependence—a perception that students either sink or swim together—while structuring individual accountability. With appropriate structure, flexible groups demonstrate more collaboration, helping behaviors, and complex problem-solving skills than when peers are less experienced in collaboration and work in unstructured groups (Gillies, 2008). The checklist in Figure 5.9 provides a framework to assist teachers' decisions of how to structure effective flexible groups for productive learning.

*Flexible Grouping*

•

*Flexible grouping is much more than students sitting together to help each other if needed as they independently complete similar work.*

Flexible grouping is a short-term grouping and regrouping of students in response to specific learning objectives and assessed needs. Group membership is fluid because we know that individuals learn best when involved in a variety of group placements that respond to the diagnosed affective and cognitive needs of students, as well as our instructional objectives. We also understand that flexible grouping is most successful when group procedures and routines are practiced and understood so all class members know how to work successfully in different group settings.

**ASSIGNMENT CARDS WITH DIRECTIONS**

When groups pursue different tasks to differentiate learning, hand out task cards to provide needed directions to each group rather than try to provide a variety of instructions in front of the whole class.

Kingore, B. (2013). *Rigor and Engagement for Growing Minds.* Austin, TX: PA Publishing.

FIGURE 5.9:
# A FRAMEWORK FOR FLEXIBLE GROUPING

❑ Task expectations, learning objectives, and schedules are clearly communicated and understood in advance of group work.

❑ Students understand and can successfully perform the individual roles necessary for group functioning.

❑ The task is authentic, interesting, and at an appropriate level of challenge for the group members.

❑ The task procedure is clearly defined, well structured, and relevant.

❑ Each group member is accountable for an equally important contribution toward successful completion of the task.

❑ Genuine collaboration rather than parallel learning is necessary.

❑ Support is available if students risk failure or deadlock.

❑ Students know what to do to document shared understanding and task completion.

*Get going!*

## SUMMARIZE GROUP TASKS

As a group task begins, tell the groups that you plan to randomly call on one student from each group to summarize the key ideas and process of the group when the group task is complete. This technique increases individual responsibility for the learning task.

## • FLEXIBLE GROUP RUBRICS

A rubric helps students establish a framework for knowing how to proceed and eventually judge their work. Working with students, develop flexible group rubrics, such as the examples provided here. Discuss ways that students effectively cooperate (work well together), collaborate (develop ideas and solve problems together), or work independently (produce separate parts of the whole).

Figure 5.10 uses simple words and meaningful illustrations to clearly convey the expectations of group work for children and young ELL students. The teacher models how students are to fill in the clock face to concretely show at what time the task should be completed. The criteria on the left signal students what is important as they work. When the learning task is complete, the groups assess their work by checking the applicable boxes on the right and completing the sentence prompt: "We think..." The prompt is purposely open-ended to elicit students' interpretations. After modeling and guided applications, small groups of children are able to use this rubric independently.

Kingore, B. (2013). *Rigor and Engagement for Growing Minds.* Austin, TX: PA Publishing.

## SELF-ASSESSMENT

Requiring groups to self-assess at the end of a task greatly increases students' levels of productivity and achievement as it helps students learn how to learn (ASCD, 2008; Stiggins & Chappuis, 2011). Provide a group rubric or reflection device as the group forms, and then, require them to complete it as the group session concludes.

Figure 5.11 shows a second example of a rubric for group assessment that promotes a more complex analysis of group work for older students. The older students enhance

productivity by reviewing the rubric and then setting goals as a team before they begin the learning task; then students return to the rubric to assess at the completion of the task. The rubric also prompts students to conclude future actions or goals based on their experiences with this current learning task.

## GENERALIZABLE RUBRICS

When possible, design group rubrics to be generalizable and then customize as needed for specific skills and concepts. Beginning with a more general tool provides a foundation to build on and decreases preparation time when a specialized version is preferred.

---

**FIGURE 5.10**
**FLEXIBLE GROUP ASSESSMENT**

Task _____

| Did your group: | | | |
|---|---|---|---|
| Listen to each other? Respond with good ideas? | | | |
| Produce important information? Share main ideas and details? Form a conclusion? | | | |
| Show respect for others? Cooperate? Collaborate? | | | |
| Use high-level thinking? Develop original ideas? Adapt and elaborate? | | | |
| Stay on task? Finish on time? | | | |

We think: _____

_____

Kingore, B. (2013). *Rigor and Engagement for Growing Minds.* Austin, TX: PA Publishing.

---

**FIGURE 5.11**
**FLEXIBLE GROUP ASSESSMENT**

Task _____ Date _____
Group Members _____
_____

| Did all members of the group: | Not Yet | Somewhat | Frequently | Consistently |
|---|---|---|---|---|
| **Cooperation and Interpersonal Skills** | | | | |
| • Respect task expectations, learning objectives, and schedule? | | | | |
| • Demonstrate respect and patience for others' ideas and property? | | | | |
| • Work and interact quietly? | | | | |
| • Take turns and include everyone? | | | | |
| • Support and encourage others as needed? | | | | |
| • Communicate diplomatically? | | | | |
| **Collaboration and Positive Interdependence** | | | | |
| • Demonstrate accountability for equally important contributions? | | | | |
| • Exert the effort required to excel? | | | | |
| • Actively listen, contribute, and build upon others ideas? | | | | |
| • Provide productive feedback to others? | | | | |
| • Persist when they encountered obstacles? | | | | |
| • Share important information and ideas? | | | | |
| • Evidence adaptability, creative problem solving, and willingness to consider new ideas or procedures? | | | | |
| **Content Information and Thinking** | | | | |
| • Complete relevant, high-quality, organized work? | | | | |
| • Apply precise academic vocabulary? | | | | |
| • Demonstrate high-level thinking and problem solving? | | | | |
| • Emphasize complex, in-depth information? | | | | |
| • Construct relevant content relationships and personal examples? | | | | |
| • Support ideas and content relationships to clarify understanding and construct deeper meaning? | | | | |
| • Summarize for closure? | | | | |

For continued learning, we intend to: _____

Kingore, B. (2013). *Rigor and Engagement for Growing Minds.* Austin, TX: PA Publishing.

---

Kingore, B. (2013). *Rigor and Engagement for Growing Minds.* Austin, TX: PA Publishing.

**Orchestrating Support Systems**

### • WHO DETERMINES FLEXIBLE GROUP MEMBERSHIP?

Group memberships vary in response to instructional objectives. Teachers, students, or random placement can determine a group's make-up. Directly assign students to groups when the learning task is specific to assessed readiness or interests. Also assign groups when your objective is to ensure a variety of group placements for all peers. However, students can select their own group membership when both the task and class make-up is well suited to peer selection, such as interest-based groups. Otherwise, create random groups with techniques such as number-off or colored dots.

When directly teaching a skill lesson, random group placements and student-selected groups can be used if we exercise some flexible thinking. Directly teach the targeted skill or learning strategy, but allow students to complete applications at different levels, using different materials. For example, everyone could be participating in a fluency lesson while reading texts at a wide range of levels for their applications; everyone could participate in instruction regarding the concept of ratio while individuals or small groups complete simple-to-more-complex authentic applications. This approach incorporates flexible groups that are mixed and varied while ensuring that students at different levels of readiness continue working at their most appropriate level.

#### CLIQUES

If you need to minimize potentially negative consequences when students self-select group members, such as cliques forming and some students feeling left out, ask students to email you their ranked preferences of four peers. Then, determine the different group memberships after taking students' input into consideration. Students will still get some of their choices, and you limit potentially negative consequences.

### • ROLES IN FLEXIBLE GROUPS

When students are experienced with group work of one kind or another, elicit their suggestions for a fresh consideration of individual roles within a group, such as these that follow in Figure 5.12 from a middle school class. Rotate roles among students as appropriate—long enough to learn a role well and provide task continuity but brief enough to maintain interest and variety. Since the most productive group size is two to four students, only some of these roles are incorporated in most learning tasks (Allington, 2008).

### • ROLE CARDS

As an authentic writing connection, have each group randomly select one group role, such as Organizer, and work together to create a role card. The card becomes the job description with an icon to visually represent the role and sound bites to guide students'

Kingore, B. (2013). *Rigor and Engagement for Growing Minds.* Austin, TX: PA Publishing.

verbal interactions. This application produces role cards for each group job. Laminate the cards for student reference as roles change.

## FIGURE 5.12:
# ROLES IN FLEXIBLE GROUPS

- **ORGANIZER**
  Leads group discussions and facilitates progress

- **DATAKEEPER**
  Records the group's actions and ideas for future information and clarification

- **RESEARCHER**
  Consults resources to check facts and word choices

- **SUMMARIZER**
  Synthesizes and organizes a summary of ideas

- **PRESENTER**
  Presents the groups' conclusion to other groups

- **ALLOCATOR**
  Keeps time and also determines who is responsible for each portion of the task

- **GRAPHIC DESIGNER**
  Represents the data graphically, such as sketching symbols for the concepts

- **TECH SPECIALIST**
  Uploads group work for others to read, pose questions, or critique online

**ROLE CARD:**
## Summarizer

The summarizer synthesizes information to guide memory of key data and process. You help the content stick in our minds.

Sound bites:
- "What do you want me to write for our topic sentence?"
- "Is that the most important idea for the end of our summary?"

**ROLE CARD:**
## Allocator

The allocator encourages the group to manage time well and guides individuals to determine tasks.

Sound bites:
- "We need that tomorrow, so who has time tonight to do this?"
- "We have five minutes left to wrap up our decisions."

Kingore, B. (2013). *Rigor and Engagement for Growing Minds.* Austin, TX: PA Publishing.

## INTELLECTUAL PEERS

A peer support system should ensure opportunities for high-ability students to interact with and learn from intellectual peers as well as age peers. Grouping is not, nor should it be, a stagnant destination inasmuch as students benefit from participating in diverse group placements during learning opportunities. To ensure continued learning growth, instruction must challenge all students to work slightly above their comfort level rather than at or below current achievement levels (Sousa, 2009). To experience challenge, high-ability students must confront a problem or situation they have not yet encountered and work with others who pose hard questions and unknowns. This level of challenge necessitates that high-ability students interact with intellectual peers as well as age peers. To minimize any counterproductive attention to intellectual peers, schedule these groups to work together while the rest of the class is also grouped in small groups using different levels of content materials or pursuing different concepts. At times, all groups could be engaged in a similar, open-ended task or problem that encourages responses at different degrees of complexity.

High-ability minds think differently. They have exceptional reasoning abilities that enable them to think abstractly with greater complexity and multidimensional applications at the same time that others are thinking concretely. High-ability children also feel differently. Their emo-

*Intellectual Peers*

•

*Intellectual peers promote the actualization of high-ability students' learning potential so they are inspired to question, adapt, and extend as much as master core curriculum content.*

tional intensity results in heightened awareness and qualitatively different ways of perceiving the world (Sword, 2001). They can experience alienation and feel lonely at school when they perceive that they are so markedly different from age peers. For their social, emotional, and academic well-being, it is imperative that teachers, families, and peers understand these differences as normal for advanced learners and help them interact with intellectual peers so they feel accepted, understood, and supported by others. (Brulles, 2010; Sword, 2001; Tomlinson, 2011; Winebrenner & Brulles, 2012).

High-ability students need to experience a culture of respect so they feel empowered to express unexpected ideas and perspectives while pursuing their academic interests and areas of passion. This culture of respect necessitates that they have ongoing opportunities with intellectual peers as well as age peers. High-ability students sense that many age peers are disinterested in their sophisticated vocabulary or deeper understanding of complex topics. In learning situations, their academic and emotional affirmation comes from intellectual peers interacting with them to ensure a balance of challenge and support. They also benefit from adults who facilitate a child's passions more than redirect that student's learning to practical applications or occupations. As Figure 5.13 elaborates, intellectual peers promote the actualization of high-ability students' learning potential so they are inspired to question, adapt, and extend as much as master core curriculum content.

Kingore, B. (2013). *Rigor and Engagement for Growing Minds.* Austin, TX: PA Publishing.

## FIGURE 5.13:
# INTELLECTUAL PEERS

Flexible groups of intellectual peers enable advanced students to:

- Pursue the intellectual risk taking needed for skill and concept adaptation as well as to succeed in advanced study.
- Experience advanced academic work that is relevant, stimulating, and intellectually challenging.
- Explore learning experiences at higher levels of complexity to extend targeted concepts and skills rather than engage in redundant work.
- Advance academically at a pace commensurate to their readiness and rate of learning.
- Use beyond grade-level resources in class as well as search out higher-level resources for themselves to satisfy their voracious appetites for specific nonfiction information.
- Pose complex questions as well as respond to hard questions from peers that require critical thinking, evaluation of advanced resources, and thoughtful reflection.
- Interact with peers who are interested in more sophisticated word choices and choose to respond with greater depth while engaging in demanding learning processes.
- Experience the social and emotional peer support they deserve while developing self-awareness and resiliency.

## *PEER SUPPORT TECHNIQUES*

Peer support techniques prove to be productive strategies in a rigorous learning environment. For example, peer editing, a central component of most writing programs, enables peers to interact and learn from one another as they perfect their writing skills. Implement additional techniques that help students support each other and solidify the principle that they are a community of learners. Peer review requests, mentors or buddies, task assistants, support assistants, and service projects are examples of simple-to-implement ways to effectively promote peer support for learning.

### • PEER REVIEW REQUEST

Students need to view classmates as sources of support and learn how to provide and receive constructive feedback. Designate an area in class or online where students can post messages and requests for assistance. This technique is useful in most classes, but is particularly beneficial when multiple sections of a course meet in the same room at different times and students do not have opportunities to discuss ideas across class sections. Provide simple templates, such as Figures 5.14 and

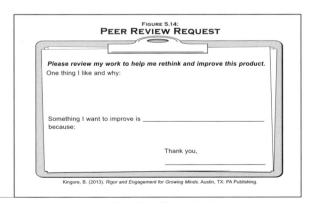

### FIGURE 5.14:
### PEER REVIEW REQUEST

*Please review my work to help me rethink and improve this product.*
One thing I like and why:


Something I want to improve is _____ because:

Thank you,

_____

Kingore, B. (2013). *Rigor and Engagement for Growing Minds.* Austin, TX: PA Publishing.

Kingore, B. (2013). *Rigor and Engagement for Growing Minds.* Austin, TX: PA Publishing.

5.15, to scaffold a framework for these student interactions and feedback.

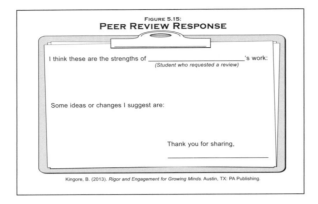

FIGURE 5.15:
**PEER REVIEW RESPONSE**

I think these are the strengths of _____'s work:
(Student who requested a review)

Some ideas or changes I suggest are:

Thank you for sharing,

_____

Kingore, B. (2013). *Rigor and Engagement for Growing Minds*. Austin, TX: PA Publishing.

### • MENTORS OR BUDDIES

The objective of mentors or buddies in a support system is not peer tutoring with a remedial focus but shared enthusiasm to extend learning about a mutual interest that is often outside the core curriculum. While educators certainly facilitate the process, mentors or buddies are most effective when self-selected by the students in response to personal interests. With teacher support as needed, the students plan their agenda, identify any potential products, access needed resources, and pursue their interest-driven topic through concepts and processes beyond grade level. Mentors or buddies may form among students within a class, between classes, or across long-distance through technology as interest-based learning attracts multiaged participants. Many members of the faculty or staff are potential mentors for students.

### • TASK ASSISTANT

Initially, teach one or two students how to complete a specific learning task or product, and post those students' digital photographs in the classroom under a sign labeled: *Task Assistant*. As individuals or small groups work, the assistant is recognized as one who can answer questions and provide help when needed. This process increases student ownership in learning, recognizes peers as resources and support agents, and is an efficient use of time for students and the teacher. Change the designated task assistant frequently as all students benefit from this opportunity.

### • SUPPORT ASSISTANT OR WELCOME-BACK BUDDY

When a student is absent, designate a classmate as a Support Assistant or Welcome-Back Buddy. The student collects an extra copy of work as it is assigned and copies the class notes so a written record is ready for the absent student. When that student returns, the buddy-support assistant is able to provide the one-on-one attention needed to reorient the student. This technique emphasizes student responsibility and collegiality as well as frees the teacher from additional details and paperwork. The process structures peer support with an in-person as well as a written record to guide the returning student's completion of missed learning opportunities.

### • SERVICE PROJECT

High school students volunteer to work with younger students as a project providing the community service hours required by some clubs and college applications. While often used with struggling students, this support technique is equally effective with high-ability learners who benefit from the advanced skills and content expected from older students.

# SCAFFOLDING FOR SUCCESS

Scaffolding is an instructional strategy providing learning support to students and then slowly retracting support as students become self-reliant. Crockett (2011) coins the term *progressive withdrawal* to explain how schools help students make a successful transition from school to life. Progressive withdrawal, however, is also a useful framework to describe the process of scaffolding. The objective is for students to decrease dependency upon adults' structure and direct involvement as they progress toward greater independence and autonomy in learning.

Willis (2011) poses an insightful analogy using digital games to explain the role of effective scaffolding. Digital games are carefully scaffolded. Game designers analyze what the gamer needs to know to be successful at each moment of participation and what they need to master in order to proceed to the next level. One of the reasons that games are so motivating is because they are planned for people to experience success early and understand that the game is designed so they can continue being successful as they work at later stages. Furthermore, students can experience trial and error relatively free from a fear of making mistakes in front of others because everyone understands that the game is designed so people learn from mistakes in order to progress to the next level.

In this sense, effective scaffolding parallels good game design. Initiate a learning task with a clear sense of purpose and appropriate challenge; then, scaffold complexity so success at each level provides the background to advance to the next. Ensure a safe environment for students to take risks and experience mis-steps along the path to success. Scaffold highly-prized social and interactive roles in learning tasks just as digital games for more than one player are incredibly social. Success in academic tasks, breeds further success and leads to a heightened sense of empowerment when students are keenly aware of their accomplishment.

## SCAFFOLDING LESSONS

Scaffolding instruction supports students so they can succeed at higher levels. Scaffold learning tasks to provide the minimum support students need to succeed. Students are expected to make errors. Your scaffolding acts as an enabler, providing the feedback and encouragement that guides students to achieve the task. Being uniquely aware of students' Zones of Proximal Development, structure a lesson so it is between the level at which students can learn without assistance and the level at which students can only learn with assistance (Vygotsky, 1962). There is an art to creating the optimal balance between supporting students learning to master a skill and pushing students to risk independence beyond their current capability.

Scaffolding fosters students' involvement in challenges just beyond their comfort zone to extend their learning growth. Skillful scaffolding is applicable to all learners. While often thought of as a strategy to provide a framework for struggling students, teachers also scaffold learning opportunities for high-ability learners to promote greater cognitive complexity.

Kingore, B. (2013). *Rigor and Engagement for Growing Minds.* Austin, TX: PA Publishing.

Scaffolding complements rigor by providing students with ways to successfully complete challenging learning experiences. It begins by focusing on students' prior knowledge and modeling applicable thinking processes and strategies in order to provide support for students as they deal with any gaps between current levels of understanding and expected levels of learning. The collaborative process of scaffolding is shown in 5.16.

Effective teachers artfully scaffold a class discussion to prepare students to be successful, increase their engagement, produce higher-level content, and model how to proceed with future discussions. Use the sequence in Figure 5.17 when scaffolding a class discussion for students.

### GRAPHIC ORGANIZERS

Graphic organizers are an appealing example to scaffold students' thinking and success, inasmuch as these visual tools provide a structure that helps students process and organize information. Scaffold applications of graphic organizers, such as charts, graphs, and outlines, to guide students' prediction, problem-solving exploration, and expansion of concepts. Scaffolding graphics not only increases students' success in integrating concepts and demonstrating skills, it also enables you to guide students toward increasing depth of content rather than simply listing accurate information. Graphic organizers are especially relevant for visual-spatial students and high-ability learners who characteristically think in relationships, prefer to organize information in unique ways, and often have a depth of understanding beyond that of their age-mates (Dean et al., 2012; Silverman, 2002).

## FIGURE 5.16:
# SCAFFOLDING: A COLLABORATIVE PROCESS

When scaffolding instruction for students, a collaborative process emerges during which the roles of teachers and students evolve.

1. Model required strategies, skills, and behaviors to students through direct instruction.
2. Students imitate the teacher's behavior.
3. Responding to observed errors, expand thinking by modeling examples and nonexamples for clarification.
4. Students practice behaviors with the your facilitation.
5. Progressively withdraw direct instruction.
6. Students continue practicing with peers and experience reciprocal teaching as they scaffold each other toward mastery.
7. The strategy, behavior, or skill is mastered and demonstrated independently by all students.
8. Some students are able to adapt the process or product to create their own examples that demonstrate new meaning and deeper understanding.

FIGURE 5.17:
# SCAFFOLDING A CLASS DISCUSSION

1. Before the discussion, propose questions for students to answer that focus concepts and terminology germane to understanding. Initially, require students to work individually to think about the topic and jot down responses to the questions.

2. Next, students work in small groups, comparing responses to produce a collective set of ideas that may be more substantial than those produced individually. As students work, they justify and explain their thinking to each other, cite text references, and correct any misconceptions in their responses.

3. Then, proceed with the class discussion. During the discussion:
   - Invite students to use any notes they accumulated as references so their input in the discussion can be more specific.
   - Suggest that students jot down new ideas as they occur so the ideas are remembered when needed at a later juncture in the discussion.
   - Encourage students to use academic vocabulary that is most related to comprehending the topic.
   - Involve students in exchanging information as you model diplomacy in language and mutual respect for ideas and differences.
   - Inject different points of view to expand students' high-level thinking.
   - Ask students to elaborate and embellish content that they or others express.
   - Encourage students to pose or respond to additional questions that arise.

4. Finally, students return to working independently to integrate new ideas into prior understanding and solidify their acquisition of concepts and skills. For example, ask students to write a conclusion that draws connections to disciplinary content and causes them to construct knowledge and deeper meaning.

Provide both simple and more complex versions of graphic organizers. After modeling experiences with these organizers, invite each student to choose between a simple or more complex version of an organizer. All students can use a graphic organizer, but a more complex graphic challenges high-ability students or those who are quite interested in the topic to demonstrate advanced levels of understanding.

As an engaging application of graphic organizers, provide a completed version of a graphic organizer with errors on it that relate to current instructional targets. In flexible groups, challenge students to locate, explain, and correct the errors. Graphics with flawed information stimulate high-level thinking and the application of specific skills and concepts as students analyze and discuss the content.

Kingore, B. (2013). *Rigor and Engagement for Growing Minds.* Austin, TX: PA Publishing.

Orchestrating
Support Systems

FIGURE 5.18:
# THINKING REFLECTIVELY

### 1. IDEAS

Identify two or more ideas you intend to apply immediately.

### 2. BE AN ENCOURAGER

Take a personal moment of reflection. In your head, voice the name of a high-ability students for whom you are ready and willing to be an unconditional encourager. Now, plan specific interventions you can do to continuing encouraging that person to maximize high potential.

### 3. CLASSROOM OBSERVATION

What evidence of a fixed or growth mindset have you observed? How might it limit or contribute to student success in your class?

### 4. SHOP TALK

> *It is engaging and often exciting to talk shop with a valued colleague. Putting your heads together produces ideas that may not have developed alone.*

Network with other professionals to create a list of suggestions and strategies to effectively support continuous learning for high-ability students. Post those suggestions on a school or district blog, and invite others to respond to and expand on your ideas.

Kingore, B. (2013). *Rigor and Engagement for Growing Minds.* Austin, TX: PA Publishing.

# Chapter 6
# Refining Assessments to Guide Instruction and Benefit Learners

Nationally, only one out of four educators think that standardized testing accurately reflects what students know or is helping to increase student competence (Neill, 2010; Scholastic-Gates, 2012). Teachers consider formative assessments, class participation, and performance on class assignments as more relevant measures of student learning (Scholastic-Gates, 2012). Neill asserts that a healthy assessment system should include limited large-scale standardized testing, extensive school-based evidence of learning, and a school quality-review process.

Educators have the power to lead this movement toward balanced assessment by clearly planning the collection of valid assessment evidence within their classes. In rigorous learning environments, educators implement multifaceted, continual assessment to guide instructional decisions and focus learning goals. Summative assessment and evaluative determinations of grades are completed as required to document achievement of those goals.

The Common Core State Standards (CCSS) requires assessments that provide actionable data completely aligned to curriculum and instruction. During initial stages of curriculum planning, educators must ensure that summative assessment is linked to the main idea of the learning target and provides opportunities for students to demonstrate conceptual levels of understanding. To implement authentic assessment, you must practice what Wiggins and McTigue (2005) call *starting with the end in mind*—starting with your learning targets. Authentic assessment procedures require you to reason-in-reverse by identifying the learning outcome and then selecting the learning experiences, resources, preassessments, and formative assessments that enable students to extend learning and reach that outcome. It is empowering to be critical thinkers rather than activity designers as we establish

Kingore, B. (2013). *Rigor and Engagement for Growing Minds.* Austin, TX: PA Publishing.

the criteria that document students' understanding of learning objectives.

# INCREASING RIGOR AND RELEVANCE IN ASSESSMENT

Assessment drives instruction. Exercise a simple way to promote rigor by implementing more complex forms of assessment. Use assessments that document achievement while challenging students to think and more fully explain demonstrations of understanding beyond simple information recall. When appropriate, include assessments that elicit beyond grade-level responses to challenge high-ability students. Assessments of work extending over time are likely to yield a far more accurate assessment of the range, depth, and quality of high-ability students' accomplishments and changes as learners. Document rigor with assessments, such as the stages of a research project, narrative assessment logs, portfolios of representative product examples, and applications of theories to solve real-world problems (Crockett, Jukes, & Churches, 2011; Neill, 2010).

To raise the level of rigor and engagement, recognize that assessment is more than administering tests and recording grades. The purpose of assessment is to gather dependable, accurate evidence that guides instruction and benefits students throughout an instructional segment by enabling them to demonstrate improvement and engage in continuous learning. We assess to inform instruction and promote learning, not solely to judge it. In other words, adopt an attitude that assessment is *for* students, not *of* students as an end in itself. In this

manner, assessment is constant, ongoing, and formative. Evaluation, judging outcomes, and recording grades to represent the level of student accomplishments are less frequent and more summative.

---

### ASSESSMENT CAUTIONS

To motivate students to demonstrate their highest level of proficiency during assessment tasks:

- Students must understand the personal value of assessment data, and
- Assessment procedures must be relevant and interesting enough to command mental and process engagement.

In reality, do we acquire valid assessment data if students perceive the evaluation process as a task to rush through so they can be done with it?

---

More authentic ways to assess must follow teachers' implementation of authentic learning tasks. When students assume the roles of authors, historians, mathematicians, or artists, for example, the question becomes: "What kinds of products should be expected from practitioners in a field of study?" Rich learning tasks, such as performances and presentations that assess how students think and respond like experts in that profession, may supersede testing as more valid assessments. Students of all ages can demonstrate learning with authors' chairs, gallery walks, digital presentations, videos, original content-related games, physical models, presentations, musical compositions or demonstrations of original experiments. The evaluation of these types of learning tasks provides information that guides continued instruction and fosters students' continued learning.

The interdependent relationship among assessment, instruction, and achievement is evident. Assessment is intended to work in tandem with instruction and correlate to the central idea of the learning segment while integrating one or more learning objectives. Employ supportive techniques, such as the standard grid in Chapter 2, to document the targeted skills in classroom learning experiences and guide the direction of assessment.

*Assessment*

•

*Assess to inform instruction and promote learning, not solely to judge it.*

During discussions regarding the role of assessment in instruction, teachers express concerns that impact assessment decisions, such as the drudgery associated with requirements to record a certain number of grades. A mountain of assignments may actually involve little learning if students are only completing different examples at the same level. It produces a losing situation—students respond negatively to *more of the same* and teachers have more paperwork to complete. Since rigor is concerned with quality, the volume of assignments is probably less significant than the merit of the tasks. Meaningful applications often require more time to complete. If a certain number of grades are required by outside decision makers, respond by breaking the long-term application into smaller units for evaluations. For example, evaluate the plan

and procedure for a grade as well as to provide formative feedback for changes before the next phase of the task continues.

Assessment is necessary to substantiate that students know more now than when this segment of instruction began. Hence assessment must document that classroom-learning experiences enabled students to *learn* and *apply* something rather than only *do* something. The CCSS does not promote assessments that focus on disconnected fact acquisition or repetitive skill practice but on helping students construct meaningful connections for themselves to promote long-term memory. Learning experiences must represent an intellectual accomplishment with personal and utilitarian value. This outcome evolves from quality assignments.

Current assessment and evaluation procedures focus heavily on the summative assessments already provided by curriculum materials and evaluations of standards. Hence, this chapter emphasizes high expectations for quality, more purposeful applications of rubrics, expanded use of preassessment, increased implementation of students' self-assessment, and an emphasis on formative assessment as procedures teachers are empowered to implement and use to influence learning. We typically cannot select which major tests are used for school or state assessment objectives. Yet, teachers do have the power to determine most of the assessments used for preassessment and formative assessment in the classroom. Preassessment

Refining Assessments

and formative assessments develop a deeper insight into high-ability students' learning-in-process and greatly augment the value of summative assessment information. Specifically address the question: "Have high-ability students demonstrated contin-ued learning or are high results on summative assessments merely reflecting their prior knowledge and skill."

## HIGH EXPECTATIONS FOR QUALITY

### EXPECTATIONS FOR EXCELLENCE

Excellence is much more than a grade or a comparison with the accomplish-ments of peers. Excellence is relative to the ways in which students change as learners from their entry point of instruction to their current achievement level.

High expectations for quality require us to conduct assessments over time to deter-mine the processes and strategies students employ as well as the products they develop. This wider view of assessment results in feed-back that fosters increasingly more sophisti-cated student work and develops students' resiliency as learners and citizens. Actively observe, question, and facilitate progress by

*Key Assessment Question*

•

*How do we determine what students know, understand, and are able to do relative to a segment of learning?*

assessing students' assimilation of targeted concepts and skills. While students are purposefully engaged in researching, adapting, and developing content.

Jones (2010) asserts that the type of assessments we choose significantly influ-ences students' level of rigor and relevance. Wolk (2009) challenges us to limit quantita-tive assessment and employ more qualitative tools, such as narratives on report cards, portfo-lios of authentic work over time, and student presentations or perform-ances. He also suggests that students are motivated to enhance the quality of their work when they are included in teacher-family conferences in which they conduct the process, present their work, and discuss strengths and areas for growth.

Communicate realistic, high expecta-tions for quality work. Work with high-ability students to generate a set of criteria that pro-motes expectations for higher quality so stu-dents can document their approximations to excellence in classroom assignments and when pursuing replacement tasks. Advanced learners need to understand that *excellence* should represent their personal best rather than a comparison with grade-level peers. Excellence is relative to their changes as learners from their entry point of instruction to their current achievement level.

Content depth, complexity, conceptual thinking, and precise vocabulary are examples of criteria communicating that content and understanding are more important than

FIGURE 6.1:
# HIGH EXPECTATIONS FOR QUALITY

| | BELOW EXPECTATIONS | GRADE-LEVEL EXPECTATIONS | ABOVE GRADE-LEVEL EXPECTATIONS | ADVANCED RESPONSE: EXCEEDS EXPECTATIONS |
|---|---|---|---|---|
| CONTENT DEPTH | Too general; some information is flawed or not accurate | Covers topic effectively; valid content; accurate facts and details but limited depth or elaboration; conveys a general idea or understanding | Extensive and detailed study; well developed; explores the topic beyond facts and details; elaborates key points; cites support for data | Precise, in-depth data; well-supported with multiple resources; concepts and relationships exceed grade-level; explores multifaceted information; insightful; thorough |
| COMPLEXITY | Too simple in content and process | Simple, basic information; limited application and critical thinking | Critical thinking is evident; compares and contrasts concepts; applies a more complicated process; supports key points | Analyzes, evaluates, adapts, and synthesizes ideas and issues across time and disciplines; logically problem solves through multiple perspectives; resources exceed grade-level |
| CONCEPTUAL THINKING | Beginning level thinking; limited | Concrete ideas; appropriate but literal; fact and event-based thinking | Concludes connections; develops relationships with some analogous thinking; infers; discusses concepts and principles; constructs deeper understanding | Symbolic or metaphorical; abstract thinking is evident; reasons beyond concrete realities or specific objects; poses principles or generalizations; idea based |
| ACADEMIC VOCABULARY | Generally accurate but basic words and descriptions | Appropriate terminology; effective syntax and semantics | Integrates specific terminology; advanced language is clear and precise in choice and application | Vocabulary enhances the communication of complex information; integrates sophisticated words and syntax; precise terminology at a professional level |

Kingore, B. (2013). *Rigor and Engagement for Growing Minds.* Austin, TX: PA Publishing.

appearance or flash value. These criteria for high quality become the main ideas for the evaluation of learning tasks. Work with students to develop rubrics, similar to the one in Figure 6.1, that incorporate these criteria and clearly communicate levels of proficiency.

In addition, provide rubrics that communicate high expectations for students' behavior during small group and individual learning applications. We use different rubrics to evaluate products and determine grades for our records. Rubrics of learning behaviors communicate behavioral expectations and guide students' reflection as they assess themselves as productive learners. These rubrics indicate how extensively students

*Learning Behavior Objective*
•
*Do everything you can to help yourself and others learn.*

exert effort to achieve. Learning behavior rubrics guide students to manage their own conduct and avoid disruptive behaviors that negatively influence the learning process of others. Students need to understand that their effort leads to higher achievement.

Use a learning behavior rubric to increase students' desire to learn and their level of achievement. Describe the levels in such a way that students understand which behaviors they are expected to demonstrate in learning applications. While it is challenging to wrestle out these delineations of productive learning behaviors, once complete, you have a powerful tool to communicate expectations to students as they work in any learning situation that you are not directly teaching. Teachers report management is greatly enhanced by this clear, communicative device. Frequently asking students to use this rubric to self-assess their learning behaviors leads them to a clearer understanding of expectations and how to have more power over their own learning. Vary the complexity and reading-level requirements of rubrics to enable this tool to be applicable for both young and more mature students as shown in Figures 6.2 and 6.3 respectively.

## AN ASSESSMENT COMMUNITY

Teaming with other teachers and school learners, dedicate some common planning time to share authentic assessment strategies, problems, and possible solutions. Building a common language and deepening understanding of assessment is a productive professional-development practice.

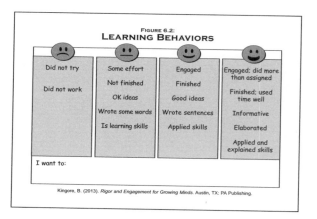

### FIGURE 6.2:
### LEARNING BEHAVIORS

| Did not try<br><br>Did not work | Some effort<br>Not finished<br>OK ideas<br>Wrote some words<br>Is learning skills | Engaged<br>Finished<br>Good ideas<br>Wrote sentences<br>Applied skills | Engaged; did more than assigned<br>Finished; used time well<br>Informative<br>Elaborated<br>Applied and explained skills |
|---|---|---|---|
| I want to: | | | |

Kingore, B. (2013). *Rigor and Engagement for Growing Minds.* Austin, TX: PA Publishing.

## *Get going!*

## COMMUNICATE ASSESSMENT TO FAMILIES

Share a copy of the class learning behavior rubric with families so they can support their child's efforts to learn.

### FIGURE 6.3:
### LEARNING BEHAVIORS

| | BELOW EXPECTATIONS | DEVELOPING LEARNER | PRACTITIONER | AUTONOMOUS CITIZEN |
|---|---|---|---|---|
| SELF-MANAGEMENT | Less self-control than expected | On task but needs some urging | Uses time appropriately with minimal supervision | Self-motivated without adult supervision |
| INTERACTION | Disrespectful | Usually respectful but interrupts others | Respects and helps others; shares; good communication skills | Respectful; encourages and redirects others; collaborator; emerging leadership skills |
| SKILL APPLICATION/ ADAPTATION | Unable to explain skill applications | Applies skills in one discipline; some inconsistencies | Accurately applies skills across disciplines | Clearly explains applications and transfers skills; transdisciplinary adaptations |
| EFFORT | Gives up easily | Works to improve when encouraged by others | Works to achieve and seeks help when needed | Works to continuously improve; goes beyond expectations |
| CONTENT DEPTH | Content is flawed and undeveloped | Accurate but basic content without elaboration | Well developed content; beyond basic facts; appropriate vocabulary | Well-supported; in-depth content; multiple perspectives; precise topic-related vocabulary |
| SELF-ASSESSMENT | Fails to assess or reflect without prodding | Generally self-assesses and reflects without prodding | Appropriate response and good analysis in self-assessment and reflection | Critical thinker; high-level, multiple-dimensional reflection and interpretation |
| To exceed expectations, I: | | | |

Kingore, B. (2013). *Rigor and Engagement for Growing Minds.* Austin, TX: PA Publishing.

Kingore, B. (2013). *Rigor and Engagement for Growing Minds.* Austin, TX: PA Publishing.

# RUBRIC APPLICATIONS

Purposeful applications of rubrics influence rigor by communicating to students what the teacher deems most significant in the learning task. While usually interpreted as a valued standard for evaluation, rubrics should also provide students with guidelines to quality by describing the requirements to achieve higher levels of proficiency on a learning task.

Think of rubrics as tools that communicate the main ideas of the learning experience. In other words, the criteria on a rubric should be main-idea statements—what is essential to high achievement. The levels of proficiency should communicate what a student is empowered to do to increase learning success. For example, when students perform at a lower level, they should read the next higher level to figure out what to do to experience higher achievement.

For a more purposeful application of rubrics, use rubrics in the following three ways to promote the personal growth and high achievement of high-ability learners.

1. **SET GOALS.**

Before beginning a learning experience, provide students with a copy of the rubric. Students set their own goals for the task by using a colored pen to mark their intended level of achievement on each criterion. Psychologists suggest that students are more inclined to work toward high achievement when they personally set the goal of reaching that objective. Intervene when students set lower goals; provide feedback that fosters their increased effort as well as offers needed support to overcome concerns or inadequacies.

2. **SELF-ASSESS.**

After students complete the task, they use a second color on the same copy of the rubric to mark self-assessments of their achievement level on each criterion. Ask them to add a reflection on the rubric comparing their goal setting with their outcome and discussing the action they envision to further their learning.

3. **EVALUATE.**

Teachers conclude the process by using a different color to evaluate the student on the same rubric copy. With well-constructed rubrics, student and teacher assessments should have very few differences, signaling that all participants in the learning process clearly understand the task requirements and criteria for higher achievement (Kingore, 2007a).

Rubrics have been widely used and perfected by teachers over the last twenty-five years. Building on prior successful experiences with rubrics, the extensions in Figure 6.4 expand the value and effective implementation of rubrics as both assessment tools (contributing information for instructional decisions) and evaluation instruments (grading learning products or processes).

*Question Outcomes*

•

*Have high-ability students demonstrated continued learning, or are high results on summative assessments merely reflecting their prior knowledge and skill?*

Refining Assessments

Kingore, B. (2013). *Rigor and Engagement for Growing Minds.* Austin, TX: PA Publishing.

FIGURE 6.4:
# EXTENDING THE VALUE OF RUBRICS

1. Use rubrics for goal setting, students' self-assessment, and teachers' evaluations to promote an atmosphere of collaboration and shared responsibility.

2. Understand that teachers' feedback to students has a direct and powerful effect on students' interpretations of what is valued in learning environments. Analyze your collection of rubrics to determine if you clearly signal to students what is expected and valued for high expectations and increased productivity. Some teachers realize that, unintentionally, their rubrics emphasize accuracy and appearance more than complexity, conceptual thinking, and depth of content.

**ASSESSMENT CRITERIA**

Instead of:
- ❑ Correct information
- ❑ Accurate application of skills
- ❑ Followed directions
- ❑ Completed on time
- ❑ Neat

Emphasize:
- ☑ In-depth information
- ☑ Conceptual thinking
- ☑ Complex ideas
- ☑ Academic vocabulary
- ☑ Extends learning for self

3. Construct generalizable rubrics that decrease the quantity of needed rubrics and increase realistic assessment applications. Endeavor to create generalizable rubrics that delineate levels for quality and high achievement while being applicable to more than one learning situation, such as the examples for graphic organizers in Figures 6.5 and 6.6. Instead of a rubric specific to a Venn diagram or concept map, consider constructing criteria that are applicable to several graphic organizers and save precious preparation time in the future. Generalizable rubrics, when carefully constructed, are a multiple-use tool to save instructional time and preparation. Students benefit as they increase confidence and understanding of high-level learning expectations through their repeated applications of a generalizable rubric.

4. Add space for action statements at the bottom of rubrics to provide opportunities for reflection and empowerment. Students conclude their self-assessment by goal setting and planning action for continued learning. With the addition of this reflective space, McTighe and O'Connor (2005, 13) conclude that "the rubric moves from being simply an evaluation tool for 'pinning a number' on students to a practical and robust vehicle for feedback, self-assessment, and goal setting."

5. Incorporate exemplars that challenge students to reach high expectations. At the highest levels of proficiency on a rubric or in the space for an action statement, include phrases, such as *exceeds expectations* or *goes beyond the assigned task,* to encourage students to risk a higher response or a personal extension to the learning experience.

Kingore, B. (2013). *Rigor and Engagement for Growing Minds.* Austin, TX: PA Publishing.

## FIGURE 6.5:
## GRAPHIC ORGANIZER

|  | DEVELOPING | PROFICIENT | EXCEEDING |
|---|---|---|---|
| Content | Simple<br>Limited<br>understanding | Well developed<br>Correct<br>Basic facts | Detailed<br>Elaborated<br>Interesting<br>Meaningful<br>Informative |
| Communication<br>Vocabulary<br>. , ? ! | Made mistakes<br>Confusing<br>Simple words | Mostly correct<br>Good words<br>Good sentences<br>Uses:<br>. ? | Skillful<br>Powerful words<br>Strong sentences<br>Uses:<br>. , ? ! |
| Thinking | Knows some facts | Understands<br>Applies ideas<br>Compares<br>Reflects | Explains<br>Analyzes<br>Unique ideas<br>Evaluates<br>Reflects and adapts |
| Neat and<br>Organized | Not neat<br>Hard to follow | Attractive<br>Organized<br>Clearly developed | Eye-catching<br>Well organized<br>Skillfully developed<br>Enhances content |
| Effort | Did not work well<br>Did not try<br>Off task | Started<br>Worked<br>Sought support<br>Effort shows | Started on time<br>Worked well<br>Finished on time<br>Encouraged others<br>Effort led to<br>achievement |

Kingore, B. (2013). *Rigor and Engagement for Growing Minds.* Austin, TX: PA Publishing.

## FIGURE 6.6:
## GRAPHIC ORGANIZER

|  | BELOW STANDARD | APPRENTICE | PROFICIENT | EXCEEDING |
|---|---|---|---|---|
| CONTENT | Little knowledge evident; reiterates facts without complete accuracy | Provides basic facts; lacks some key ideas; valid but little depth | Informative; well-developed major ideas and concepts; explores beyond facts; appropriate substantiation | Meaningful and interesting; relates in-depth concepts and relationships; well supported; examines issues; constructs original understanding and connections |
| COMMUNICATION AND VOCABULARY | Serious errors make reading and understanding difficult; limited vocabulary | Errors are evident but content is readable; emerging skills; appropriate but basic vocabulary | Communicates clearly; minimal errors in mechanics and spelling; descriptive language is appropriate with elaboration | Skillfully communicates; fluid; enhanced by error free application of mechanics; uses specific terminology; precise, advanced syntax and semantics; rich imagery |
| THINKING AND COMPREHENSION | Vague; basic | General understanding; limited questioning or examination of evidence; lacks support of thinking | Critical thinking; understands scope of problem and at least one issue; conclusion reflects examination of information; explains and supports thinking | Critical and creative thinking; understands scope and issues; conclusions based upon thorough evaluation of evidence; evaluates consequences and reasonable alternatives; original and thorough |
| ORGANIZATION AND APPEARANCE | Unclear; lacks organization; little care evident; incomplete | Attempts to organize but is hard to follow; wanders; appearance is adequate | Organized effectively; a good beginning and ending; well structured; attractive and visually appealing | Coherent; skillfully planned; logically organized to communicate well; eye-catching; aesthetically pleasing; beyond expectations |
| EFFORT | Did not try; off task | Tried to work and learn; appropriately sought assistance when needed | Effort is evident; used time well; exchanged support with peers as needed | Effort led to high achievement; resourceful; autonomous; supported others when needed |

Kingore, B. (2013). *Rigor and Engagement for Growing Minds.* Austin, TX: PA Publishing.

Assessment development tools, such as a digital rubric generator (Kingore, 2007b), allow teachers and students to select among thousands of criteria combinations to construct customized rubrics and other assessment devices appropriate to the readiness levels of students in different grade levels, including pictorial rubrics to communicate quality to young and ELL learners. RubiStar (rubistar.4teachers.org) is another favorite tool for creating scoring guides. In addition, these resources are particularly useful for enabling students to produce their own rubrics to assess their projects and inquiry. Student-developed assessment tools help to solidify students' understanding of quality, foster self-assessment, and increase achievement.

## PREASSESSMENT

Preassessment is nonnegotiable. It should precede instruction in every topic to increase learning success by illuminating what students know and need to know. A potential benefit of preassessment that surprises some teachers is a trade-off in time. Specifically, the class time it takes to preassess can actually save instructional time later. Armed with preassessment data, teachers substantiate which skills or concepts to emphasize and which to delete from instruction because students already demonstrate mastery.

Preassessment techniques provide the baseline data that enlighten potential insights from formative assessments, empowering students and teachers to analyze growth and changes as learners. The CCSS and

Kingore, B. (2013). *Rigor and Engagement for Growing Minds.* Austin, TX: PA Publishing.

standards-based curricula stress more extensive use of preassessment and formative assessment to provide feedback over time of students' responses during a learning segment in order to increase the students' learning and their success on summative assessments. The preassessment results enhance the value and depth of information from the formative assessment.

Preassessment guides the pace and level of instruction. Decisions of instructional pace and level based on data from preassessment techniques ensure that all students engage in learning at their highest readiness level. Preassessment is particularly crucial for high-ability students who frequently enter a segment of learning knowing some or all of the targeted concepts and skills. Use preassessment results to enable these students to experience continuous learning and avoid the less meaningful repetition of known content. When we recognize and are responsive to what students have previously mastered, students are more motivated to exert the effort required to excel. Students are seldom bored when learning tasks match their readiness and interests.

Testing is certainly a form of preassessment—using summative tests before the segment of learning begins or employing benchmark tests to evaluate readiness for targeted standards. However, I suggest the term preassessment rather than *pretest* to emphasize that the process of determining learning readiness can be accomplished in so many ways beside tests. Since many teachers and students are weary of testing, effective teachers use a variety of purposeful tools and procedures to gather assessment information, such as the examples in Figure 6.7.

## FIGURE 6.7:
# PREASSESSMENT TOOLS

- Anecdotal records
- Auditions
- Checklists reviewing skills and concepts
- Discussions
- Graphic organizers
- Interest inventories
- Learning logs
- Observations
- Performance tasks
- Problem solving samples
- Process interviews
- Products from the prior learning experiences
- Questioning
- Records of independent reading of both fiction and nonfiction
- Students' self-assessments
- Writing samples

### PREASSESSMENT IS AN ASSET

Preassessment potentially saves some students from frustration when the skills and concepts exceed their readiness; other students are saved from boredom and allowed the right to extend their learning.

## CAUTIONS

1. **DO NOT GRADE PREASSESS-MENTS.** Review them to guide instruction. Grading a preassessment risks penalizing students for prior experiences and is counterproductive to their motivation to learn.

2. **NOT SURE.** Rather than students guessing at a response when they complete preassessments, ask them to use a question mark to signal any skill or idea they do not understand well. I assure them that the question mark is not a negative about them; it tells me what to teach by indicating skills and concepts for which additional instruction and learning experience would be beneficial. Students usually enjoy telling me what to teach, so they eagerly use the question mark.

*Get going!*

### INTERNET ASSESSMENTS

In addition to rubrics, a variety of assessment tools are available on the Internet to deliver timely, specific feedback to help students experience academic gains. Since these resources are subject to inconsistent and flawed information, be a critical consumer. As you gain expertise in evaluating assessment tools, survey web sites to add to your repertoire of applications.

# STUDENT SELF-ASSESSMENT

Many students view grades as something totally determined by teachers. Students signal this interpretation through frequent comments, such as "The teacher *gave* me an *A-,*" or a *91* or a *check-plus*. Obviously the more appropriate interpretation from students would be to acknowledge and discuss what they *earned.* Being responsible for self-assessment increases students' use of the verb *earned* instead of *gave*.

Embrace self-assessment to enable advanced students to more concretely view their progress and assume ownership for their growth. The core of assessment, particularly when authentic learning experiences are involved, is student ownership. Students must assume responsibility for their own learning in order to maximize learning potential. As Costa and Kallick warned in 1992, if we allow students to graduate from our high schools still dependent on others to tell them if they are completing inadequate, good, or excellent work, we have failed to prepare them for their future.

Expand applications of students' self-assessments. Using self-assessment formats, such as rubrics, reflective thinking, learning logs, narrative responses, and checklists of concept and skill applications, escalates achievement as it necessitates students' increased involvement in their own learning. Through consistently evaluating their own achievement, students become better achievers with a greater incentive to improve (Marzano, 2010b; Stiggins, 2007). Wolk (2009) recommends that students assess most of their work before teachers review it; he also endorses

Kingore, B. (2013). *Rigor and Engagement for Growing Minds.* Austin, TX: PA Publishing.

asking students to complete a photocopy of a blank report card before teachers fill it out. The International Baccalaureate program (2007) advocates students' self-assessment to extend their thinking, metacognition, and foster habits of a rigorous examination of evidence for potential bias or other inaccuracies.

Demonstrate both high-quality and lower-quality learning responses to build students' understanding of expectations and help them formulate more concrete targets for quality. When appropriate, provide a rubric and facilitate as groups of students practice assessment. They discuss the criteria and work together to reach consensus using the rubric to evaluate high-quality and lower-quality products presented as examples.

> Involve students in self-assessing homework.
> - "Draw a star beside three examples you like. Check one example you would like to improve and write why."
> - "Draw a happy face by something you did really well. Check something you would like to improve."

## STUDENT REFLECTION

Reflection is a metacognitive process. It is an authentic way that students practice and develop cognitive skills, particularly when they analyze their applications of basic knowledge to complex, unique situations. The very act of reflection further develops cognitive skills.

Students' reflective thinking is crucial to higher expectations and their growth toward becoming autonomous learners. Students need to reflect on the merits and demerits of their own work. Frequently, expect students to conclude a segment of learning by reflecting on their experiences, conclusions, methods of reasoning, and quality. Reflective thinking elicits their perceptions which may differ from the perceptions of observers.

I had an opportunity to talk with a former student recently who is currently completing his Ph.D. As we recalled his days in my classes, he commented on the process of reflection: "That was my least favorite responsibility and something you always made us do. You seemed to think it was so important." His comments caused me to reflect! I continue to believe that reflection after a lesson helps students process information at a personal and deeper level. I believe that reflection elicits understanding or reveals misconceptions that are not perceived by merely finishing the lesson. However, his perspective reinforced three principals that influence the effectiveness of reflection.

1. ***MODEL MORE THAN TELL.***
   Rather than only explain, demonstrate instructional processes you consider extremely important. Demonstrate to students the personal relevance of reflection by clearly and convincingly confirming how reflection furthers their understanding and guides continued instruction. Model a think aloud of your reflective process. Ask students to volunteer to share a think aloud of their processes. Involve students in debriefing after completing a reflection to emphasize the results, new insights gained from the reflection, and salient points of the process.

Kingore, B. (2013). *Rigor and Engagement for Growing Minds.* Austin, TX: PA Publishing.

## 2. ACTIVE ENGAGEMENT TRUMPS PASSIVE LEARNING.

Do not merely tell students to reflect, engage them in reflection. Endeavor to make reflection more interactive and peer-based in contrast to always requiring an individual written response. Work to alleviate what some may perceive as the *drudgery* of reflection.

## 3. ASK THE LEARNERS.

Frequently, ask students for their reactions to instructional procedures. (Do not risk waiting until they are adults who explain changes that might have improved instruction when they were your students.) Elicit their reactions more regularly and follow through by using as many of their suggestions as feasible.

Reflection and formative assessment are symbiotic in classroom learning situations. Formative assessment stimulates student reflection, and reflection provides formative assessment insights. Student reflection about core-curriculum, class-assigned learning tasks facilitate our instructional decisions. Actively observe students as they work; employ simple reflective responses to ensure they are engaged in relevant learning and not *twiddling thumbs* over mastered concepts and skills. For example, ask students to discuss or briefly write about what they gain from a lesson.

> *Reflection and Formative Assessment*
>
> •
>
> *Student reflection and formative assessment are symbiotic. Formative assessment stimulates student reflection, and reflection provides formative assessment insights.*

Student reflection about independent projects or replacement tasks enhances their achievement. As they pursue replacement tasks and research projects, require high-ability students to maintain a daily log self-assessing and reflecting on their goals, learning behaviors, effort, and results. Periodically, review these self-reflections and debrief with students as appropriate to facilitate and support their learning as well as motivate more sophisticated work. It is important to ensure that high-ability students maintain records of progress and personal changes as learners rather than solely gauge their results through comparisons with grade-level peers.

Reflective questions, similar to the following, are frequently used and prove fruitful to guide some students' reflections. Additionally, the Questioning for High-level Thinking document in Figure 4.8 of Chapter 4 includes many prompts appropriate for stimulating student reflection. To guide their progress and enable more productive conversations with others about potential changes for continued learning, request that students record their thoughts and feelings as they complete each phase of an independent project. Reflection leads students to discover alternative ways or solutions to problems and determine adaptations to their process.

- "What are some aspects of your learning task that are going well?"
- "What is something that is causing a problem for you? Why?"

Kingore, B. (2013). *Rigor and Engagement for Growing Minds.* Austin, TX: PA Publishing.

• "Is there some part you would like to discuss with someone else? Why?"
• "What is your advice to someone starting a similar project?"

Reflecting with a peer is more engaging for some students. They adapt their process or products better when they talk over ideas with someone else and often produce ideas that may not have developed alone. The Peer Review Request in Chapter 5 is one device for organizing reflection between peers. Peer editing is another well-used strategy that authentically fosters reflection.

Schedule time for student reflection. In today's busy classrooms, what is not specifically scheduled is less likely to occur. Set aside time at the conclusion of a lesson or learning task for students to reflect on their process or progress, particularly when these reflections need to be written so they can be shared and reviewed at later times. The reflections help students celebrate current success, organize their thinking, identify beneficial changes, and recognize which direction to pursue to foster their continued learning progress.

Whenever students are assigned to watch an instructional video, for example, whether in class or as part of a flipped classroom, schedule interactive, reflective activities to reveal their perceptions and support their cognitive processing of the concepts and information. Students need time for metacognition to prime the cognitive processing required to connect known to new knowledge, connect content to learning objectives, and discern personal relevance to the information.

## FORMATIVE ASSESSMENT

Formative assessment evaluates real-time learning–a timely assessment of what students do and do not comprehend during a lesson so accommodations can be immediately initiated. This data enables teachers to adjust instruction and provide students feedback about accomplishments or specific errors and conceptions or misconceptions, to facilitate higher levels of success. It is *formative* when the evidence is used to form instructional adaptations that promote learning, such as adjusting the pace and level of instruction or forming groups of students for coaching or extensions. As McTighe and O'Connor (2005, 10) assert: "Waiting until the end of a teaching period to find out how well students have learned is simply too late." You have already missed opportunities to adjust the pace, depth, and complexity of students' learning.

Formative assessment data helps teachers plan different ways to use instructional time, collaborating with students to bridge the gap between current achievement and where students need to be relative to significant learning targets. It enables the kinds of feedback students require to develop and maintain a growth mindset (Dweck, 2006).

The formative process is cyclical. It encourages students' self-regulation of their learning by helping them to understand the learning objective, determine how close their current work approximates it, and collaboratively plan with the teacher what to do next to progress their learning (Hattie & Timperley, 2007). As the instruction continues, this cycle is repeated until the time for summative assessment.

Use formative assessment to conclude a learning segment with content reflection. Sousa's (2009) concept of *recency* tells us that students remember best what they experience last in a lesson. Formative assessment effectively elicits students' perceptions of learning opportunities and acquisition of skills as it fosters students' high-level thinking through their analysis and review of current learning.

During any formative assessment procedure, complete an overview assessment of the achievement and understanding of all students before concentrating on individuals who need assistance. Ginsburg (2012) cautions teachers to assess all students before assisting individuals in order to avoid assessment misconceptions that result from interacting with only a few students. Asking one student to answer a question posed during a whole-class lecture does not provide valid assessment information regarding the state of learning for the other students. Use observation, every-student responses, and variations of checking-in for immediate feedback of all students' understanding of a current segment of the lesson before initiating assistance with individuals.

## OBSERVATION

Observation is a significant means to monitor students' learning and gather formative assessment information. As students engage in the learning task, circulate to jot down observations of students' approximations to the learning objective to guide instructional adaptations and decision-making. Problem-solving conversations among group members also provide formative assessment opportunities as teachers and students alike can watch, listen, and infer students' levels of

understanding and cognitive processing strategies. Rigorous learning environments, in keeping with the CCSS requirements, focus on developing and assessing conceptual understanding as students apply previously learned content.

In addition to technological notation devices, an observation checklist of skills and concepts, as shown in Figure 6.8, is an efficient tool that supports teachers' focus on pertinent skill and concept applications and helps limit distractions from students' sidebar conversations and behaviors. Keeping the checklist brief promotes an efficient documentation of students' capabilities, progress, and achievement. For this jot down, list the names of the students in a small group and note observed skill and concept applications or reteaching needs as part of your formative assessments. Use the checklist during direct instruction or

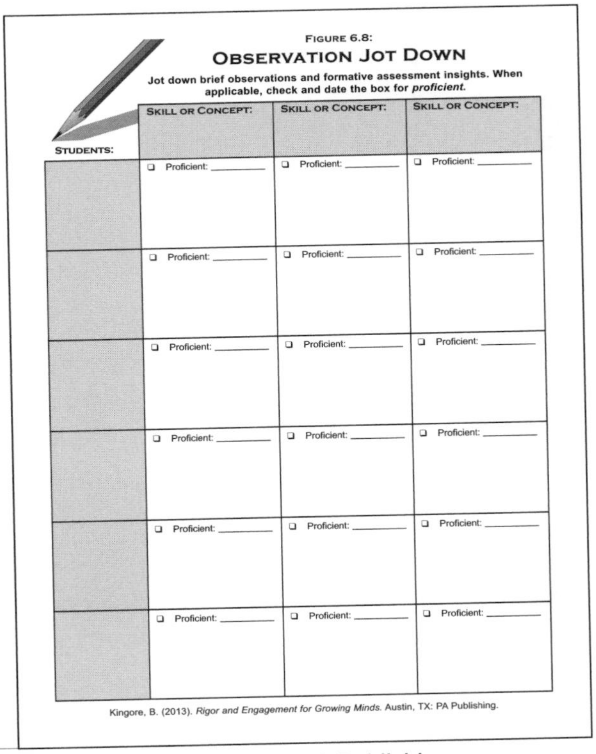

**FIGURE 6.8:**
**OBSERVATION JOT DOWN**

Jot down brief observations and formative assessment insights. When applicable, check and date the box for *proficient.*

Kingore, B. (2013). *Rigor and Engagement for Growing Minds.* Austin, TX: PA Publishing.

Kingore, B. (2013). *Rigor and Engagement for Growing Minds.* Austin, TX: PA Publishing.

when observing students engaged in group or independent application tasks.

## QUESTIONING

Questioning is a favored, productive means to generate formative assessment data. However, we want to ensure that we are eliciting information about students' levels of understanding rather than intimidating students with an atmosphere of interrogation. Implement the suggestions in Figure 6.9 to increase the formative assessment value of productive questioning.

## FORMATIVE ASSESSMENT APPLICATIONS

Consolidate preassessment and formative assessment data to document continuous learning. As an ongoing, insightful assessment task for learners, combine preassessment and formative assessment in a sequenced assessment process. After students complete a preassessment in one color ink, they return to that same document later in the learning cycle, using a second color ink to review, change, correct, add, and elaborate content on their preassessment. Encourage students to compare and contrast their learning results thus far, and then set goals for their next step in this learning segment. Students either revisit this assessment again as appropriate later in the learning cycle or file their results as documentation of mastery and readiness before beginning replacement tasks to continue learning.

## COMMUNICATING ASSESSMENT INFORMATION WITH FAMILIES

Use the results from the previously described preassessment and formative assessment combination when conducting parent or family-member conferences. This integrated process enables the families to more concretely understand the continuous progress of their children.

*Teachers' efficiency with formative assessment is a key to students' proficiency with summative assessment.*
–Ginsburg, 2012

Implement frequent and purposeful formative assessments to determine the state of students' learning. Substantiating student achievement in relation to learning goals clarifies our subsequent instructional decisions—we understand more clearly what to do next to help students move ahead. Teachers who strategically implement formative assessment are seldom surprised by students' performance on summative assessments. As Ginsburg (2012) observed, teachers' efficiency with formative assessment is a key to students' proficiency with summative assessment.

---

Kingore, B. (2013). *Rigor and Engagement for Growing Minds.* Austin, TX: PA Publishing.

## FIGURE 6.9:
# QUESTIONING FOR FORMATIVE ASSESSMENT

**✦ QUESTION WITH FAIRNESS**

Instead of promoting anxiety, encourage intellectual risk taking and higher responses by only asking students questions that they should be prepared to answer from classroom learning experiences. It is not helpful to play *gotcha* by posing questions that students do not have the background to tackle.

**✦ STIMULATE THINKING WITH A GRAPHIC**

Share a completed content-related graphic organizer and ask students what they notice, what similarities and differences they can identify, or what conclusions they can make. You will conclude a clearer sense of what they understand as you solicit their perceptions.

**✦ POSE THE QUESTION FIRST**

Insert the student's name at the end of a question since some students tune out as soon as they know they're not being called on (Ginsburg, 2012). Ask the question, pause about thirty seconds for cognitive focusing time, and then identify the student who is to respond.

**✦ ALLOW WAIT TIME AND ENCOURAGE PLANNING**

Pose a question and ask students to plan a response. Wait a minute while all students jot down notes to prepare a response, and then call on a student to answer. This process only takes an extra minute but dramatically increases the likelihood that all students are thinking and processing related information.

**✦ PAIR-SHARE**

Pose a question and allow students to work in pairs and put their heads together to generate a response before randomly calling on one pair to respond. Increase assessment value by calling on one or more additional pairs to build on the initial response. Challenge students to incorporate specific academic vocabulary as they plan. As students interact to share particulars and develop a response, they cognitively process information from multiple perspectives and increase their development of meaning.

**✦ TEACH, DON'T TELL**

Avoid answering your own question when students are slow to respond. Otherwise, students learn to wait, knowing you will eventually just tell them what you wanted to hear.

**✦ DEMONSTRATE SENSITIVITY**

Brain-based learning reminds us that healthy social and emotional conditions are paramount to achievement; when students feel anxious, the amygdala blocks learning (Willis, 2007a). There are instances when you should request volunteers rather than cold call students you observe demonstrating anxiety about questioning, reading aloud, or other tasks that they may feel self-conscious performing in front of others (Ginsburg, 2012). When possible, seek out those students later to discern reasons for their anxiety and determine what can be done.

Kingore, B. (2013). *Rigor and Engagement for Growing Minds.* Austin, TX: PA Publishing.

Refining Assessments

## FORMATIVE AND SUMMATIVE ASSESSMENT

Some assessment procedures are applicable as both formative and summative tools. For example, incorporating peer editing or including a revise-and-resubmit step when students work on research, graphics, and written tasks provides students with feedback for recommended revisions (formative assessment) prior to submitting the final product (summative assessment).

## EXIT TICKETS AS ADVANCED ORGANIZERS

Pose the exit ticket question at the beginning of a lesson to prime students' active listening. Then, students write a response at the end of the lesson.

Formative assessment is a major focus in rigorous learning environments and prominent in the language of the CCSS. It challenges students to reflect upon their academic achievement thus far in a learning segment and their comfort level regarding current learning targets, not how interesting they find the topic. With formative assessments, students reveal what they currently understand about the topic or skills to guide the teacher's decisions about pace and level of instruction as well as small group applications.

As I work with schools across the nation, a reoccurring theme is teachers' need for specific and effective kinds of formative assessments. Educators are convinced of the value of these assessments as important measures of student learning (Scholastic-Gates, 2012) but lack an applicable repertoire of tools that work effectively and efficiently. Multiple assessment procedures provide valuable formative assessment information, such as revise-and-resubmit, student reflections, exit tickets, peer editing, quizzes, and constructed responses that mirror the question format of high-stakes tests. Despite that, teachers express serious concerns about the use of class time; they want to assess learning and progress but feel they cannot afford time-consuming assessments.

The applications that follow respond to educators' requests for examples of formative assessments that streamline preparation and implementation time. Teachers need to feel empowered to implement formative assessment without compromising the precious time needed for instruction. It is important to remember, however, that the ultimate objective is information about the learning in progress. There is often an inverse relationship between the efficiency of the assessment procedure and the instructional value of the data secured by the process.

Numerous educators recommend the following assessment techniques as efficient and effective formative assessment procedures. I categorize these techniques as either *in-the-moment* or *more expanded* feedback.

In-the-moment techniques are more instant feedback devices providing brief but immediate assessment information. The more expanded devices potentially increase the assessment information but involve three to five minutes of students' time and require a bit more time to review after class for assessment conclusions. Combinations of both are applicable and desirable during many segments of instruction. Each of the following formative assessment procedures is preceded by a check box. As you read these techniques, ease decisions of future applications by checking any techniques you intend to use.

Adding quick notes on a pad or checklist enhances formative assessment information. Circulate among students to more closely observe their responses and interactions. When possible, write brief notes to heighten the value of information related to the achievement and capabilities of specific students.

*Formative Assessment*

•

*There is often an inverse relationship between the efficiency of the assessment procedure and the instructional value of the data secured by the process.*

## IN-THE-MOMENT FORMATIVE ASSESSMENTS

### TECHNOLOGY

Technology offers several ways for students to provide instant formative assessment feedback to teachers. Review potential applications available with your technology packages and network with others to determine useful assessments.

### EVERY-STUDENT-RESPONSE TOOLS

Individual wipe-off boards, laminated cardstock, or technological devices invite each student to respond to a formative assessment prompt or question, immediately supplying assessment information that informs teachers of in-the-moment comprehension of individual students. Observe and note which students quickly record their responses, whose responses exceed expectations, who looks around for help before responding, and who would benefit from reteaching or additional practice to increase their understanding.

The every-student-response assessments are best used with short-answer, often single-word or quick-graphic responses to compensate for differences in students' writing speeds. The technique invites a wipe-off, sloppy-copy feature that emphasizes a more risk-free response. (See Risk Taking in Chapter 5.)

### FORTUNATELY/UNFORTUNATELY DISCUSSIONS

This interactive assessment requires students to briefly discuss a designated topic or process, such as conducting a science experiment or completing and checking a math problem. Initially, read aloud the book *Fortunately* by Remy Charlip—a humorous picture book exploring how the many events in one's life can be interpreted from a fortunate or unfortunate perspective. This point-of-view response is effectively applied to content by

Kingore, B. (2013). *Rigor and Engagement for Growing Minds.* Austin, TX: PA Publishing.

challenging students to reorganize the current topic or the problem into a series of *fortunately–unfortunately* statements, as in the following example.

Teacher: "Fortunately, coal is a sedimentary rock in large supply as a fossil fuel in the USA."

Student 1: "Unfortunately, when burned, it emits toxic gases and liquid chemicals that are harmful to our global environment."

Student 2: "Fortunately, coal consumption in the US is decreasing and the industry is exploring ways for coal to burn cleaner."

Student 3: "Unfortunately, it remains the dominant source of electricity in the US and is the fastest growing fuel worldwide."

Student 1: "Fortunately..."

To begin the application, announce a content-related fortunately statement. Students stand in groups of three, face each other, and determine who goes first. A trio is important so the same student does not always create the *fortunately* statements. In their groups, students proceed to take turns responding to that initial statement, continuing the pattern with alternating points of view. Their statements must switch perspective for every response. The rounds continue among students until the designated time is spent; typically, two or three minutes produce an appropriate quantity of content.

For added assessment value, require students to use the most specific academic vocabulary related to the topic. This interactive formative assessment requires students to reprocess known information from multiple points of view. They have to cognitively process the content for deeper meaning, as this form is quite different from the original resource.

Circulate among the groups, coaching and informally assessing by writing brief notes. The process requires students' to actively listen and respond to each other's information. With this quick assessment, engagement is increased by fast pacing and by holding students accountable for learning. For example, conclude by randomly drawing one or more students' names and ask each to summarize their group discussion.

As a variation, use this technique as an interactive application of reading comprehension or content understanding. The trio of students retells a story or event in sequence as a fourth student uses a checklist of the content as an assessment tool and checks off each correct event or detail the trio is able to incorporate.

## ◼ CHECKING-IN

Checking-In is a technique with multiple variations that provide student engagement and formative assessment information. The objective is for students to share their current state of understanding and confidence about a topic or skill. Cue Cards, Feedback Numbers, Action Responses, as well as Assessment Sticks are worthwhile check-in applications.

## ◼ CUE CARDS

Cue Cards are an instant response technique in which all students are asked to display a colored card to provide quick feed-back about levels of understanding regarding the current instructional content (ASCD, 2008). Each student has three cards: *C* for *clarify*, *U* for *I understand*, and *E* for *I have an example* or *I can elaborate.* Students hold up a card to cue the teacher to the students' levels of understanding and questions. The cue cards are colored to aid immediate visual recognition.

As a formative assessment technique, stop at a juncture of learning and ask students to use the cue cards. State or display key terms, key points, or pose an essential question and then say to the class: "I want you to use your cards to respond. Show me which terms or key points you need clarified, which ones you know and understand, and the ones for which you can provide examples or elaborate." Each student holds up the most appropriate card to reflect current learning level and specify the action needed to continue to learn. If students don't understand something, they hold up the *C* card; if they understand, they extend the *U* card or *E* card. Use this data to quickly assess and vary instruction to respond to students' conceptions and misconceptions. Students displaying the *E* card can be called upon or elect to respond to other students to help them better understand the material by elaborating or enriching the content with examples.

Additionally, invite students to use the cue cards at any time throughout instruction to signal needs for clarification. This system may prove faster than students raising their hands and the teacher having to stop and ask what is

needed. For example, sometime during a lesson, a student extends an *E* card to inject a personal example or insight.

### FEEDBACK NUMBERS

A Feedback Number invites students to provide feedback regarding their level of confidence with topic content and skills as well as where they are in the learning cycle (Kingore, 2008). The class discusses a scale similar to the example provided in Figure 6.10. At a juncture in a lesson, students close their eyes and hold up the number of fingers that indicate their feedback number relative to their current level of understanding. Having students close their eyes helps ensure more accurate individual reflections.

## FIGURE 6.10:
# FEEDBACK NUMBERS

**5** I own this! I understand information and connections beyond what was taught.

**4** I get it! I understand what was taught and can apply this without making mistakes.

**3** I know some parts. I don't understand all of it yet.

**2** I understand some of this. I need some help to do this well.

**1** I need another way to learn this.

Kingore, B. (2013). *Rigor and Engagement for Growing Minds.* Austin, TX: PA Publishing.

When asking students for a feedback number, tell them that the curriculum plan suggests that they should be at a *one* or *two* or *three* at this point. This information is important so students do not misinterpret that a feedback number of *four* or *five* is the present goal.

A feedback number guides instruction by clarifying students' perspective of their learning needs. It facilitates decisions regarding which students would benefit from a different approach, reteaching, continuing guided practice, faster pacing, or extensions.

### ACTION RESPONSES

Action Responses are a checking-in assessment particularly enjoyed by younger students but effective to activate engagement from students of many ages. During instruction or for closure of a lesson, state an action for children to demonstrate to assess content or skills, such as: "Raise both arms over your head if..." or "Stand up if..." Then, specify the assessment prompt:

*   "...this is making sense to you."
*   "...you can do this now."
*   "...this seems hard to do."

As a variation during instruction, state a response for young children to demonstrate as content is shared. Say:

*   "Clap two times when the shape I hold up is a square."
*   "Thumbs up if the statement is true. Thumbs down if it is not true."
*   "Touch your nose when I point to a capital letter."
*   "Use your fingers on both of your hands to show me the solution to this math word problem."

### ASSESSMENT STICKS

For immediate formative assessment with primary children, provide craft sticks with a construction paper shape stapled at the top. The paper shape has a different face on each side–a happy face on one side and a questioning expression on the other face. At a learning juncture, ask the children to hold up the face that shows how they feel about their level of understanding for this information. The intent is to elicit their comfort with the learning target, not whether they like the topic.

## MORE EXPANDED FORMATIVE ASSESSMENTS

### I NOTICE... I FEEL... I WANT... I THINK...

These open-ended thinking prompts elicit students' written reflections and perceptions. Assigning two or more of the sentence stems usually provides more information; however, assign only one of the prompts when time is of the essence. Students can complete this reflection when concluding a discussion, ending a direct-teaching lesson, finishing a small group task, completing silent reading, or reviewing homework.

### CONSTRUCTED RESPONSE

The Northern Nevada Writing Project (2011) explains a constructed response as a written answer to a question that is structured to document students' understanding. In a constructed response, students are taught to answer the question, cite supporting text or graphics, and then examine their response for thoroughness and accuracy. A constructed response is framed in high-level thinking and includes a student's restatement of the question, simple answer, supporting evidence, and concluding thoughts. It is particularly effective for nonfiction information.

(http://writingfix.com/RICA/
Constructed_Response.htm)

### THREE-WAY VENN

In small groups, students draw a large three-way Venn to compare the similarities and differences of three examples of a topic, such as three different biomes, carnivores, explorers or events during the Civil Rights movement. When students arrive at the point where they develop the information for the center of the Venn, they have to determine similarities that actually identify the essence of the concept. For example, they conclude which attributes make a biome a biome.

### ANALOGIES OF KEY TERMINOLOGY

Design analogies as formative assessments. Analogies require students to analyze and demonstrate their understanding of vocabulary that is essential to a topic and apply it in a new context. Asking students to figure out incomplete analogies provides formative assessment information to guide instructional decisions regarding students' readiness for extensions or the need for clarifications.

- Square is to 90 degrees as _____ is to 60 degrees.
- _____ is to atom as core is to earth.
- Superlative is to the highest degree as _____ is to exaggeration.

- Manifest Destiny is to a covered wagon in Oregon as _____ is to the Great Wall in China.

After students gain experience completing analogies using key terminology, increase the complexity of the formative assessment by asking individual or pairs of students to create their own analogies using assigned key vocabulary terms.

### 3-2-1 SUMMARY

Use the familiar 3-2-1 technique to promote summarization and provide formative assessment information. Students respond to the prompts in Figure 6.11 the last few minutes of a planned lesson. The teacher reviews the results after class to guide instruction and grouping decisions for the next lesson.

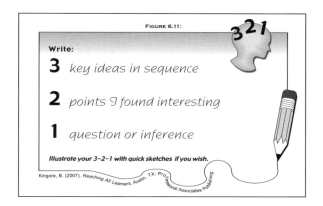

FIGURE 6.11:

Write:

**3** *key ideas in sequence*

**2** *points I found interesting*

**1** *question or inference*

*Illustrate your 3-2-1 with quick sketches if you wish.*

Kingore, B. (2007). *Reaching All Learners.* Austin, TX: Professional Associates Publishing.

If expanded use of the data is warranted, facilitate the next day as the group combines all of the different ideas and organizes the responses on a four-column chart with category headings of *Key Ideas, Interesting Points, Inferences,* and *Questions* to promote further discussion. Students prioritize the most significant points by noting how frequently some ideas appear. The process invites high-level thinking and skill integration, such as identifying main ideas, sequence, inference, or recognizing cause-effect relationships.

### ERROR INVESTIGATION

Use Error Investigation as a formative assessment following a specific skill lesson. Provide content with skill errors purposely planted in it that relate to the current skill instruction. Students are challenged to think about the skill as they identify, explain, and correct the errors. For closure, inform the class that there is misinformation or mistakes in the content you are now showing them without revealing how many errors are included. By not revealing the number of errors, students must continue actively processing the content rather than stopping when they identify a specified quantity. Working in pairs, students jot down on a sticky note which errors they can identify and explain. This assessment technique is engaging, as many students respond enthusiastically to finding others' errors. After two minutes, ask students to share and compare what they found or have them post the sticky notes on the board or door as they exit for you to review after class.

Error Investigation is particularly applicable with math problems, a science process, historical information, story retelling, vocabulary, grammar, and spelling skills. The novelty of flawed information is an effective device to stimulate students' attention to key concepts and skills (Kingore, 2007c).

### THE HAMBURGER

As described by the Northern Nevada Writing Project (Harrison, 2011), a hamburger paragraph has a topic sentence and conclusion representing the two pieces of bread and three supporting detail sentences for the meat and condiments. It is not a particularly authentic writing format as one would not expect such a structured paragraph in real-world text, but its application as a formative assessment has value. Conclude a lesson by asking students to "make a hamburger response" to demonstrate their understanding. Students produce a summary of the content through this structured written response.

### ACROSTIC

As a formative assessment, present a concept or topic word essential to current study and have pairs of students complete the assessment by writing key ideas organized for each letter of that word. Academic conversations result as students determine which words or ideas they think most essential to the prompt. Emphasize that the objective of this acrostic is for them to organize the most significant content they know and understand. This is not the time for frivolous or humorous responses.

Limit the number of letters in the acrostic word so the assessment can be accomplished in a few minutes. If the key topic word is long, generalizable terms such as KNOW or THINK can be used as the acrostic prompt for any topic or text.

### SO FAR

Inasmuch as brain research advocates the significance of students' social and emotional responses to learning opportunities, use formative assessment to unearth what students think or feel about a new topic and instruction (Willis, 2011). Students' perceptions may be particularly fruitful for adjusting instruction or planned learning experiences and individual applications early in a learning segment.

After an initial lesson or two for a topic or skill, pause and request that students reflect how they feel *so far* to guide your instructional adjustments. The intent is to elicit their perceptions and increase relevancy. Respecting students' ideas and taking appropriate actions

signals our mutual efforts to advance learning. The following questions are examples of prompts to assess *so far*.

*   "What suggestions do you have to make this content relevant and interesting to you?"
*   "How could we learn this another way?"
*   "What is an unanswered question you leave class with today?"
*   "What skills or concepts require more explanation or practice?"

FIGURE 6.12:

# APPLICATION TIME:
# THE TOP TEN FORMATIVE ASSESSMENTS

Begin developing a list of the top ten formative assessments most applicable to you, your students, and your teaching situation. Select from those shared in this chapter as well as any additional, personal favorites. Add to your list over time and edit your selections for their degree of effectiveness as you implement the assessments.

**TOP 10!**

A top ten list becomes a checklist enabling you to scan and select varied formative assessments to maintain interest in the assessment process for students and yourself. Strive to determine assessments that are quick and fruitful—simple to prepare and apply but result in actionable data to facilitate immediate adjustments to instruction.

1. _____
2. _____
3. _____
4. _____
5. _____

6. _____
7. _____
8. _____
9. _____
10. _____

Kingore, B. (2013). *Rigor and Engagement for Growing Minds.* Austin, TX: PA Publishing.

**Refining Assessments**

FIGURE 6.13:
# THINKING REFLECTIVELY

### 1. IDEAS

Identify two or more ideas you intend to apply immediately.

### 2. QUALITY CHECK-UP

Review your current rubrics to assess their main ideas—your messages of priorities to students. Expand your emphasis of complexity, depth, thinking, and vocabulary; lift criteria above appearance and basic accuracy as extensively as appropriate.

### 3. A ROUND OF APPLAUSE TO VALIDATE AND CELEBRATE YOUR CURRENT PRACTICES

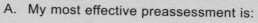

A. My most effective preassessment is:

B. I intend to involve students in self-assessment by:

### 4. DON'T WONDER ABOUT IT—ASK THE LEARNER.

Conduct a discussion with students to elicit their perceptions and suggestions for improving assessment procedures.

- "Which tools or procedures do you think are most beneficial?"
- "How might we more effectively use rubrics to communicate learning goals?"

Specifically, ask students for examples of interactive tasks to make assessment and reflection more engaging and beneficial.

Kingore, B. (2013). *Rigor and Engagement for Growing Minds.* Austin, TX: PA Publishing.

# Chapter 7
# Fostering Rigorous and Engaging Environments for Learning

Academic rigor should guarantee students' continuous learning at the deeper levels of cognitive processing that foster conceptual understanding. However, students' construction of meaning is quite individual and highly personal. Therefore, rigorous learning environments need to respond to a key differentiation principle: students' readiness, interests, and different ways to learn must be recognized and responsively addressed in instruction.

## Readiness, Interests, and Ways to Learn

### Readiness Is Significant

If we fail to adjust instruction to students' readiness levels, they do not learn. Vygotsky (1962) has been right all these years. If education intends to ensure continued learning growth, instruction must begin at students' current level of readiness and challenge them to work slightly above this comfort level rather than at or below their present achievement level.

Readiness is not synonymous with ability; it is a result of prior experiences and opportunities to learn. Children of poverty and cultural diversity, for example, can have gifted potential yet not be ready for a particular skill level because of a lack of prior learning opportunities. Attention to their readiness is vital to successful skill instruction, and teaching to students' highest levels of readiness is vital to their growth and continuous progress.

### Interests Are Significant

If we fail to adjust instruction to students' interests, they are less engaged in learning. Students are more willing to exert the effort required to acquire and process information when they perceive the work as personally relevant and interesting (Sousa, 2009; Willis, 2010; Wolfe, 2010).

Responding to students' interests does not imply that students have license to unacceptable behaviors, such as refusing to learn standards that do not appeal to them. It is, however, an asset when you know students' interests and are skilled at determining ways to incorporate them as frequently as is feasible. For example, a social studies teacher working with a high-ability student passionately interested in steam power and trains can facilitate the boy's study of the ways in which topography, natural resources, and social structures influenced the completion of the transcontinental railroad.

### DIFFERENT WAYS OF LEARNING ARE SIGNIFICANT

If we fail to adjust instruction to students' best ways to learn, they experience less individual success. Incorporate multiple learning pathways because the more ways information is introduced to the brain the more dendritic pathways of access are created to enhance memory (Willis, 2011). Providing different ways of learning responds to a learner's profile and increases the likelihood that instruction engages the varied natures of learners in today's classes. Moreover, different ways to learn are significant as a student may exhibit different preferences, strengths, and needs in different contexts, further affecting how learning proceeds.

A learning profile is not synonymous with learning style. Tomlinson (2012) defines a learning profile as the combination of gender, culture, intelligence preference, and learning style. Rather than over-promoting inventories of learning styles, Tomlinson advises that teachers emphasize multimodality instruction to provide learning options to engage students and help them understand themselves as learners (Tomlinson, 2012). Understanding and accommodating learner differences makes learning more authentic and relevant.

## CURRICULAR MODIFICATIONS FOR HIGH-ABILITY STUDENTS

Differentiated curriculum is imperative to ensure instruction that is responsive to the readiness, interests, and learning profiles of high-ability students. Many curricular modifications for these students are discussed and applied throughout this book, including:

*   Inquiry and in-depth study,
*   Acceleration of pace and level,
*   Curriculum compacting,
*   Mentors,
*   Flipped classrooms,
*   Grouping intellectual peers,
*   Cluster grouping,
*   Tiered instruction, and
*   Problem-based learning.

Combinations of these modifications should be evidenced in learning environments that endeavor to foster rigor and engagement in learning. A rigorous learning environment that promotes learning beyond core standards is particularly significant for high-potential students from under-represented populations. When high-ability or potentially gifted children from diverse backgrounds or poverty experience open-ended, instructionally challenging learning experiences, their potential is stimulated and more likely to be recognized (Ford & Harris, 1999; Slocumb & Payne, 2011).

Research recognizes cluster grouping, acceleration, and curriculum compacting as paradigms with positive, sustained effects on continuous learning for advanced and gifted children. Each of these models is supported by abundant research and realistic implementation, and each is dependent upon classroom teachers who differentiate skillfully. I encourage you to continue to explore these models as features in your plans for academic rigor.

### CLUSTER GROUPING

To clearly understand cluster grouping, read Susan Winebrenner's and Dina Brulles's definitive book entitled *Cluster Grouping Handbook: How to Challenge Gifted Students and Improve Achievement for All.* With cluster grouping, several high-ability students are clustered full-time in one mixed-ability classroom so a teacher can more consistently adjust instructional pace and level to their readiness. It allows gifted students to interact and learn together part of the day while encouraging a variety of grouping arrangements with all class members for the rest of the day. It is a full-time, financially sound response to the learning needs of advanced students.

### ACCELERATION

Download the research from Nicholas Colangelo, Susan Assouline, and Miraca Gross entitled: *A Nation Deceived: How*

*The Classroom Environment*
•
*Classrooms need to be exciting, stimulating laboratories for learning experiences.*

*Schools Hold Back America's Brightest Students.* It is an outstanding report discussing the multiple kinds and significant aspects of acceleration related to high-ability students.

(http://www.accelerationinstitute.org/ Nation_Deceived/ND_v1.pdf)

### CURRICULUM COMPACTING

Joseph Renzulli's and Sally Reis's respected work on compacting is explained in *Curriculum Compacting: The Complete Guide to Modifying the Regular Curriculum for High Ability Students* and *Curriculum Compacting: An Easy Start to Differentiating for High Potential Students.* Curriculum compacting is a differentiation strategy that is highly applicable to advanced students. It is designed to eliminate further instruction in mastered curriculum and streamline the instructional pacing of content commensurate with students' readiness. It affords students who demonstrate high levels of achievement the time to pursue personally relevant continuous learning.

### QUALITY INSTRUCTION

Instruction enables or limits academic rigor through curriculum content and instructional decisions. Sousa and Tomlinson (2010) believe that a rich classroom-learning environment is such a significant influence on students that it actually impacts brain development and levels of intelligence. In an academically rigorous environment, high-quality instruction is characterized by behaviors that are observable, continuous, and orchestrated to maximize learning. Be proactive with the instructional priorities listed in Figure 7.1 to promote quality instruction in your classroom. A teacher's enthusiasm for teaching and personal love of the subject matter is a model that motivates students and ultimately influences their achievement (Stronge, 2012).

Rigorous learning environments ensure that standards remain high and teachers provide the support and quality instruction that enable students to learn how to reach high standards. The classroom environment is a reflection of your educational philosophy and expectations. Next to students, you are the crucial human element in a rigorous and engaging learning environment, forming the bonds and connections that enable classroom learning to be richer and more stimulating. A close examination of classroom environments and schedules will signal what is most valuable for children and learning.

Consider what your classroom environment suggests about your priorities. Classrooms need to be exciting, stimulating laboratories for learning experiences. Through quality instruction that integrates social and emotional learning into the curriculum, you empower students with strategies that help them develop the resiliency to respond to future challenging situations and authentically extend learning beyond the classroom.

Ferguson (2010, 7) describes instructional quality measures as the Seven C's. He proposes that students engage more deeply and master lessons more thoroughly when teachers:

- Care about them,
- Control the classroom well,
- Clarify complex ideas,
- Challenge them to work hard and think hard,
- Deliver lessons in ways that captivate,
- Confer with them about their ideas, and
- Consolidate lessons to make learning coherent.

I propose that an eighth *C* for instructional quality should be *collaborate*. Students benefit and improve academically when teachers are engaged in meaningful collaboration with their peers (Leana, 2011). A partnership of teachers built on mutual trust and concern for students can network to problem solve, share, and support one another as we attend to the little stuff—conflicting individual policies such as students chewing gum in class—and the larger, more professionally significant issues that facilitate school-wide achievement.

Ultimately, is it the heart and skill of insightful, dedicated teachers that enable the positive future changes and construction of new understandings to evolve from a student's intellectual work. Quality instruction is significant.

*Skilled Teachers*
•
*It is the heart and skill of insightful, dedicated teachers that enable the construction of understandings to evolve from students' intellectual work.*

Kingore, B. (2013). *Rigor and Engagement for Growing Minds*. Austin, TX: PA Publishing.

## FIGURE 7.1:
# PROMOTING QUALITY INSTRUCTION

**TO PROMOTE RIGOR AND QUALITY, TEACHERS MUST:**

❏ Establish and communicate clear learning goals and high expectations that are both realistic and relevant.

❏ Make personal connections with each individual and set expectations for all class members to interact respectively and frequently.

❏ Actively respond through personal interactions and instruction matched to individuals' readiness, interests, and needs for different ways to learn.

❏ Implement preassessment and formative assessment to guide and adjust lesson planning as well as initiate accommodations for individual students.

❏ Commence varied and frequent flexible groups for collaborative problem solving and real-world applications.

❏ Collaboratively develop rubrics to focus learning and communicate the specific attributes that enable high achievement.

❏ Support learning by acknowledging students' efforts as well as their products; support their questions, needs, and differences in a positive, sensitive manner.

❏ Promote a growth mindset and expect each student's personal best—students in competition with self rather than peers.

❏ Target important ideas and standards in each lesson with relevant, meaningful content and applications authentic to the world outside of the classroom.

❏ Focus on students' high-level thinking and development of conceptual understanding.

❏ Encourage intellectual risk taking, imaginative thinking, and originality with real-world problems and issues that involve multiple perspectives and solutions.

❏ Preside over a learning climate with a student-supported management plan that builds relationships, productivity, and leadership.

❏ Use closure for meaning construction and formative assessment to gauge learning and plan adjustments for continued instruction.

❏ Do everything they can to facilitate continuous learning for each student.

Kingore, B. (2013). *Rigor and Engagement for Growing Minds.* Austin, TX: PA Publishing.

# INTELLECTUAL WORK

Rigor is not characterized by more work but by more meaningful work that is intellectually challenging and thought provoking, relative to the age of the child. Traditional school assignments document students' competence in their acquisition of standards. Rigorous intellectual accomplishments represent personal and utilitarian worth that impacts others.

The Center for Authentic Intellectual Work (AIW) frames intellectual work with three criteria: construction of knowledge, disciplined inquiry, and value beyond school. AIW explains that authentic intellectual work requires original application of knowledge and skills, rather than routine application of facts and procedures. It entails careful study of a topic or problem, resulting in a product or presentation that has meaning beyond success in school (Carmichael & Martens, 2012, 22). Cognitive skills, interpersonal skills, and intrapersonal skills are components in intellectual work.

Intellectual work is an intended outcome of academic rigor. In a rigorous learning environment, educators must promote intellectual work, and students must aspire to engage in learning in a manner that displays distinctive attributes of intellectual work similar to those listed in Figure 7.2.

Intellectual work challenges learners to exceed core standards and minimum competencies. It leads children of all ages to develop higher levels of skills and deeper, more complex understandings. Relevant to older students, Washor and Mojkowski (2007) characterize intellectual work as deep immersion in a subject over time with the guidance of expert practitioners or mentors using sophisticated resources. Mature students function more like academicians and clinicians who remain committed to their work as they encounter complex, unpredictable problems and are subject to peer and public scrutiny. The demands of their academic process cause them to continuously expand their levels of skills as they construct deeper, more complex understanding and develop self-awareness. They increasingly assume ownership of their ideas and actions.

Students' intellectual work, however, shares a reciprocal relationship with quality instruction and support. In reality, no one succeeds totally alone. Educators and peers support and encourage all learners to higher aspirations through respectful interactions sensitive to learners' profiles. Without support and feedback, high-ability students may:

- Be reluctant to take intelligent risks.
- Not challenge themselves to expand their potential for nuanced, sophisticated, conceptual understanding.
- Fail to identify non-routine, unstructured questions or generate strategies to determine solutions to unpredictable problems.
- Appear less intellectual.

Without quality instruction and support, we risk students developing a fixed mindset and not

*A Rigorous Environment*

•

*In a rigorous learning environment, educators exhibit a greater concern for quality rather than quantity as well as conceptual thinking rather than memorization.*

FIGURE 7.2:
# ATTRIBUTES OF INTELLECTUAL WORK

In developmentally appropriate ways, students of all ages benefit when they engage in academic rigor and intellectual work. Their work should demonstrate variations of these distinctive attributes that enable them to grow as resilient learners who adapt current knowledge to prepare for future academic and workplace cultures.

## STUDENTS' INTELLECTUAL WORK IN A RIGOROUS LEARNING ENVIRONMENT:

❑ Is meaningful, high-quality, intellectually-challenging work accompanied by appropriate support.

❑ Has an authentic purpose relevant to the learner that motivates a reason to exert effort and strive for a remarkable accomplishment.

❑ Requires substantive peer and adult interactions with elaborated communication through complex, multifaceted forms of verbal, written, graphic, symbolic, and visual communications as processes and products of learning.

❑ Incorporates prodigious experiences with informative writing and strategic reading of non-fiction texts to assess and support their construction of deeper meaning.

❑ Represents an intellectual accomplishment with personal and utilitarian value.

❑ Communicates ideas and authentic problem solving pertinent to real-life issues that impact others and contribute to the community beyond the classroom.

❑ Leads students to become producers, constructing new knowledge and conceptual, in-depth understanding. They extend beyond knowing and reporting information to applying known information and conceptual understanding in different ways that establish new relationships and clarify issues or problems. In so doing, they exhibit increasing sophistication as they identify similarities and differences, use analogies, summarize, use inferences to draw conclusions, and form generalizations.

❑ Develops a structure of knowing rather than only memorizing known details.

❑ Demonstrates the intellectual openness, creativity, and commitment that can lead to a state of flow with a contagious excitement for learning and deep immersion in a content or topic over time.

❑ Sets a standard for scholarship.

❑ Increasingly develops students' skills to self-monitor and self-reflect to scrutinize for accuracy and continuous improvement.

❑ Promotes continuous learning.

Kingore, B. (2013). *Rigor and Engagement for Growing Minds.* Austin, TX: PA Publishing.

Fostering Rigorous Environments

benefiting from challenges to exceed grade-level expectations.

As a personal example, my high school history teacher excused me from class for the entire semester and sent me to the library to structure my own learning. Without parameters or guidance, I aligned my own inquiry to the allotted time and content represented by the regular class syllabus. My semester grade resulted from the learning log I kept for myself and the substantial paper I was asked to produce to represent my learning accomplishment. I remember much of what I did because it was personal. But I suspect that my construction of meaning would have been deeper and more complex if I had experienced guidance and supportive feedback, challenging me to refine my emerging understandings and to perfect original problem solutions to present to a real-world audience. Feedback and encouragement from teachers and peers enhance the likelihood that advanced students reach higher levels of intellectual work as they become self-directed and self-corrective. The academic process is richer when high expectations are accompanied with scrutiny and support.

Intellectual work in a responsive learning environment enables high-ability learners to evolve to personal and autonomous learning as they interact with and learn from students like themselves and students dissimilar in backgrounds and interests. Intellectual work from high-ability students is observable in

their learning processes as well as their products. When a rigorous learning environment is functioning at responsive levels, expect to observe advanced, even brilliant, behaviors.

*Get going!*

### BIOGRAPHIES AND AUTOBIOGRAPHIES

Organize book studies in which each student reads biographies or autobiographies of people eminent in a field of interest to the student. This nonfiction is an individual choice or flexible group engagement if all members of the group are personally interested in a book study about this person. The objective is for students to identify and relate to the personal qualities that enable individuals to develop a personal vision for the future, persevere, overcome challenges, and succeed. Challenge students to draw conclusions and generalizations that connect their studies and their lives.

> *Rigorous Assignments*
>
> •
>
> *Rigor is not characterized by more work but by more meaningful work that is intellectually challenging and thought provoking, relative to the age of the child.*

## HIGH-ABILITY LEARNERS: RIGHTS, RESPONSIBILITIES, AND INSTRUCTIONAL DIFFERENTIATION

Initially, I intended to advocate for the rights of high-ability students. Based on discussions and work with thousands of advanced students, I wanted to promote understanding from the students' perspectives about the ways high-ability children think, feel, learn, and experience self-actualization. However, as I pursued this topic, it became evident that advanced students' rights are interdependent with their related responsibilities and instructional implications for differentiation. In Figure 7.3, a parallel comparison of students' rights, responsibilities, and implications for instructional differentiation are proposed for discussion among advanced students and adults. Stimulating discussion rather than fostering agreement is the goal.

*Collaborative Classroom Management*

•

*The quality of student-teacher relationships is the most significant factor in effective classroom management.*

As you share these ideas with other adults, high-ability students, and parents of advanced students, elicit their perceptions and encourage productive communication through an exchange of ideas. Students and adults have the ability to change personally and change instruction. Advocate for best practices in our rigorous learning environments. The first step is communication and shared understanding.

## MANAGING A COLLABORATIVE CLASSROOM

The term *classroom management* connotes the kind of teacher control related to the former industrial model of education—rows of students completing the same tasks as the teacher directs from the front of the room. In

contrast, a rigorous learning environment is characterized by collaboration among all participants, requiring a climate for learning and relationship building. As Jones (2008, 8) explains, today's classroom consists of "...a group of students who desire and deserve high-quality personal relationships with adults and peers. It is the quality of these relationships that drives their behavior and leads to learning." Thus, the climate and management for learning is determined by the collaborative relationships mutually agreed upon by teachers and students. Inasmuch as the quality of student-teacher relationships is the most significant factor in effective classroom management (ASCD et al., 2008; Elias, 2012), management decisions should focus on productivity and methods to nurture students who care about others while thinking for themselves.

Classroom management should not imply control; it is more importantly concerned with routines, organizing procedures, and an agreement of a clear social contract between all class members. Tomlinson (2012, 129) advises that "students learn best in a classroom that is organized to make room for their differences, where they understand and contribute to the rationale for the classroom, and in which routines are predictable."

Understand the value of involving students in setting rationales and routines. In a collaborative classroom, never doubt the impact that insights from even young students offer. A number of years ago, a primary child taught me a management strategy I use to this

## FIGURE 7.3: HIGH-ABILITY LEARNERS: RIGHTS, RESPONSIBILITIES, AND INSTRUCTIONAL DIFFERENTIATION

| HIGH-ABILITY LEARNERS HAVE THE RIGHT TO: | HIGH-ABILITY LEARNERS HAVE THE RESPONSIBILITY TO: | HIGH-ABILITY LEARNERS NEED INSTRUCTION DIFFERENTIATED TO: |
| --- | --- | --- |
| 1. The identification and nurturing of their advanced potential as early and consistently as possible regardless of age, special needs, language, or background experiential gaps. | 1. Share their high-level ideas and unique problem-solving responses. They need to exert the effort required to demonstrate complex ideas and products so educators observe their potential in learning contexts. | 1. Avoid the barriers to attainment that limit some individual's opportunity to demonstrate outstanding potential. Provide open-ended, problem-based experiences. Be alert to potential demonstrated through learning behaviors as much as products or test results. |
| 2. A learning environment with developmentally appropriate high expectations and intellectually challenging work aligned to advanced capabilities at and beyond core standards. | 2. Work productively while pursuing intellectual work with critical thinking, curiosity, passion, effort, and persistence that yield the life skills and habits of mind for success and achievement in multiple pursuits. | 2. Implement curricular modifications, such as acceleration, cluster grouping, curriculum compacting, tiered lessons, problem-based learning, and individual inquiry. Communicate expectations for a greater degree of complexity and depth to promote students' excellence. |
| 3. Teachers who have esteem for advanced students and are quite accomplished at differentiating instruction to elicit beyond grade-level achievement, personal satisfaction with learning, and autonomy. | 3. Respect and be responsive to the culture of learning teachers work diligently to provide. They should respond productively as teachers demonstrate empathy for them and their impassioned learning interests as well as achievements. | 3. Select instructors with a passion to teach advanced students, skill in differentiation, ability to facilitate individual inquiry, and understanding of beyond grade-level content. Avoid assignments based on scheduling convenience or a teacher's *turn for* a gifted section. |
| 4. Interactions with intellectual peers and age peers to experience a real-world balance between academic challenge and the social and emotional support that promotes resilience and joy in learning. Academic rigor and socialization skills are mutually beneficial. | 4. Practice active listening and the language of diplomacy when interacting with others and responding to hard questions. They must model respect during social interactions to communicate *with* others rather than *to* others. | 4. Artfully use flexible grouping for continuous learning. Base peer interactions on mutual needs and interests more often than peer tutoring or cooperative tasks that enable others to conclude solutions to problems previously understood by high-ability students. |
| 5. Experience continuous learning by pre-assessing out of previously mastered work and advancing academically at a pace and level responsive to their learning profile and readiness. | 5. Expend effort to learn while understanding that excellence should represent personal best rather than a comparison with grade-level peers. They should maintain records of personal progress and changes as learners. | 5. Use preassessments and formative assessments to ensure a pace and level of instruction that fosters continuous learning. Evaluate curricula for the degree of challenge to engage intellectually demanding learning processes. |

Kingore, B. (2013). *Rigor and Engagement for Growing Minds.* Austin, TX: PA Publishing.

| # | | | |
|---|---|---|---|
| **6** | Effectively reverse underachievement by ensuring replacement learning tasks based on interests and strengths. Promote rigorous intellectual accomplishments representing personal and utilitarian worth that impacts others. | Engage in intellectually demanding tasks rather than settle for easy accomplishments. They should avoid calling undue attention to themselves when engaging in replacement tasks. | Replacement tasks that enhance conceptual understanding and construction of deeper understanding rather than "enrichment" tasks that merely treadmill learning by focusing on different applications of understood concepts and skills. |
| **7** | Ensure a positive, collaborative climate that tiers the complexity of questioning and interactions so all students explore the topic in an intellectually stimulating manner. Allow students to prepare responses in pairs; randomly call on one pair to respond. | To participate, interact, and collaborate by actively listening to build upon others' ideas rather than interrogate or intimidate peers. They need to understand and encourage the perspective of others as often as they share their point of view. | Be called upon to respond in class proportionately to other students. They should not dominate class discussions or flexible group interactions nor should they be ignored. |
| **8** | Encourage unique perspectives and complex responses by providing extensive opportunities for conceptual thinking involving open-ended problems related to change, issues, and ethics. | Risk asking a provocative question, sharing a complex idea, and applying more sophisticated vocabulary rather than clam up and dumb down responses as a way to better fit in the class. | The encouragement of diverse, content-rich, and appropriate but unexpected ideas rather than only simple, right-answer responses. They should feel inspired to question, adapt, and extend as much as accept the current wisdom. |
| **9** | Promote authentic learning applications with technology, mentors, and in-person or online advanced classes to build upon students' learning passions, even when their topics are outside of the current curriculum. | Develop a structure of knowing that fosters development of insightful generalizations as well as accumulation of vast amounts of information. They should experience higher levels of intellectual work as they become self-directed and self-corrective. | Become experts investigating interests that may seem unusual for their age. They seek specialized content at an early age, are intrinsically motivated by personally relevant topics, and experience joyful learning pursuing their topics for an extended time. |
| **10** | Mutually respect all learners while reinforcing that differences are natural and valued. Respond to effort and social-emotional needs as well as foster achievement and giftedness. Facilitate gifted students' self-understanding and interactions with intellectual peers so they feel welcomed to use their intellect. | Demonstrate respect for peers as well as seek respect from them, understand others' perspectives as well as expect others to understand their perspective, and develop a richer understanding of every person's worth. They should seek and interact with at least one person who can support their intellectual and personal progress. | A culture of respect enabling them to feel understood, accepted, and supported while maintaining their uniqueness, idealism, and intensity. They flourish with unconditional encouragement from at least one person who facilitates passions more than redirects learning solely to core curriculum or today's occupations. |

Kingore, B. (2013). *Rigor and Engagement for Growing Minds.* Austin, TX: PA Publishing.

Fostering Rigorous Environments

day in elementary classrooms. As she observed two boys enmeshed in a conflict, she noted: "It seems to me that when somebody hurts someone, they should be responsible for them until they feel better." From that day forward, when a conflict emerged, the participants stayed together until they worked it out, typically progressing from quiet resignation, to attempts at diversion, to conflict resolution. While perhaps not applicable to situations with older or more hostile students, the idea of collaborative conflict resolution is appealing.

## MANAGEMENT STRATEGIES FOR A COLLABORATIVE CLASSROOM

The most effective curriculum and the best planned lesson are of little consequence if instructional practices fail to establish a productive and responsive learning environment organized with effective management details that everyone knows and understands. While management practices must be structured to your individual style, explore some specific strategies shared in this section to ensure that instruction proceeds smoothly and individual needs are addressed.

Building upon established management practices and processes, set your environment for learning rather than control. In a collaborative classroom, students are empowered to act because they understand and concur with the management details for productive engagement in learning.

*A Classroom Social Contract*

•

*Management should not imply control; it is more concerned with routines, organizing procedures, and agreement of a clear classroom social contract among all class members.*

A management plan for a collaborative classroom works most effectively when it is clearly articulated and consistently practiced. Students are better able to focus on constructing understanding and deeper meaning of content when an established range of routines and management structures are in place. Students who clearly understand and comfortably operate within agreed management guidelines can better promote their own learning and work toward developing autonomy. Consistent, predictable routines enable us to prevent most difficulties before they occur.

## • ESTABLISH ROUTINES.

As a collaborative classroom, establish routines with students that vest power with everyone in the classroom to ensure that all members work productively and efficiently. Productive classroom routines and rituals give students a sense of stability and control (Johnston, 2012); students develop the sense that *this is how we do things around here.* Communicate and consistently apply the routines that students need to feel empowered and competent as well as provide structure for the class when students work in flexible groups. Once established, routines enable you to instruct small groups or confer with individuals, assured that the rest of the class can and will proceed productively with their learning responsibilities.

Consider developing a digital presentation of class expectations and routines. Developing the digital presentation helps you refine and clarify your expectations. Stop after each slide and engage students in modeling and practicing each new procedure. The digital presentation can be replayed when needed as well as help new students more quickly acclimate to class routines.

Students can dramatize routines as another way to ensure that productivity and organization become a habit. Role-play is a novelty that captures attention and matches many students' best ways to learn as they use auditory, kinesthetic, and visual modalities to interactively demonstrate understanding of management expectations. Role-play the routines that make the learning climate work, such as interacting with peers, documenting the quality of their work, working quietly, accessing assistance, cleaning the work area, displaying work, and moving between learning locations.

Establish routines for getting materials. Since students complete work at different times, empower individuals to be responsible for getting their own materials as needed. As a class, establish when and how to get materials and determine storage locations with a place for everything and everything in its place. This management procedure prevents students from having to wait as a few helpers pass things out, avoids teachers doing it all, and makes better use of class time. Throughout the day, this procedure is also a welcomed movement for bodily-kinesthetic learners.

Establish routines for assessing quality. Every day, students should self-assess the quality of their learning process and products through a variety of assessment techniques, such as writing reflections of learning experi-

ences. This action is authentic, informative writing that also provides useful formative assessment information.

- **ESTABLISH WAYS TO GAIN ASSISTANCE.**

Empower students with ways to access assistance during independent work. Confer with students to generate a set of procedures to use when they feel stymied and need help. As a class, implement agreed upon ideas for a trial period, and then, debrief and select those most beneficial and comfortable. To prompt your thinking, Figure 7.4 is a reminder of frequently implemented procedures for assistance.

- **POSITION YOURSELF AT THE DOOR.**

As frequently as possible, stand in the doorway as students enter and exit the classroom to build personal contacts. This routine guarantees that you take the opportunity every day to use their first names, smile, and offer at least a brief individual recognition.

- **USE YOUR VOICE AS A MANAGEMENT TOOL.**

A teacher's voice is a powerful thing in a classroom. It can soothe a tempest or stimulate enthusiasm for a segment of learning. Avoid any tendency to raise your voice. Instead, model a volume level and tone that you want students to use. Modulate your tone for variety and interest, and sometimes lower your volume to invite closer, more personal listening.

Kingore, B. (2013). *Rigor and Engagement for Growing Minds*. Austin, TX: PA Publishing.

FIGURE 7.4:
# GAINING ASSISTANCE

As they work on assignments, procedures for students to implement when stymied and techniques for gaining assistance are important. Otherwise, students waste precious learning time and risk forgetting a good idea because they had to stop thinking about content to secure help. Implement routines and techniques that encourage on-task behavior and independence while still enabling students to gain needed assistance during independent applications. These techniques are applicable for individuals and flexible groups.

## ✦ PROXIMITY

Rather than waste time waiting with a raised hand, teach students to mark a difficult item or problem area and continue working until a solution occurs to them or until you or another student is near to help. As students work, move around the room. A student raises a hand to signal a need for help only when help is nearby.

## ✦ I NEED A HAND

Students trace their hand, cut it out of both red and green paper, and glue the two colors together making one hand shape. (Laminate the hands for long-term use.) Students display the green hand on their desks as long as the learning task is proceeding smoothly. When a student has a question or needs help, the student displays the red side of the hand and continues working until you or a classmate can assist.

## ✦ 3-BE-4

Students ask three students for assistance before requesting help from the teacher.

## ✦ THE POWER OF 3

Students consult their notes, textbook, or another student before approaching the teacher with a question.

## ✦ PEER ASSISTANTS

Student task assistants and support assistants, discussed in Chapter 5 as peer support techniques, prove useful when peers need assistance.

## ✦ RESOURCES

Do not ignore the obvious. Ensure that resource materials are readily available so students can independently search for needed clarification of a skill or concept. Online searches, software, and books designed for efficient referencing are most likely to actually be used by students.

Kingore, B. (2013). *Rigor and Engagement for Growing Minds.* Austin, TX: PA Publishing.

- ### ESTABLISH A CLASSROOM SOCIAL CONTRACT.

At the beginning of the year, include students in creating a classroom social contract to define the rights and duties of each participant in the classroom. Discuss how to treat each other, interact positively, and disagree diplomatically as part of an effective learning community.

- ### INSTILL RESPECT.

Respect for others and respect for self is a mandate in effective learning environments. Greet each other in a positive manner. Challenge adults and children to practice the art of language diplomacy, filtering how they phrase ideas and responses to avoid alienating listeners. Constantly model and promote culturally responsive interactions among all class members.

- ### BELIEVE STUDENTS WILL LEARN.

Believe in students; care about them, and respect them even when their behaviors or attitudes do not seem to deserve it. Our responses model what is preferred in our classroom. If we allow ourselves to become sarcastic or give up on students, what can we realistically expect from them?

- ### GET STUDENTS' ATTENTION.

Traditional, simple techniques are often the best to focus attention. Try flicking the lights, using a particular sound as a signal, or clapping hands in a repetitive pattern for young children.

- ### MODEL ACTIVE LISTENING.

Face students, maintain eye contact, and quietly attend to them as they offer what they perceive as an important point. Call on students to paraphrase, summarize, review, or respond to positive ideas from peers during a discussion. Provide a reason for peers to listen to each other through advanced cues, such as: "As _____ shares, listen to be able to build upon one key point." Books, articles, and online resources offer a wealth of active listening techniques you can investigate and teach to students less experienced in the process.

- ### CONFIGURE FURNITURE FOR COLLABORATION.

Ask students to help design different desk or table configurations to create more inviting collaboration areas and foster students' ownership of the learning environment. Clusters of students facing each other foster the student-centered problem solving and collaboration advocated by core standards and are certainly more conducive to peer interaction.

- ### ESTABLISH CLEAR COMMUNICATION CHANNELS OUTSIDE OF THE CLASSROOM.

Initiate a variety of communication avenues for you and students to contact one another. Ask students to supply you with their best contact times and share times when you are most available. Use a class blog, school-based email accounts, interactive logs, or a suggestion box in the classroom to connect to students and their families. Some teachers prefer lunchtime meetings or phone calls for communicating with students and families.

Kingore, B. (2013). *Rigor and Engagement for Growing Minds.* Austin, TX: PA Publishing.

Fostering Rigorous Environments

- ## USE CLOSURE FOR BUILDING A COMMUNITY OF LEARNERS.

When students work in flexible groups or simultaneously engage in a variety of different learning tasks, close with a whole-group time that brings everyone together for debriefing, summarizing, and sharing. Students benefit from hearing peers' perspectives and learning about what others in the class are pursuing. Students also benefit by recognizing that we do not all learn in the same way, at the same time, all of the time.

### STUDENTS DO NOT WAIT WELL

Implement routines for students to begin replacement tasks if they finish quality work early or are waiting for you to assist or confer with them. (See Chapter 8 for a discussion of replacement tasks and ideas that work.)

### LABEL THE LEARNING ENVIRONMENT

When appropriate, involve children in labeling materials and storage areas. Words and symbols provide young and special-needs children with the graphic support to successfully read the labels and manage materials better.

# MANAGEMENT CONCERNS AND POSSIBLE SOLUTIONS

A well-designed, engaging lesson is a powerful, preventative technique for classroom behavioral problems. Sometimes, however, in spite of careful planning and engaging instruction, issues can develop. Today's complex society may model less civil behaviors, and television and popular online videos can certainly reinforce poor listening habits and rude, disrespectful behaviors.

Multiple books and online resources articulate management techniques and practices. In particular, beginning teachers benefit from reviewing those ideas and selectively determining which ones accommodate their teaching situation and personal preferences. Initially, develop a management plan to implement and constantly monitor; then, eagerly make adaptations to that plan as classroom experience grows or the needs of the class change.

Management concerns are relevant to veteran as well as less experienced teachers. Peruse some of the following concerns that emerge in rigorous learning environments, and explore possible solutions offered by colleagues to expand effective management practices.

*"HOW DO I HELP STUDENTS KNOW WHAT CONTENT IS MOST IMPORTANT DURING A LESSON?"*

✓ Switch colors as you write. "I'm writing this idea in purple ink so that you know it is important."

---

Kingore, B. (2013). *Rigor and Engagement for Growing Minds.* Austin, TX: PA Publishing.

✓ Use cue cards (discussed as a formative assessment technique in Chapter 6). "This information is quite important. Hold up a cue card to signal your understanding right now."

✓ Establish a physical signal that students understand indicates significant information, such as holding your index finger to your forehead.

✓ Elementary students respond well when you make a physical change in your appearance, such as putting on a tiara to signal a key point. "The queen wants you to think about this."

✓ Use highlighters. Before the lesson, students highlight what they interpret as significant. At the beginning of the lesson, discuss and compare highlighted text. Avoid excessive highlighting as students conclude that you mark a lot or just mark every first sentence. Encourage students to mark key words and phrases more than highlight sentences.

✓ Jensen (2003) recommends what I characterize as giving unexpected, staccato directions: "Grab a pen. Write this down. This is a key idea today." State that key point and then pause. "Now, look at your shoulder-partner's paper. If the idea is written down correctly, say: 'Great Job!'" Use this technique infrequently so it remains a novelty rather than a common practice.

**"WHAT CAN I DO TO PROMOTE LEARNING AND LIMIT WASTED CLASSROOM TIME WHEN STUDENTS ARE NOT PREPARED FOR CLASS OR DO NOT WORK DURING CLASS?"**

✓ Ensure authentic audiences for students' work. Make certain they have a reason to produce.

✓ Ask the class: "How do you feel when some people are not prepared? When might it affect your attitude or learning in any way?" Elicit students' ideas regarding the problem and potential solutions; implement their suggestions as much as is feasible.

✓ Have students work in small groups so it is harder to hide or mentally disengage. Post the group memberships just before the learning discussion begins so students cannot rely on grouping with friends who will not hold them accountable if they are not prepared.

✓ Use modified Socratic Seminars in which you pose reflective questions and purposely do not tell answers nor tell them what information is important. Encourage an exploratory dialogue to stimulate students' active and thoughtful interchanges of ideas more than an answer.

✓ Allow students some choice in what they do and how they demonstrate it. "Your choices when preparing for tomorrow's class are to write answers to the chapter questions, highlight key points in the text, jigsaw with others, or prepare three-minute videos to teach others."

Fostering Rigorous Environments

Kingore, B. (2013). *Rigor and Engagement for Growing Minds.* Austin, TX: PA Publishing.

✓ Announce an audience and reason for students to be prepared. "Tomorrow, I will randomly draw seven names. You will be our group leaders who guide a discussion of this content in your group as I write notes."

✓ Winebrenner (2012) recommends a random technique she calls Roll the Die that simultaneously results in less grading for you. Over several days, students work in flexible groups to complete different assigned and numbered tasks in class and as homework. On a predetermined day, a random roll of a die designates the one learning experience that you will evaluate for each group to determine the grade for the entire segment of assignments. Students increase their concern for accuracy and preparedness since no one knows in advance which assignment represents the entire grade.

✓ Tomlinson (2012) suggests that students who have not completed the homework or assigned preparations move to a designated area of the room and work individually to complete the assignment. As you monitor the entire room, the remaining students interact in flexible groups to clarify, discuss, and reach agreement of the strongest answers or key points of the content. All students mark their work for agreement or disagreement, write explanations to correct a wrong response, and sign it to indicate agreement as a group. To promote ownership and accuracy, all group members' responses are turned in together and the teacher spot checks only one response.

## "HOW CAN ACADEMIC RIGOR BE EFFECTIVE WITH STUDENTS WHO ARE LESS INDEPENDENT, LESS RESPONSIBLE, OR FREQUENTLY OFF-TASK?"

✓ Strive to make learning personally relevant to each learner.

✓ Identify which specific skills of an autonomous learner are most significant in your classroom. Then, model and teach those skills. Students' prior experiences may have precluded developing autonomy.

✓ Post a rubric or list of the class expectations for the behaviors students exhibit when they are working to learn. Make students responsible for daily self-assessment of the merits of their learning effort in response to those behaviors. (See Chapter 6 for examples of learning behavior rubrics.)

✓ Individually, ask a disengaged student how you can make the learning assignments more interesting. Ask the student to share different ways that learning could be more engaging. Then, share how and when you intend to follow up on one of the suggestions and ask the student to provide feedback to you about how well it worked.

✓ Provide authentic audiences of peers and adults who will scrutinize and respond to the product.

✓ Try the flipped classroom approach discussed in Chapter 5.

## "WHAT ARE POSITIVE WAYS TO RESPOND WHEN STUDENTS SAY THEY DO NOT KNOW AN ANSWER?"

Sometimes you can avoid the problem by requiring students to use planning sheets before they speak or use every-student-responds techniques so you know in advance who is having difficulty. (See formative assessment in Chapter 6.) When a student responds to an inquiry with: "I don't know," scaffold for the kind of success that fosters students' continued engagement and learning success.

✓ Maintain eye contact and a positive tone to your voice so the interaction is not perceived as punitive.

✓ Use inquiry to facilitate the student toward a correct answer. "What is one thing about this content that you know right now?"

✓ Challenge them to ponder how to progress. "What might you do to begin to figure this out?"

✓ Ask students to repeat an effective previous answer. "I know you have been listening well. So what do you think is a good response or partial solution that has already been expressed?"

✓ Invite students to consult with a shoulder partner. "Discuss this with a shoulder partner for one minute and then share your ideas."

✓ Enable students to refer to relevant text information. "Check your textbook and we will come back to share what you think."

✓ Avoid counterproductive strategies.
   A. If you tell the student an answer, you may be teaching students to wait until you provide the solution.
   B. If another student is called on to answer for the first student, you risk students inferring that they are not as able as others.

## "HOW MIGHT I RESPOND TO WRONG ANSWERS WITHOUT STYMIEING THE STUDENT'S THINKING?"

✓ Acknowledge mistakes without being too critical. Our response models how to handle errors while establishing the truism that everyone makes mistake.

✓ Equally question students when their responses are correct or incorrect to probe for more information, examples, or citation from the text to substantiate the response. Equal questioning helps avoid any peer stigma when less accurate responses are questioned.

✓ Select one key word from the task and ask the student to begin thinking about that word. Student: "Is 5/4 an example of an equivalent fraction?" Teacher: "What does equivalent mean?"

✓ Incorporate ways to provide a rescue.
   A. Have IOU slips to hand out. "You owe the class one idea. Signal me when you have an example or idea to share."
   B. Offer a time extension. "Think about it. I'll come back to check with you in two minutes" (and then absolutely remember to return).

Kingore, B. (2013). *Rigor and Engagement for Growing Minds.* Austin, TX: PA Publishing.

C. "Do you want to use a lifeline?" A lifeline is an idea from a television show that most students seem to understand. The student can choose input from another student or resource but remains responsible to determine how or if to use it. "Use your lifeline, and I will return to you for your conclusion."

## "HOW DO I RESPOND TO STUDENTS WHO QUESTION DIFFERENCES IN ASSIGNMENTS FOR DIFFERENT PEERS?"

✓ Learning environments of the past conditioned students to expect the same tasks for everyone in the class. Explain your reasons for different assignments. "We will engage in different tasks, in different ways of learning, because that is what helps you the most. Understand, however, that everyone is always graded fairly."

✓ Believe that it is crucial to address student differences when increasing learning opportunities. If you do not believe in the necessity of different learning experiences to address student readiness, interests, and learning profile differences, it will be most difficult to convince students. You must practice what you preach—authentically incorporate as well as model.

✓ Promote differences as an asset rather than a question of fairness. Try a think aloud with your class to share your reasoning.

✓ Elicit students' perceptions and ideas to promote learning. "Write and quickly sketch ideas to me about how to best help you learn. What do you do best? What do you most and least enjoy doing in learning situations? What could others do to help you learn?" Later, discuss with the class the range of different ideas that emerged. "You are different and so are your ideas for your best ways to learn."

✓ Inventory students' interest and preferred ways to learn. Have them fold a paper into thirds to write and illustrate in each section respectively what they do well, not well, and want to learn at school.

## "WHEN DO I ASSIGN LEARNING TASKS AND WHEN IS STUDENT CHOICE THE BETTER IDEA?"

✓ Assign or select the learning tasks when:
   A. You conduct direct instruction and applications, whether in whole class or flexible group lessons.
   B. You target individual or flexible group tasks to specific readiness levels.
   C. Students are not skillful in selecting the appropriate level of a tiered task relative to their readiness.

✓ Students select learning tasks when:
   A. Interests are targeted.
   B. The tasks are open-ended and successfully accommodate a range of readiness levels.
   C. They are able to self-select the appropriate level of a tiered task relative to their readiness.
   D. They are working on replacement tasks.

✓ You can skillfully combine your assignments with students' choices by providing a student with two or three choices of tasks. In this way, the student retains the power of choice, but you limit the choices to the most relevant tasks for that student.

### "WHAT CAN I DO IF A STUDENT SELECTS A LEARNING TASK THAT IS TOO DIFFICULT?"

✓ Provide peer support by encouraging two students to quietly work together on the task. Peer support is an excellent motivational tool and encouragement for struggling students. It also builds the communication skills of both children.

✓ Post a picture of the task assistant so students understand who to ask for clarification or help.

✓ Briefly talk with the student to elicit his or her perceptions and to share your own perceptions.

✓ Contract with the student for specific tasks to select from when working individually. Limit the choices to those most applicable to that student's readiness, interests, and best ways to learn.

### "HOW DO I RESPOND IF A STUDENT SELECTS LEARNING TASKS THAT ARE TOO EASY RELATIVE TO THE STUDENT'S LEARNING CAPABILITIES?"

✓ Ignore the situation if it happens occasionally. Everyone deserves some time off now and then. For example, even bright adults have been known to read a magazine that is beneath their intellectual level.

✓ Communicate with students that any choice is acceptable sometimes but they are expected to demonstrate continuous learning. Lead them to understand that they learn more when they predominantly strive for challenge.

✓ Intervention is recommended if a student consistently chooses tasks that are too easy. Briefly talk with the student to elicit his or her perceptions and to share your perceptions. Achievement does not increase when students work at a level below their potential. Furthermore, students develop negative habits of mind when no struggle or persistence is required when learning.

✓ Contract with the student and specify several challenging tasks as options. Limit the choices to those most applicable to that student's readiness, interest, best ways to learn, and need for challenge.

✓ Color-code tasks by their complexity level and require students to work at a certain color-coded level. Be sensitive to the danger that students and adults may perceive this color-coding as labeling by ability.

✓ Require students to write a response about why they chose the task. Leave the prompts open-ended to elicit the student's perception. "I choose this task because..." or "I think this learning task is..." Briefly meet with the student to discuss the response and motivate appropriate future action.

Kingore, B. (2013). *Rigor and Engagement for Growing Minds.* Austin, TX: PA Publishing.

**"STUDENTS GET TOO NOISY WHEN I AM NOT DIRECTLY INSTRUCTING THEM. WHAT CAN I DO TO CONTROL NOISE LEVELS?"**

✓ Ask students: "How is the noise level affecting your learning in our classroom?" Identify if noise levels bother them and risk their work being less productive. If the level is not disruptive to this class or to other classrooms, the noise may simply be our problem and not a problem for them.

✓ There is a difference between chaos and a learning buzz. Concretely establish the desired range of volume. Role-play the different levels of sound on a continuum from what is preferred to what is out of control. Noise problems tend to reoccur, so be prepared to revisit earlier discussions and role-play again.

✓ Conduct a class problem-solving meeting to elicit students' ideas. They may feel more responsible about noise control when they help establish the parameters and signals for volume adjustments.

✓ Talk softly at times to encourage students to listen more carefully. Deliberately lowering the volume of a voice can invite attention.

### ANYTHING YOU HEAR

My favorite way to limit noise was taught to me by a student in my class years ago. As we discussed individual roles in cooperative learning groups, she shared that her job was to listen and get ideas from the other groups! Now when group tasks begin, I announce: "You can use anything you hear from another group." I smile as the students draw closer together and talk softly to prevent others from taking their ideas.

**"HOW CAN I RESPOND TO DISRUPTIVE BEHAVIOR ISSUES WITHOUT ALIENATING THE STUDENT?"**

✓ Endeavor to resolve conflicts or disruptive behavior quickly, quietly, and unobtrusively. Making a student feel defensive is extremely counterproductive. When addressing a conflict with one or more students, move to the back of the classroom, standing away from others as much as you can. Rather than challenge the student, act naive and positive so students have to speak up and explain rather than mentally disengage from the conflict. "How might I help you?" or "How could this lesson be more engaging to you?"

✓ Offer a positive observation before addressing the disruption. "As I watch you work, one thing I really like about what I observe is... What is something I may have noticed that is less productive?"

Kingore, B. (2013). *Rigor and Engagement for Growing Minds.* Austin, TX: PA Publishing.

## "HOW CAN I DO IT ALL?"

✓ Don't get lost in the forest; focus on one tree. Initially, select one idea or technique you want to try ASAP and do it! Decide on one action and follow through on that plan before assuming any additional change.

✓ Prioritize implementation. Be selective and give yourself permission to move forward slowly. We know that any change that is worth doing will take time. Choose three strategies or applications you are interested in implementing. Then, plan and set into action those three changes.

✓ Adapt rather than start from scratch. If a prior learning experience was fairly effective but engaged less of the relevant complexity and depth you now seek, adapt it. Consider how to vary that learning experience for increased rigor and relevance. (Revisit some ideas for increasing complexity and depth in Chapter 4 to prime your changes.) Adaptation is a powerful, productive tool.

✓ Actively communicate with other teachers who share your vision of instruction. Collaboration with others provides positive opportunities for problem solving and idea generation as it validates that you are not alone with your objectives. The collegiality and collaboration can be quite engaging and productive.

✓ Do not feel guilty for not differentiating enough. Make an honest, professional effort to enable every child to experience continuous learning and celebrate every success. Even one forward step is a step closer to a rigorous and differentiated learning environment.

*How can I do it all?*
*...One step at a time*

*Implement!*

Implement one good idea and let that success lead you to another.

Kingore, B. (2013). *Rigor and Engagement for Growing Minds.* Austin, TX: PA Publishing.

FIGURE 7.5:

# THINKING REFLECTIVELY

### 1. IDEAS

Identify two or more ideas you intend to apply immediately.

### 2. QUALITY CHECK-UP

Ponder which characteristics of quality instruction or attributes of intellectual work are most significant to you. Use the checklists in Figure 7.1 and Figure 7.2 to mark your priorities. Now, extend your thinking. What additional aspects of quality do you deem important to either teachers or students?

### 3. SHOP TALK

*It is engaging and often exciting to talk shop with a valued colleague. Putting your heads together produces ideas that may not have developed alone.*
Management issues inevitably occur. Talk with colleagues to discuss management experiences and challenges. Share what has worked well for you. Develop two or more positive, specific strategies to implement for change. Later, meet again to mutually celebrate successes, pose continued questions, and brainstorm additional applications.

# CHAPTER 8
# ENGAGING LEARNING EXPERIENCES

Academic rigor necessitates engagement. Rigor is only possible when students are engaged in a deeper exploration of the content, such as when actively problem solving, often with peer collaboration. Student engagement is the result of a complex interaction of factors, including pedagogy, relevant topics, students' backgrounds, peer collaboration, and students' mental, social-emotional, and process connections.

Engagement is critical to learning and higher achievement since students retain more when they are engrossed. Engaged students are on task in their thinking and actively participating in the process of learning–the opposite, for example, of trying to learn the game of football strictly from lecture and the playbook. Indeed, how students engage in the work is more significant to long-term memory and learning dispositions than the number of assignments students complete (Sousa, 2009; Willis 2007a).

Brain research provides insights into many aspects of engagement or the lack of it in classrooms. To ensure a productive level of engagement in learning environments, guide instructional decisions with implications from brain research, such as the:

- Value of novelty to shift brains to full attention.
- Importance of a healthy social and emotional learning environment.
- Advantage of physical activity to boost brainpower.
- Significance of students' actively applying or incorporating information in order to retain it.
- Necessity of organizing concentrated lecture into multiple segments of less than fifteen minutes with student engagement and applications in-between segments.

(The summary of brain-based instruction in Chapter 4 elaborates and provides references for these insights.)

Kingore, B. (2013). *Rigor and Engagement for Growing Minds.* Austin, TX: PA Publishing.

When students are deeply engaged in learning tasks, it is apparent to educators who can simultaneously interpret the quality of that engagement. Observe students' alert attention and meaningful contact with others as they discuss, paraphrase, interact, write content notes, move, explain, experiment, perform, problem solve, ask questions, and draw to illustrate a point or connect ideas with symbols. The ultimate engagement is when students feel in charge of learning and are intrinsically motivated to learn. The Hungarian psychologist, Mihaly Csikszentmihalyi (1990), refers to that level of engagement as a *state of flow.*

# FLOW

Flow is the intrinsic motivation you experience when physically, mentally, and emotionally absorbed in a personally relevant task with a potential for personal success. This advanced level of engagement produces a sense of personal achievement and active contribution to a worthwhile result. Csikszentmihalyi (1993, 178-9) identifies the conditions necessary to achieve a state of flow as:

* Focused concentration,
* Clear and attainable goals,
* A balance between high challenge and personal skill level,
* Immediate feedback from the process or from people, and
* A merging of action, effort, and awareness in a self-rewarding experience.

Ultimately, a state of flow results in a loss of conscious awareness as when you hear students' comment that they had no idea what time it was.

Since a state of flow is the highest level of engagement, the Depth and Complexity Framework in Chapter 3 Figure 3.1 can be adapted to accommodate flow at the top of the graph, as depicted in Figure 8.1. Csikszentmihalyi interprets optimal experiences in the state of flow as moving outward with graduated involvement as skills are gained that generate new skills. In a state of flow, students' cognitive processing is engaged at and beyond the targeted areas of assimilating ideas and concepts. Flow extends toward students' adapting relevant depth and complexity to formulate principles and generalizations in both existing and unpredictable real-world situations.

Once you experience flow, you understand the elated feeling of engagement and understand why it is a prime target for students in their individual learning pursuits. As Csikszentmihalyi (2002) explains, when the characteristics of flow are present, a person wants to continue with whatever produces that feeling. The experience is so rewarding that it becomes almost addictive; you strive to repeat it and that action produces more learning. He added that schools and families can promote these optimal learning experiences by first supporting and then challenging learners. Support is significant because students' fear of how they appear to others or what others might think of them can place a constraint on experiencing a state of flow.

Engagement in school-based learning means that students primarily like what they are doing, as in extracurricular activities and interactive projects, so it is doubtful that students experience flow when completing a skill sheet. Likewise, no matter how cleverly and

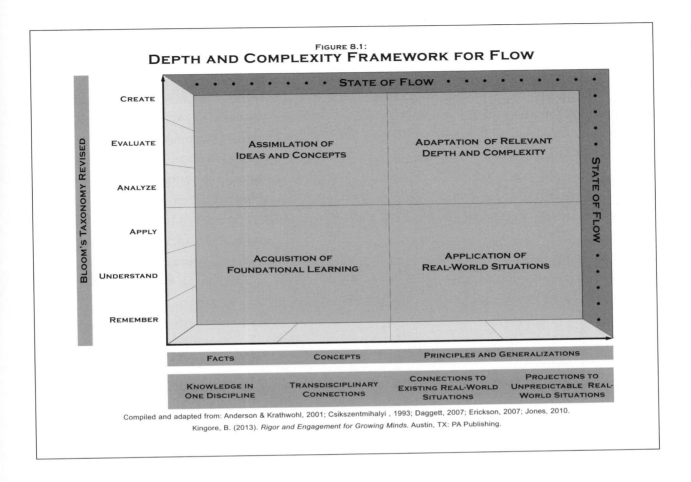

FIGURE 8.1:
## DEPTH AND COMPLEXITY FRAMEWORK FOR FLOW

Compiled and adapted from: Anderson & Krathwohl, 2001; Csikszentmihalyi , 1993; Daggett, 2007; Erickson, 2007; Jones, 2010.

Kingore, B. (2013). *Rigor and Engagement for Growing Minds.* Austin, TX: PA Publishing.

creatively we deliver a lecture, if it only requires students to listen, it is a passive action. For deeper learning meaning, we must increase students' mental and process engagement as well as physical involvement with the content. Information must be applied and incorporated rather than only heard in order for it to be retained and retrieved (Sousa & Tomlinson, 2010; Willis, 2011; Wolfe, 2010). Tomlinson (2011, 22) emphasizes: "By manipulating new learning in a variety of ways, learners build neural networks leading to better retention and retrieval of the new information."

The kinds of interactive, authentic learning experiences that we incorporate into our instruction directly influence students'

engagement. Fair or not, we bear the main responsibility to establish student engagement. Our instructional decisions help students achieve flow or disengage from instruction. As Jones (2008) noted, it is primarily the teacher's responsibility to engage the students, as opposed to the teacher expecting students to come to class naturally and automatically ready to engage. When students are truly engaged in learning, teachers are engaged with the students, and all experience the joy that accompanies positive learning experiences. Thus, the promising return for our sometimes hard-fought efforts toward the students' engagement is that when they experience flow, we do as well.

## ENGAGING LESSONS

In the classrooms of the past, adults endeavored to prevent students from being off-task and noisy. The predominant voice was the teacher's—engagingly dispensing information while quelling students' talking to increase their listening and note taking. This practice sometimes resulted in disengaged students because there is a significant difference between a teacher being engaging and students being engaged. Engagement results when students are mentally, emotionally, and socially interested and involved in the process of learning. Understand the difference between a learning buzz and noisy chaos.

Students are more responsive to high expectations when interactive learning applications are valued in classrooms. Many students are tired of just sitting and listening; they want to be more involved in their learning—similar to the feelings teachers may experience during some lecture-based professional development. In classrooms for students or adults, lecture is appropriate when it involves important information that is relevant, interesting, carefully prepared, and brief. Since humans actively attend to concentrated information for only eight to fifteen minutes or less before becoming distracted (Medina, 2009; Sousa, 2010; Willis, 2011), plan opportunities that switch students from focused listening to more active participation to activate understanding. The incorporation of engaging and hands-on tasks requires minds-on applications that enhance learning

*Keep Lectures Brief*

•

*Lecturing is appropriate when it involves important information that is relevant, interesting, carefully prepared, and brief.*

within a rigorous, relevant curriculum (Wolfe, 2010).

Ponder this question when planning direct instruction: "How can I engage students in constructing meaning and applying the knowledge and skills we are learning?" The answer is not to determine some tangentially related activity for them to do for a few minutes; the answer is to connect content and engagement for more rigorous results.

For example, student reflection or responses to questions is more engaging, richer, and more meaningful if students first think together to prime their brains. Additionally, when we ask students to figure out an example, invite engagement and simultaneously honor introspective learners by announcing: "You may work by yourself or with one or two other students." As an example in math, rather than merely give students a set of problems to complete, engage them in flexible groups to formulate their own examples of real-life problems that apply targeted skill and concept sets.

Engaging lessons must integrate students' mental, social-emotional, and process connectedness. Mental engagement means that students are actively and mentally involved in the learning opportunity. A nonexample of mental engagement is students writing spelling words ten or twenty times as they talk to peers about a television program or music group they like. Obviously, they are not totally engaged in the intended spelling skill. Learning experiences without mental engagement may squander precious class time and result in students becoming cynics who think of school assignments as busywork.

Social and emotional connectedness does not imply that learning experiences must entertain students. Rather, social and emotional connections mean that students view the learning experience as relevant and interesting to them. It implies that students feel connected to and affirmed by others as a learning community. Brain researchers remind us that student attention increases and long-term memory is activated when pleasure is associated with the learning situation (Willis, 2007b).

Process engagement incorporates the metacognitive strategies teachers use to elicit students' long-term memory. Asking students to think aloud and unpack their thinking about the task requires them to process the task at a deeper level.

What does it look like when mental, social-emotional, and process engagement are active in a lesson? Consider an example of a direct-instruction lesson for the comprehension of nonfiction. When assigned to silently read nonfiction text, students' minds wander, and they turn pages more than they comprehend text. Yet, knowledgeable teachers and the Common Core State Standards (CCSS) emphasize the importance of students interacting with text to figure out exact meaning and cite specific examples to support that meaning. The sequence in Figure 8.2 engages students in comprehending nonfiction and is adapted from Reeves' (2012) discussion of

reading instruction. Model the strategy and encourage students' applications.

An advantage of this sequence is that it anticipates and responds to students' differences in pacing. Some students need the time to complete the task for a single page while others have time to continue reading additional pages. Mental engagement is encouraged by the brief, specific task and by high-quality reading material. Process and social-emotional engagement activate as students analyze the text for a main idea and details, share their perspectives with a peer, and then reflect on the process. The sequence can trigger higher comprehension of non-fiction within most content areas or grade levels. Students' responses furnish an immediate formative assessment, revealing who would benefit from additional direct assistance with reading comprehension. The process sends a clear message that reading is about comprehension rather than speed. As Reeves (2012, 4) notes, "...good reading is about getting it—understanding what you read and, when it's really good, wanting to learn more."

Engaging lessons promote transfer, and transfer is a keystone skill. Transferable knowledge builds on content knowledge and process knowledge—knowing when, why, and how to apply this information. How students use data, answer questions, and formulate problem solutions demonstrates transfer. A student's ability to transfer and apply existing understanding to a new context promotes

*Engagement*

•

*Learning experiences without mental, social-emotional, and process engagement may squander precious class time and result in students becoming cynics who think of school assignments as busywork.*

FIGURE 8.2:
# READING COMPREHENSION: A LESSON FOR NONFICTION TEXT

1. **HELP STUDENTS FOCUS ON THE TASK RATHER THAN MERELY ASK THEM TO READ SILENTLY.**

   Introduce nonfiction text that is interesting and relevant. Tell students that you are going to work together using a strategy to promote deeper comprehension of the information. Emphasize: "One of our objectives when reading is to clearly comprehend and be able to cite information in the text to support our thinking."

2. **GIVE THEM A CLEAR, SHORT-TERM TASK.**

   "Working alone, please begin reading page 32 of our text. When you finish that page, jot down quick notes of the main idea and two or more supporting details. That is what I am going to ask you to explain and discuss in four minutes. When you are certain you understand that page, continue reading but stop to jot down the main idea and supporting details of each page."

3. **AFTER THE DESIGNATED FOUR MINUTES, CHECK FOR UNDERSTANDING.**

   Invite students to pair-share their notes from page 32 before engaging in a group discussion. As a group, compare main ideas and details before reaching a comprehension consensus.

4. **REPEAT THE SEQUENCE FOR ADDITIONAL PAGES AS NEEDED.**

5. **CLOSE THE LESSON BY INVOLVING STUDENTS IN ANALYZING CONTENT AND PROCESS.**

   Initially, work together to summarize key points of the content. Then, ask students to reflect about the process as a strategy for comprehending nonfiction. "Even though it takes a couple of minutes to write the main ideas and supporting details at the end of each page, are there ways this strategy may save you time in the long run?" Encourage them to implement the strategy when reading on their own and report back what they conclude about the effectiveness of this strategy and their suggestions for adaptations for their personal applications.

Kingore, B. (2013). *Rigor and Engagement for Growing Minds.* Austin, TX: PA Publishing.

long-term memory and the construction of deeper understanding. In the preceding nonfiction lesson, students are challenged to continue the strategy and report back to the class regarding their personal conclusions of the effectiveness of the strategy.

*Get going!*

## WRITING TO COMPREHEND

When students engage in silent reading for a scheduled period of time, as with the silent sustained reading strategy (SSR), have them conclude by writing for two to five minutes about what they read. The depth and quality of their response is an immediate formative assessment providing feedback about their level of engagement and need for different techniques or support for reading comprehension. Continuing this process throughout a novel or expanded nonfiction text results in a content log summarizing key information for review.

# FACTORS IN STUDENT ENGAGEMENT

To ensure productive engagement in learning, view instruction through the eyes of students. Discern which learning experiences induce the greatest engagement from your students. In a spirit of relevancy and student ownership, survey students regarding their perceptions of engagement. Invite them to share what engages or dissuades them in learning situations. Have interested students

compile and categorize the responses into useful patterns to present to the class for further discussion. Facilitate as the class draws conclusions regarding what they value most in engaging learning environments. Then, act on their input and incorporate as many of their engaging ideas as are feasible.

While specific responses are unique to different students and different contexts, anticipate some of the following responses as characteristic of today's students. No single aspect magically ensures engagement, but combinations of these factors effectively heighten student engagement in learning. The intent is to plan learning experiences that are so engaging that students feel compelled to participate.

## PERSONAL RELATIONSHIPS

Students seek and deserve satisfying personal relationships with teachers and peers in a classroom. It is the quality of those relationships that drives their behavior and learning dispositions (Jones, 2008). With high-ability students, for example, social and emotional difficulties diminish and intellectual risk taking accelerates when students feel respected by both intellectual peers and age peers. In classrooms characterized by a commitment to personally satisfying relationships, students take a proactive interest in supporting others rather than merely assisting others when assigned to do so.

## PEER INTERACTION

Liberate students to talk and problem solve with each other for more engaged learning. All learners want to interact with peers.

Conversing and interacting in problem solving applications of content, concepts, and skills helps students and teachers promote relevant connections. Individuals come to realize that their input contributes to everyone's construction of new understanding and conclusions.

## TECHNOLOGY

Technology is inherently engaging to today's digital learners. Skillful applications of technology bridge academics to the real world, including accessing extraordinary quantities of resources and expanding the learning situation to include people outside the classroom. Through technology, high-ability learners experience more cognitively demanding work as they collaborate on virtual teams, have access to mentors beyond the classroom, and participate in advanced online classes.

## INTERESTS

Enhance engagement by taking advantage of every opportunity to link student interests to curriculum learning targets. Transdisciplinary connections and interest-based groups weave student interests into our content. Superior learning occurs when classroom experiences are relevant to students' interests and experiences (Willis, 2007a).

## CHOICE

Offer choices in learning experiences and products so students can select an option

that is more relevant to them and their best way to demonstrate learning. Providing choices increases students' ownership in the task and their motivation to exert the effort required to excel.

## INQUISITIVENESS

Curiosity fosters engagement. Build students' strong desire to know and then couple that with something different or unexpected to spark attention and pique interest. Inquisitive interactions elicit strong reactions among students or between a student and content materials.

## AUTHENTIC, PERSONALLY RELEVANT, REAL-WORLD WORK

Meaningful work elicits engagement and helps students make connections and construct meaning for themselves in the process. Incorporate the phrase *in the long run* to help students envision the future applications of current concepts and skills (Edwards, 2010). Guide them to perceive that this investment of effort and concentration is worthwhile now because in the long run it ensures them an advantage. Ask students to express how this learning can serve them in their future. "How might this be worth your effort in the long run?" "What is a major benefit to you in the long run?"

## ENGAGED, KNOWLEDGEABLE TEACHERS

Engaged teachers more effectively engage students. When teachers clearly love

*Learning ExPEERiences*

•

*In a rigorous learning environment, learning experiences should be spelled expeeriences to denote the importance of peer interactions in real-life situations.*

this profession, obviously care about who they teach, and enthuse a fascination with what they teach, they connect with their students.

## ACTIVITY

Physical movement, hands-on learning tasks, and project-based learning are engaging. When you increase students' activity, their mental awareness and engagement increases. Frequently, ensure that students physically do something and immediately apply the concepts and skills as they are learning.

## VISUAL APPLICATIONS

Inasmuch as digital learners are so accustomed to visual connections to content, incorporate visual applications as frequently as feasible. Graphic organizers, photographs, art, videos, and technology are some of the ways to include visual connections.

## VARIETY, NOVELTY, OR HUMOR

Including variety, novelty, or humor in learning situations is not asking teachers to deliver comic routines but to incorporate the unexpected or humorous with content connections when possible. These elements wake-up the brain (Willis 2010; 2011). Research also confirms the value of humor to increase endorphins in our bodies so we literally feel better (Cousins, 2005). Appropriate novelty or humor in the classroom builds relationships and increases personal accessibility by making everyone more comfortable with each other. It is a call to attention and memory as students are more inclined to remember an unexpected or funny example rather than a list of facts. Laughter and surprise often invite

students to examine information from a different perspective.

Engaged students will learn and retain more. Build on the factors in student engagement that best captivate your students. Provide an array of learning experiences that are challenging, relevant, and ensure opportunities for all students to flourish as they expand their unique interests and capabilities. Explore this chapter to ponder the multiple opportunities for engagement inherent in:

- Replacement tasks,
- Project-based learning,
- Academic conversations,
- Tiered learning stations,
- Academic games,
- Art and non-linguistic connections, and
- Physical activity.

## REPLACEMENT TASKS

Replacement tasks are learning experiences that are not in the core curriculum. They are engaging because they represent high-quality learning options that students can self-select. They go beyond keeping students busy by ensuring alternative learning experiences in response to the following objectives.

- Provide meaningful learning options to ensure that students continue to learn.
- Support learning beyond core curriculum by providing alternatives to redundant work while connecting to curriculum content and instructional objectives.
- Enable a teacher to directly instruct others while some students proceed with individual or small group learning objectives.

Replacement tasks are options negotiated and agreed upon by you and the class so students can select tasks without asking permission or interrupting others. As a management routine, these tasks are designed to ensure student access to engaging alternatives when class time is available. Students proceed with replacement tasks when they:

- Complete assigned work early,
- Wait for your input as you assist others,
- Preassess above grade-level expectations on a specific topic and require alternative learning experiences in order to continue learning, or
- Demonstrate mastery of core curriculum for an academic discipline and need to pursue learning experiences beyond the core curriculum.

Replacement tasks provide learning opportunities that are relevant, generalizable, and engaging so they afford all students meaningful, interesting learning options. These tasks empower students with choices and independence as they consider which possibilities might provide the most interesting and productive ways to pursue their learning interests and capabilities. The tasks are often transdisciplinary to incorporate students' preferred academic disciplines.

Post a list of replacement tasks to provide a rich pool of learning opportunities that students may choose as they work without direct instruction. Since the tasks are learning opportunities rather than an entertaining break, everyone needs to understand the expectations in Figure 8.3 that accompany replacement tasks.

## FIGURE 8.3:
# REPLACEMENT TASK EXPECTATIONS

✓ Students are accountable for their behavior and quality of work.

✓ It is not permissible to disrupt others or interrupt their learning.

✓ Students work at levels conducive to their continuous learning capabilities.

✓ The learning tasks must connect to students' interests and learning objectives.

✓ The tasks can be pursued independently or occasionally in self-selected, flexible groups.

✓ All students have opportunities to engage in replacement tasks when they complete assigned work at an appropriate level of quality or document mastery of core curriculum.

As a strategy in rigorous learning environments, replacement tasks can be either short-term or ongoing learning opportunities. When used as brief tasks, such as when students complete assigned work early, replacement tasks must possess certain attributes in order to be a productive component that supports learning. During short blocks of time, effective replacement tasks must be designed to:

- Involve minimum mess,
- Be quick to set-up and put away,
- Be interesting,
- Avoid disrupting others,

- Avoid calling undue attention to self,
- Ensure respectful and personally relevant learning, and
- Apply important learning targets.

When replacement tasks are used for ongoing, long-term projects or inquiry, the first two attributes are not applicable.

As a class, brainstorm and display replacement task options for ready access when students need an alternative learning task. Initially, limit these learning activities to a small number of tasks, processes, or graphics with which students have previous experience so they are capable of completing the tasks independently. As needed, teachers may also designate the parameters of the task to guide students' progress.

Ultimately, however, as students gain experience and self-management skills, they should assume more or most of the determination of the process and products of replacement tasks. Encourage students to view replacement tasks as their opportunity to learn what they are excited to know. Students should select tasks that are so personally interesting they feel inspired to invest the time and depth that great work deserves. At this juncture, high-ability students benefit from ongoing, long-term replacement tasks they design for inquiry and in-depth study. These tasks should be responsive to their intellectual curiosity, problem-solving interests, and construction of deeper understanding. Figure 8.4 provides examples of potential replacement tasks.

## FIGURE 8.4:
# REPLACEMENT TASKS

These suggestions for replacement tasks are arranged from short-term to long-term applications. The tasks listed first require only a brief amount of time. The tasks in the middle are options that may continue across several learning segments. The list concludes with the long-term opportunities associated with projects and disciplined inquiry.

- Sneak reading—individually selected silent reading
- Quick sketch to illustrate
- Work with content-related manipulatives
- Listening stations
- Journals or learning logs
- Academic games
- Develop graphics to organize content
- Compose content-related songs or poems
- Create materials or learning tasks for flexible groups, learning stations, or younger classrooms
- Create and display a content-rich, classroom bulletin board
- Computer applications and web searches appropriate to topics or skills
- Problem-solving investigations
- Write fiction or nonfiction
- Self-selected, content-based learning projects
- Self-selected, independently-developed inquiry

## ELICIT STUDENTS' REPLACEMENT TASK SUGGESTIONS

After developing and displaying a list of replacement tasks, continue to elicit student additions to the tasks. As a serendipitous connection to multiple learning skills, when students question why a specific task is not included on the list of potential replacements, suggest that the student write a persuasive proposal to present to the class for their consideration. Plan a two-minute window for the student's presentation in class, inviting peer questions and promoting a peer consensus of the fate of the proposal.

## PROJECT-BASED LEARNING

Project-based learning (PBL) is based on interactive, engaging, and often hands-on learning tasks for flexible groups. Yet, it is instructionally useful only if we incorporate and build upon core concepts. The objective of these projects is to investigate real-world questions and discover new concepts and skills in the process. Effective projects hold individuals accountable for learning targets while honing the 21st century skills of communication, collaboration, critical and creative thinking, consensus development, and problem solving. At their best, these projects have an impact on others beyond school rather than merely serve to demonstrate success in a school-learning task.

PBL uses contextual investigations and transdisciplinary applications to develop multifaceted understanding. Transdisciplinary projects engage learners in understanding how ideas from two or more disciplines are related while increasing the likelihood that their interests and talents connect with a current topic. For example, a group of students who disliked math and were more interested in writing became quite engaged in math when their teacher challenged them to write stories teaching targeted math concepts to peers. They researched children's literature that incorporated math concepts, integrated class learning targets, and completed books illustrating four different math concepts. A fortuitous by-product of project-based, transdisciplinary study is that everyone is more engaged in the learning as students and teachers alike discover that interactive tasks connecting across disciplines provide a more interesting approach to learning.

Project-based lessons incorporate students' mental engagement, process engagement, and social-emotional connections through quality relationships among peers and adults. Feedback from peers, the teacher, and the lesson process provide evidence to students that their contributions to the group are needed and respected.

To build the collaboration and research skills required in PBL, initially present students with a clearly defined project and specify the parameters, process, and time schedule of the task. At this beginning level, all students work on the same or similar project. As soon as it is feasible, focus on open-ended questions or problems with multiple pathways to solutions in order to challenge different individual

Kingore, B. (2013). *Rigor and Engagement for Growing Minds*. Austin; TX: PA Publishing.

groups to function at higher-levels of cognitive processing as they explore the project.

Eventually, increase cognitive processing and opportunities to construct new understandings. Present students with an authentic, multi-step problem that is less structured, undefined, complex, and has multiple solutions. Students proceed to analyze the problem, collaboratively investigate, and pose solutions through applications of a problem-solving sequence. In the process, they apply basic skills, enlarge prior understanding, develop research competence, and construct new understandings and skills.

---

### DIFFERENTIATION FOR HIGH-ABILITY STUDENTS

While most often organized into mixed-ability groups, PBL is also an effective way to increase differentiation through groups of intellectual peers. These groups are advantageous when the project requires an advanced level of background knowledge and skills to successfully initiate the task.

---

When students feel they are stuck in their problem-solving process, a rich pool of resources may help prompt new perspectives and directions. As much as is feasible, use project-based opportunities to develop their independence in acquiring resources. Pose questions to facilitate their consideration of available resources.

- "As you look about the room, what do you notice about colleagues or materials that might prove helpful?"

- "What interesting databases might you be able to access quickly?"
- "I'm curious which resources you might be able to list if everyone stops to brainstorm together for two minutes."

Reflection, self-assessment, and formative assessment are essential components of PBL. Individuals and groups periodically reflect on the different stages of a project to continue progressing, problem solve, and set personalized learning goals.

During PBL, engage in facilitating groups and providing mini-lessons as needed to promote continuous learning. Additionally, participate in brief oral conferences with groups or individuals, encourage originality, and conduct formative assessments. When it is advantageous to do so, use questions to prompt high-level thinking, challenge assumptions, and build students' tolerance for ambiguity. Increase accountability by announcing in advance that you will randomly select a student in each group to summarize the process or explain the group's solution at the closure of today's work.

## ACADEMIC CONVERSATIONS

Academic conversations are purposeful communications among peers and teachers that incorporate academic vocabulary, thoughtful ideas, and skills connected to school-related topics. Rather than only as social exchanges, conversations during group work is invited in the context of learning discussions that elicit diverse perspectives and encourage new understandings.

---

Kingore, B. (2013). *Rigor and Engagement for Growing Minds.* Austin, TX: PA Publishing.

Academic conversations in flexible groups increase students' conceptual understanding and enhance their social and emotional growth as they respectfully exchange intellectual ideas with peers. Informal and structured conversations among students affirm equity of voice, mutual support, and respect for others as well as elicit numerous cognitive skills (Zwiers & Crawford, 2011). Substantive classroom conversations are authentic and relevant as students think aloud to unpack their reasoning and share strategies. These conversations also provide formative assessment opportunities as others listen and infer students' levels of understanding.

Academic conversations among group members enable students to practice and extend prominent interactive and cognitive skills desired by both educators and employers. Specifically, as they model positive interpersonal skills in their group, students should:

- Offer encouraging feedback,
- Share original thinking,
- Elaborate,
- Clarify,
- Support ideas with examples,
- Paraphrase as they build on and question input from others,
- Synthesize, and
- Reach decisions as group work concludes.

Research documents that the degree of learning during group work improves when academic conversations brim with respect for others' ideas (Sullo, 2009; Zwiers & Crawford,

*Academic Conversations*

•

*Academic conversations in small groups increase students' concept understanding and enhance their social and emotional growth as they respectfully exchange intellectual ideas with peers.*

2011). Brainstorm with students how to respectfully encourage elaborations and explanations from peers as they work together. Develop a pool of sound bites as class examples.

- "Tell me more so I can understand your thinking."
- "Elaborate that idea."
- "Help me picture that."
- "Give me an example and nonexample so I understand what you mean."
  - "Help me find more about that in the text."
  - "Explain the reasoning behind the decision you made."

Explicitly integrate time for academic conversations during most lessons and applications of skills and concepts. Create a culture of explanation instead of a culture of correct answers by using questions and tasks that invite multiple strategies to reach successful outcomes (De Frondeville, 2009). Encourage students to use key vocabulary in context, actively listen and learn from one another, ponder multiple points of view, and extend meaning beyond prior knowledge.

Children internalize academic language when they are immersed in meaningful opportunities to use language for real-life purposes. To maximize vocabulary development, all students benefit from ongoing opportunities to listen to and speak with others. Indeed, conversations among students in classrooms is fundamental to extending knowledge of academic words in multiple contexts, appreciating the nuances of words, and reinforcing newly developing vocabulary. Research supports the value of students collectively analyzing content and communicating by applying the specific terminology related to a field of study (Marzano & Pickering, 2005; Zwiers & Crawford, 2011). The CCSS advocates academic discussions one-to-one and in small groups, as well as in whole class settings so students collaborate to answer questions, build understanding, and solve problems.

## MOTIVATE CONVERSATIONS AND PROBLEM SOLVING

Incorporate novelty to wake-up the brain and motivate discussion. Drop a different set of coins in the center of each flexible group and ask each group to work together to respond to questions incorporating current concepts and skills. For example, ask:

- "What coins do you need to add or subtract to total exactly one dollar?"
- "Determine two other sets of coins you could have that would total this same amount."
- "If you can only keep part of this, would you want 5/8 or 2/3 of the total?"
- "This is the change from $10 that paid for lunch and sales tax. What was the total cost of the bill?" or "What was the total cost of the food before the sales tax was calculated?"

## COMMUNICATION STRATEGIES FOR STUDENT ENGAGEMENT

Experienced teachers use discussion techniques in whole class and small groups to actively engage students in discussing content and applying skills. Add peer discussion as a follow-up to many familiar learning strategies to increase learning. With silent reading, for example, researchers conclude that having students discuss what they read is crucial in developing their ability to construct meaning and support ideas by citing textual references (Cooper, 2011).

Begin with strategies you already know and use well. Then, vary those strategies by incorporating elaborated communication strategies that foster students' construction of deeper meaning and enable more instructional mileage out of the familiar. Conclude learning applications by requiring peer groups to discuss newfound insights to extend concepts and relevant connections. Have students summarize, judge the best ideas that emerge, write a conclusion, or rank the significance of the information. Figure 8.5 shows effective ready-to-use variations of several well-known learning strategies.

## TIERED LEARNING STATIONS

Tiered learning stations are highly appealing and engaging to students of all ages. They represent an effective way for students to interact with supportive peers while pursuing significant learning objectives away from their desks. Instead of all students completing the same learning task, tiered stations

FIGURE 8.5:

# LEARNING STRATEGIES VARIED FOR ENGAGEMENT AND RIGOR

These well-known strategies interface with differentiated lessons to increase student engagement and promote students' construction of in-depth understanding. Pause periodically during a lesson to elicit students' responses specific to current content and foster their construction of deeper meaning. Incorporate these variations multiple times to ensure elaborated communication that enhances achievement.

| STRATEGY | VARIATIONS FOR ENGAGEMENT AND RIGOR |
|---|---|
| Cooperative Learning | • Advanced students work in the same group<br>• Incorporate key academic vocabulary<br>• Jigsaw using advanced-level materials<br>• Elaborate ideas with symbols and quick sketches<br>• Groups randomly select a student to summarize<br>• Groups evaluate to determine a group achievement that could not have been achieved individually |
| Sustained Silent Reading (SSR) | • Read material that is personally selected and at an individual readiness level<br>• Maintain a log of interesting, relevant vocabulary<br>• Conclude with a follow-up reflection in writing or an oral discussion with a peer |
| Think-Pair-Share | • Incorporate key academic vocabulary<br>• An ELL and bilingual peer pair for language support<br>• Advanced students pair for intellectual support and increased content complexity and depth<br>• Pairs conclude by determining their two best ideas<br>• Each person must be able to summarize the ideas of the other |
| Pair-Share-Square | • Reach a consensus of the best ideas that emerged<br>• Rank the key points in order of their significance |
| Role-Play | • Incorporate key academic vocabulary<br>• Create a conversation between two concepts<br>• Create a conversation between the antagonist and the protagonist<br>• Explore the conflict of interests between Manifest Destiny and states' rights<br>• Discuss which is more useful in real-life: fractions or percentage<br>• Debate which is more significant to life: the sun or rain; osmosis or photosynthesis<br>• Students end the experience by writing a brief conclusion based on the presented perspectives |

Kingore, B. (2013). *Rigor and Engagement for Growing Minds*. Austin, TX: PA Publishing.

provide variations of essential academic skills and concepts adapted to the skill levels and learning styles of students. Students are engaged by the empowerment to select among learning options and by peer interaction.

Learning stations are not only for primary grades. When stations are tiered, all grade levels can use them to flexibly group students for maximum achievement. The tiered learning experiences make it realistic for individuals demonstrating a range of readiness levels to learn at the same station. This mixed-ability grouping ensures that high-ability children have opportunities to interact with both intellectual peers and age peers. Tiered instruction safeguards uninterrupted academic growth for advanced students while all students interact to practice or extend learning targets (Kingore, 2011).

Tiered learning stations must provide challenging learning opportunities that students pursue with peer support, thus freeing teachers to conduct direct lessons with other students. Tiering does not make the work easier; it provides appropriate levels of challenge so students thrive (Wormeli, 2006). It customizes how students learn concepts and skills; it does not compromise what is learned. To promote continuous learning for all students at a tiered learning station:

✓ Allow students to focus on targeted concepts and skills at different levels of depth and complexity,

✓ Provide meaningful tasks at varied levels of complexity aligned to individuals' readiness and best ways to learn,

✓ Incorporate different support systems and structures to expedite learning, and

✓ Include high-interest, relevant tiered tasks that engage students.

Tiered learning stations are only realistic in today's busy classroom schedules when they further students' learning but do not burden teachers with unrealistic requirements for preparation. Select learning experiences for stations that provide a range of meaningful applications using targeted skills and concepts while minimizing extra preparation time (Kingore, 2011). Figure 8.6 shares ideas for quick starts to tier your learning stations and includes several suggestions to make learning stations relevant and practical.

> *Target Learning Standards*
>
> •
>
> *Learning stations that fail to focus on essential academic content and students' learning profiles have little effect on achievement and squander valuable learning time.*

## SKILLED TEACHERS TIER INSTRUCTION

Teachers who are skilled in differentiation and quite knowledgeable of content and students' diverse learning levels are best prepared to effectively tier learning tasks and create tiered learning stations.

Kingore, B. (2013). *Rigor and Engagement for Growing Minds.* Austin, TX: PA Publishing.

# Quick Starts to Tiered Learning Stations

The applications that follow are ideas for the kinds of tiered learning stations that enable teachers to make the most efficient use of their instruction time while providing significant learning experiences for all students. The intent of these examples is to promote your decisions about tiered tasks appropriate to students' interests and capabilities. Explore how to best use learning stations to foster students' continuous learning of essential concepts and skills while minimizing additional preparation time.

✦ **Familiar Graphics**

Provide new and different applications of the graphic organizers and learning tasks students already know how to complete. Using the known in a new way continues learning applications with a minimum of instructional preparation time.

✦ **Standing Stations**

Find room for tiered stations in crowded classrooms by using standing stations. A windowsill or a shelf allows space for selected problems and simple materials that students use for high-level thinking investigations while standing in the area.

✦ **Logic Station**

Provide a problem-solving station that assumes a detective-style ambience. Content-based logic problems are one example that works well at this station. Multiple examples of logic tasks are readily accessible online.

✦ **Reading Corner for Nonfiction**

Nonfiction text is significant to the CCSS and applicable to all content areas. A corner of the room with a few floor pillows becomes an invitation to explore a range of provided nonfiction, high-interest materials relevant to current topics and students' interests. Many students are eager to read silently when comfortably surrounded with peers instead of isolated at a desk. Provide simple response options or time for academic conversations as a way for students' to share what they learn when they finish reading.

✦ **Academic Games**

Since academic games increase student achievement, provide a game-playing station that incorporates board, card, and computer games that apply targeted skills. Students interact to complete a game and develop a list of the skills and concepts they apply.

✦ **Direction Cards**

Use direction cards in tiered stations to provide a framework and directions for the varied learning experiences as well as to support students who would benefit from repeated reading of directions. Direction cards enhance student management and independence without direct teacher intervention.

Kingore, B. (2013). *Rigor and Engagement for Growing Minds.* Austin, TX: PA Publishing.

## ACADEMIC GAMES

Games are a part of the lives of digital kids. They have instant appeal and decidedly engage students. Consequently, extending games into classrooms seems a natural fit. However, the effectiveness of games as academic tools is directly related to how skillfully we correlate them to essential learning targets. Limit classroom applications of games to those that focus on significant skills and concepts related to your academic content.

When games are aligned to learning targets and used purposefully, research studies confirm that they increase achievement gains and build academic vocabulary (Marzano, 2010a). Students are most motivated to excel when the game process is perceived as fun competition rather than a high-stakes winner-loser designation. Provide a small number of different card games, board games, and digital games with academic connections appropriate to the readiness levels of the students. When the game is finished, require students to debrief with one another to share perceptions and extend their construction of understanding.

Games that require two or more players combine concept and skill applications with social practices, collaboration, problem solving, and team building. The most effective games present a clear sense of mutual challenge to each player.

To extend learning and apply creative thinking to current skill levels, invite students to adapt commercial games, particularly card and board games that students can actually access for adaptation. Students build upon the original game to design a new game that is specific to a current topic of study. Challenge students to develop their game adaptations to incorporate appropriate terminology, involve a more complex process, and be engaging to play while extending beyond basic information. For example, three gifted middle school students used the Monopoly™ game board to develop a game about Egypt. They creatively designed Egyptian sites on the board and developed cards that related to events, the diverse perspectives of historical peoples, and the causes and effects of several Egyptian cultural changes over time.

In rigorous learning environments, respond to students as they engage in games and propose additional game-related ideas to enhance learning potential. Figure 8.7 lists several ideas to increase academic challenge as students play games in classrooms.

## ART AND NON-LINGUISTIC CONNECTIONS

Art and non-linguistic representations play a significant role in academic engagement. Most students enjoy engaging in the visual and performing arts, and visual-spatial learners thrive when learning experiences integrate art or graphics. Recent research continues to support that art and non-linguistic connections lead to higher comprehension and vocabulary development (Dean et al., 2012). Associating an image with a new word has a powerful effect on retention. Additionally, the Developing Reading Education with Arts Methods (DREAM) found substantial gains on state standardized reading tests for elementary

# INCREASING THE EDUCATIONAL VALUE OF ACADEMIC GAMES

✦ List the skills and concepts targeted in a certain game; then, ask students to explain how they applied or extended those skills as they played that game.

✦ Ask students to describe what they are doing as they play a game so you access students' perceptions, academic vocabulary, and problem-solving strategies. Most children have a lot to say when asked about their game-playing process.

✦ Invite students to analyze and alter one rule or aspect of the game that might effectively increase the challenge level and make it even more engaging to play. Have them experiment with that change and report their results.

✦ Incorporate authentic writing tasks. When students create an original game that teaches or applies targeted skills and concepts, have them write directions so others can play the game independently.

✦ Ask students to teach a digital game to their family, a peer, or another adult at school. This invitation provides an effective opportunity for children to guide adults and peers into their digital world. Ask these students to present a brief oral or written report of their experience.

✦ Challenge students to determine ways they can connect the ideas and skills they develop from games to other learning opportunities, such as with books, discussions, or personal interests. As one example, students might generalize that they need to continue trying when learning something new as one skill builds to a higher level.

✦ Post a short list of approved websites that are sources of games with academic connections. In pairs or as individuals, students explore one or more of the sites to assess its engagement potential and educational value. Students write recommendations to peers based on their assessment. When possible, they post their reviews on the game website.

✦ Invite students to propose additional online sites they discover that offer appropriate games with skill applications. To nominate a site, a student writes a proposal explaining the academic value of the site and includes reasons why classmates will benefit from the site. A class committee and the teacher review all proposals and research a site before it is added to the recommended list.

✦ Deconstruct what it is about a game that entices students to practice and apply particular skills or ideas. Use gained insights to provide learning opportunities with value-added potential for your content.

Kingore, B. (2013). *Rigor and Engagement for Growing Minds.* Austin, TX: PA Publishing.

students in classrooms integrating arts with language art instruction. DREAM reports that art infusion, singing, and performance help children construct meaning from print and retain what they learn (Flynn, 2012).

To connect with targeted learning skills and concepts, art and non-linguistic representations must go beyond drawing a neat picture of something, as in: "Draw a picture of the main character." The purpose of these representations is to engage students in identifying the most critical information, elaborating prior knowledge, or illustrating key understandings from the content, as in: "Sketch the antagonist displaying the resulting emotions in the scene at the resolution of the conflict."

Art and non-linguistic representations comprise multiple formats to engage learners. Some examples include:

- Pictures, illustrations, and pictographs,
- Dramatizations and pantomimes,
- Graphic organizers,
- Photographs,
- Computerized graphics and simulations,
- Flow charts,
- Symbols,
- Maps,
- Sketches,
- Graphs, and
- Concept maps.

Actively constructing physical models, such as a representation of a DNA ladder, is another example of an effective use of non-linguistic connections.

Art and non-linguistic representations entice students to gather, interpret, and organize information. The imagery mode supports and elaborates what students know in a linguistic form. Hence, students' art and construction of non-linguistic representations deepens understanding. The process of relating linguistic to non-linguistic information increases transfer as students form connections to new situations. The following suggestions elicit greater complexity in students' cognitive processing of information.

✓ Challenge students to think abstractly and develop symbols that interpret and connect content.

✓ Integrate linguistic and non-linguistic responses by asking students to explain their non-linguistic representations. The act of explaining helps deepen their understanding and shares different perspectives.

✓ Enhance understanding by having students revisit their representations as more information is learned. Students return to embellish their original work with additional insights or to correct earlier misconceptions.

✓ Invite students to create original versions of graphic organizers and other non-linguistic representations. A plethora of software programs and online sites provide tools that students can use to develop visuals to represent content.

Increase student engagement through frequent incorporation of specific learning experiences using art and non-linguistic representations. Several learning experiences follow as reminders of the many ways visual representations can enhance students' applications of targeted concepts and skills. In each case, it is significant to ask students to explain their representations to someone else,

Kingore, B. (2013). *Rigor and Engagement for Growing Minds.* Austin, TX: PA Publishing.

particularly through a pair-share. This oral interaction extends learning as students rehearse their thinking, use relevant vocabulary, and deepen understanding in the process. The skills and understandings of both students increase.

## INFERENCE AND OBSERVATION

To introduce a new topic, display a related photograph, completed concept map, or graph to the class. Students work in pairs or trios to determine two things they observe and two things they infer. After two minutes, have students share and compare observations and inferences. Use that discussion to establish interest and curiosity about the new topic.

## QUICK SKETCH

When using content-related vocabulary and concepts in context, ask students to quickly complete a sketch to demonstrate understanding by illustrating a concept or key word. For example:
- "Quickly sketch a way to show 1/6."
- "Sketch an example of a magnetic field."
- "Sketch the shape of our state and put a dot to locate where we live."

The term *quick sketch* frees students from worrying about the quality of their art talent and focuses instead on a personal interpretation of content. Multiple applications are possible and offer a joyful, meaningful interlude for students of all ages.

## WORD VISUALIZATIONS

Word Visualizations are a familiar technique in which words are written in a manner to look like what they mean. In simple to more elaborate ways, students illustrate a word so others can denote its meaning. Students must understand the word well and think about it in unique ways to represent it in a drawing. Explaining their interpretation to others elaborates understanding.

Develop a class dictionary of Word Visualizations. Provide a list of key words and invite students to draw one of them to help others visualize its meaning. Students can illustrate the words on index cards and sort them alphabetically in an index card box. The box makes it easy to add new words to the developing visual dictionary.

petite    *facetious*    **TOWERING**    *elongated*

## PANTOMIME

- ### WHAT HAPPENS NEXT

As an engaging application of sequence or cause-effect skills in multiple disciplines, small teams of students pantomime a content-related scene or event for others to decipher. Students who successfully determine the depiction do not reveal what it is; rather, they call out: "This is what happens next," and proceed to pantomime the next scene or the effect of the event. Invite the class to discuss the pantomimed content before proceeding with another scene or event.

- ### Adverb Actions

Pantomime engages students in developing proficiency with some difficult aspects of English, such as adverbs. Adverbs are particularly challenging for young children and learners whose first language is not English. However, even middle school students benefit from richer applications of adverbs.

Using a familiar verb, such as *move*, provide three adverbs on index cards. Hold up a selected card for students to read and pantomime the action, such as *move quietly* or *move boldly*.

Next, involve the class in brainstorming a more extensive set of adverbs for the verb and write each of those on a card. Individuals take turns randomly selecting a card and pantomiming the action as others identify the adverbial phrase.

Finally, increase skill applications and assess student responses using a means for every student to respond, such as a technology tool or an individual wipe-off board. As one student pantomimes an action, others write a sentence describing that action on their boards. Provide encouraging feedback about sophisticated sentences and vocabulary as you observe applications. Continue the process at another time using a different verb.

### Symbols or Pictographs

Symbols and pictographs represent knowledge by abstractly illustrating and interpreting information.
- "Create a symbol for the protagonist that reveals a key trait."
- "Create a symbol that represents *subterranean*."
- "Research and compare ancient pictographs in Europe and the United States."

Pictographs use symbolic pictures to represent relevant information, as with a picture graph of animals aligned to show the results from a class survey of favorite African animals or the results from researching the most endangered African animals.

### Symbol System

Students create a set of symbols to translate content or represent a process. For example, students create symbols for the key characters in the novel and storyboard the cause-effect conditions that lead to the conclusion. In science, students can develop a symbol system to explain the catalyst and reaction in an experiment. Students might also develop unique symbols and a legend to represent content on their original maps.

### Word Clouds

Students access computer software or hand-draw word clouds to delineate the rela-

Kingore, B. (2013). *Rigor and Engagement for Growing Minds*. Austin, TX: PA Publishing.

tionships of key words connected to a topic or field.

### NONFICTION ILLUSTRATED BOOKS

Creating nonfiction illustrated books is an authentic, transdisciplinary task with several potential audiences. Individuals or groups of two or three students refine their understanding of a discipline concept or a topic of personal interest by writing and illustrating a nonfiction book for others to read. Extensive attention to content area vocabulary enhances the educational value of the book.

It is important to keep group size small to ensure a more equal responsibility and input in the work. Individuals are motivated to expend effort and be productive when their contributions to this composition are clearly needed and respected.

Students can complete nonfiction books by hand or by using computer software programs. At the minimum, most groups employ word processing for the text and then scan or digitally photograph their original art or graphics to incorporate.

For an especially relevant audience, arrange for students to interview an interested teacher of younger children to determine a concept or topic in a chosen discipline that would provide useful information needed by these young learners. It is powerful for students to know that their work will be used to potentially benefit a classroom of children. This audience motivates extensive time-on-task and disciplined inquiry. If possible, arrange for the authors to personally present and share their work with the younger classroom.

### ABC BOOKS

As a specific application for elementary students, engage them in creating books in an ABC format. This format appeals to audiences and requires students to organize content by using the letters of the alphabet as starting points to interpret information.

Students research the styles and structures of available alphabet books for multiple ages to guide their original thinking and use of non-linguistic representations. After determining their topic, they research to determine a key concept or vocabulary term for each alphabet letter and proceed constructing text and illustrations for their ABC book.

## PHYSICAL ACTIVITY

Movement engages students and is a welcome alternative to the extensive amount of seat-time in the classrooms of the past. Research supports that movement enhances both learning and memory and that the brain is more active when physical activity increases the flow of oxygen-rich blood to it (Medina, 2009; Sousa, 2010). Marzano (2010b) reports that engaging in kinesthetic activities helps students illustrate ideas and retain knowledge, such as children using their arms to demonstrate the diameter of a circle or an obtuse angle or a large group of students pantomiming the different parts of cellular division simultaneously. Physical activity, such as physical exercise and moving to music, boosts brainpower and heightens students' ability to concentrate. Movement, such as simulations and dramatizations, engage students in kinesthetic activities to develop higher comprehension.

Movement is natural in effective student-centered learning environments. With all students, purposefully build physical movement into class routines and learning experiences, such as:

- Getting needed materials,
- Accessing and using manipulatives in math and science,
- Moving to a different location to form groups,
- Standing to conduct science experiments and lab tasks,
- Participating in creative dramatics and role-play, and
- Engaging in learning experiences at tiered learning stations.

Additionally, design specific learning experiences incorporating physical activity. Four Corners and Math Fingers are two examples of the many ways movement can enhance students' work with targeted concepts and skills.

## FOUR CORNERS

Use the four corners or the perimeters of the classroom for students to share information and conduct demonstrations in self-selected groups (Kingore, 2007c). Students relocate to one of the corners to form small groups for designated academic purposes that encourage active engagement. Four Corners is a worthwhile strategy in busy classrooms. Less class time is required for more students to benefit from increasingly frequent opportunities to present their work to a peer audience. As groups work in the four corners, freely

move about the classroom to attend to the ideas, encourage, and jot notes for formative assessment information.

- ### WALK ABOUT

Post one or more pieces of blank chart paper in each corner. Label each paper with a topic-related category, such as different elements, characters, countries, or issues. On a two-minute rotation, each group writes responses on one paper before advancing to the next paper. Have each group write in a different color to clarify in the subsequent discussion who wrote which ideas.

- ### DEMONSTRATIONS

In each corner, two or three students work together to demonstrate a science concept or how to complete a math problem they have prepared to present to a small group. The process takes less than ten minutes. If this strategy is used once a week, every student has the opportunity to complete a demonstration every three or four weeks.

- ### AUTHOR'S CHAIR

Literacy skills authentically develop in classrooms that serve as a literary community in which students discuss favorite books or articles and share their writing with peers for reflection and enjoyment. For a fresh application of Graves's and Hansen's influential 1983 concept of the Author's Chair, invite four students to simultaneously present their written work to small groups of peers in different corners of the classroom. Author's Chair encourages students to see themselves as real writers with interesting ideas to share with others. By using

Kingore, B. (2013). *Rigor and Engagement for Growing Minds.* Austin, TX: PA Publishing.

four corners, opportunities to participate in literacy presentations exponentially increase with less investment of class time.

- **OPINION POSITIONS**

Each corner has a sign to designate an opinion position, such as *strongly agree, agree, disagree,* or *strongly disagree.* In response to a content-related, provocative statement, students move to the corner that best represents their opinion. Each group discusses their opinions for two minutes before you randomly call on one person from each group to summarize that group's position.

## MATH FINGERS

As a mathematical finger-play, students use fingers and hands to demonstrate math solutions. Initially, the active responses build number concepts. However, more complex applications using mathematical vocabulary, symbols, and higher math concepts are also possible and prove quite engaging. The following steps illustrate using Math Fingers from quite simple to more complex applications.

1. Tell and Show.
   Bring your hands out from behind your back to reveal some extended fingers. Ask children to tell you the number of fingers and then show you that amount with their fingers. Put your hands behind your back and continue producing a different number each time for their response.

2. Another Way.
   Change the activity to require another way. When you bring your hands out to reveal a number of extended fingers, children are

to use their fingers to show you the same number another way.

3. Silent Display.
   Students work in pairs to mentally complete the math problems you present. For each solution, no talking or writing is permitted and all four hands of the pair of students must be used to display parts of the solution. Initially, announce the problem orally. For more complex applications, write problems on task cards or on a board for students to read and then respond. As solutions are revealed, ask students to stop and debrief. Inquire about their process and point out the different ways they represented the solution.

Orally prompt Silent Display by incorporating operations and vocabulary in the problem. Some examples follow.
- "What is the product of four and five?"
- "Show me the difference of forty-three and thirty-six."

Written examples of Silent Display can incorporate a wide range of math concepts, formulas, symbols, and vocabulary. Some examples follow.
- $42 \div 21$
- $\sqrt{121} + 8$
- (2 X the prime # between 7 and 13) - 2
- $X + 2 - 3X + 4 = 0$

Silent Display requires collaboration, understanding, cognitive processing of concepts, and engagement. With fast pacing and appropriate applications, middle school students are as engaged as elementary learners in this learning experience.

Each level of Math Fingers is simple-to-use and an instant application when variety during a lesson is an advantage. Our limitation is designing problems with solutions that do not exceed either ten or twenty, depending on which level of the game we are using. Math Fingers affords in-the-moment formative assessment as you observe every student responding.

## INCREASING YOUNG LEARNERS' ENGAGEMENT AND ATTENTION SPANS

Young children particularly benefit from physically active engagement in learning situations. When children are active participants in the learning process, they both uncover and receive information. They are more physically and mentally absorbed, satisfying developmental needs. Specifically, physical engagement for children increases their attention spans, intensifies their interests in learning, and promotes their long-term retention of information.

Active engagement techniques are valuable for young children and teachers. They help guide students to process and react to information, and they give children a reason to listen more attentively so they can respond appropriately. These techniques also guide instruction by serving as effective formative assessment devices that provide immediate feedback regarding the comprehension and content acquisition of each child.

## ACTIVE ENGAGEMENT TECHNIQUES FOR YOUNG CHILDREN

### 1. ACTION REACTIONS

During the second reading of a good book, invent a simple action for children to demonstrate in response to a character, event, or repeating idea. For example, when reading Leo Lionni's *Alexander and the Wind-Up Mouse,* have children wiggle one index finger like a scampering mouse when Alexander is involved in the story. Children put their index finger and thumb together and twist their hand as if they were winding something whenever the Wind-up Mouse is involved.

### 2. WORD PUPPETS

Provide each child a simple puppet to use when continuing a story or discussion. Create these puppets with minimum effort by stapling laminated cards to craft sticks. The cards might be index cards, geometric shapes, or even shapes cut out to correspond to the topic being studied, such as character figures or woodland animals. To increase efficiency and applications, laminate blank shapes so you can reuse them with other words.

Write words on the puppets and divide the puppets among the children so every child has one. Children hold up the puppet when that word is used in oral discussion or read in a story. Some applications include:
- High frequency words,
- Parts of speech, such as adjectives,
- Word wall words, and
- Names of children or characters.

### 3. ORAL CLOZE

Omit words or patterns for the children to fill in to complete the idea. This works particularly well for rhyming words: "Hickory dickory dock, The mouse ran up the _____." It is also useful for retelling sequence: "First of all, he saw a _____."

Kingore, B. (2013). *Rigor and Engagement for Growing Minds.* Austin, TX: PA Publishing.

## 4. LOLLIPOPS

Lollipops (laminated circles stapled to craft sticks) are a variation of every-student-response techniques that young children greatly enjoy. Lollipops have letters, numerals, symbols, or words written on them. Children can hold them up appropriately to respond as they interact during teacher-directed instruction. For example, leave out a word as you read a sentence to children, and they hold up the lollipop with the correct word. In math, pose a word problem, and they show the lollipop bearing the correct number for the answer.

Lollipops are also effectively used for more physically active responses by inviting children to walk around and *sell* their lollipop to another child if that child can correctly identify the information on the lollipop. As children move about the room, they quietly sing or chant, "Lollipop, lollipop, who will buy my lollipop?" Another child answers: "I will," and then states what is on the lollipop.

## FIGURE 8.8:
# CREATING REPLACEMENT TASKS

Create a list of replacement tasks to provide students with learning options in your class. Ensure that your options are relevant to students' needs and learning targets. Later, collaborate with a peer to share successes and brainstorm new learning opportunities for students.

1. _____

2. _____

3. _____

4. _____

5. _____

6. _____

7. _____

8. _____

9. _____

10. _____

Kingore, B. (2013). *Rigor and Engagement for Growing Minds.* Austin, TX: PA Publishing.

# Sometimes It Just Takes One

Children's picture books provide such wonderful opportunities to make metaphorical connections. A charming book entitled *One* by Kathryn Otoski tells the story of Blue—a quiet color who was picked on by a hot head named Red. Blue began to feel bad about himself, and the other colors did not rise to support him. Finally, One came along—a number with a different shape and bold ideas. He modeled to the colors that they should support each other and stand up to say "No" when someone is mean or picks on them. Eventually, the colors began to change their ways until even Red learned to get along. The book ends with the observation: "Sometimes it just takes One."

Many people will appropriately use this book to prompt class discussions about bullying. Equally important, however, is the embedded moral of this book that one person with a unique idea or perspective can take action to make a difference.

Abundant research cannot change classrooms into rigorous learning environments if we fail to translate research into classroom practices. You are the one with the power to do that. Despite what actions others may or may not take, establish your priorities for a nurturing, rigorous learning environment that engages your students in relevant, authentic learning opportunities. Guarantee students' continuous learning at the deeper levels of cognitive processing that foster conceptual understanding. Sometimes it just takes one to make a difference and promote life-long learning for our students.

Kingore, B. (2013). *Rigor and Engagement for Growing Minds.* Austin, TX: PA Publishing.

FIGURE 8.9:
# THINKING REFLECTIVELY

### 1. IDEAS
Identify two or more ideas you intend to apply immediately.

### 2. DON'T WONDER ABOUT IT—ASK THE LEARNER.
What engages them? Conduct a discussion with students to elicit their perceptions and suggestions for engagement in learning. Specifically, ask them for examples of tasks or techniques that appeal to them and entice them to be more engaged.

### 3. SHOP TALK
*It is engaging and often exciting to talk shop with a valued colleague. Putting your heads together produces ideas that may not have developed alone.*
Together, reflect upon the many professional development sessions you have experienced. Describe why you did not appreciate some of the sessions; then, determine and list the specific components that led to your frustration or disengagement. What can you conclude? Which factors might relate to student engagement in your classroom?

APPENDIX A:

# CHARACTERISTICS OF A RIGOROUS LEARNING ENVIRONMENT

**STUDENTS ACHIEVING AT GRADE LEVEL**

**ALL STUDENTS**

**HIGH-ABILITY STUDENTS**

**Students Achieving at Grade Level**
- Grade-level instructional pace and content
- High-level thinking is more concrete, linear, single-dimensional
- Expectations for depth and complexity when appropriate

**All Students**
- Realistic and relevant learning experiences
- Respectful
- High expectations
- Supportive teachers and peers
- Authentic, real-world applications as frequently as possible
- Concerned with the ways current instruction affects students' academic careers and future roles
- All students experience continuous learning

**High-Ability Students**
- More rigorous, beyond grade-level instructional pace and level
- High-level thinking is more complex, abstract, multi-dimensional
- Expectations for depth and complexity in most learning experiences and responses

**SUMMARY:** All students benefit from a respectful support system in a rigorous environment that emphasizes realistic, relevant learning. While most students benefit from grade-level instruction and high-level thinking, high-ability students only experience continuous learning when the instructional pace and level is more rigorous and when challenged to engage in high-level thinking that is more abstract, complex, and in-depth.

Kingore, B. (2013). *Rigor and Engagement for Growing Minds*. Austin, TX: PA Publishing.

## APPENDIX B:
# RECOMMENDED WEBSITES

✦ The Center for Authentic Intellectual Work (AIW) develops and shares criteria and standards for authentic pedagogy and student work.

**http://centerforaiw.com**

✦ The Common Core State Standards Initiative provides information about the academic content standards for the United States.

**http://www.corestandards.org**

✦ Common Sense Media is a nonprofit organization providing free classroom lessons and parent education resources to guide kids to safe, smart, and ethical decisions online.

**http://www.commonsensemedia.org**

✦ A constructed writing response is a structured written response to a question and usually used as a formative assessment tool.

**writingfix.com/RICA/Constructed_Response.htm**

✦ Edutopia, *s*ponsored by the George Lucas Educational Foundation, is dedicated to improving the K-12 learning process by disseminating comprehensive assessment, integrated studies, problem-based learning, social-emotional learning, teacher development, and technology integration.

**http://www.edutopia.org**

✦ Hoagies' Gifted Education Page is a respected and relevant resource for parents, educators, and gifted students.

**http://www.hoagiesgifted.org**

✦ International Baccalaureate Organization (IBO) is a non-profit educational foundation in 143 countries with schools and programs for students aged 3-19. IB strives to develop the intellectual, personal, emotional, and social skills students need to live, learn, and work in a rapidly globalizing world.

**http://www.ibo.org**

✦ Khan Academy provides a free library of thousands of K-12 videos for math, science, and humanities to help students learn or extend their skills.

**http://www.khanacademy.org**

✦ My Group Genius, a project of the Bill and Melinda Gates Foundation, seeks to improve education through collaboration and invites teachers to explore best teaching practices and specific examples integrating the Common Core State Standards into math and literacy curricula.

**http://www.mygroupgenius.org**

✦ *A Nation Deceived* from the Belin-Blank Center reports the disparities between the research on acceleration and the educational beliefs and practices that may run contrary to the research.

**http://www.accelerationinstitute.org/Nation_Deceived/ND_v1.pdf**

✦ The National Association for Gifted Children (NAGC) is an organization providing information and resources about gifted children and youth for parents, teachers, and educators.

**http://www.nagc.org**

✦ The National Council of Teachers of Mathematics (NCTM) is the national voice of mathematics education to support educators' highest quality of mathematics learning and standards.

**http://www.nctm.org**

✦ The National Writing Project (NWP) is a network of sites focusing K-college educators on sustained efforts to improve writing and learning for all learners. Began in 1974, it is the only federally funded program focused on the teaching of writing.

**http://www.nwp.org**

✦ The Northern Nevada Writing Project (NNWP) freely shares hundreds of lessons to inspire teachers and students with authentic writing projects.

**http://writingfix.com**

✦ RubiStar is a free online tool to help teachers and students create quality rubrics.

**http://rubistar.4teachers.org**

✦ The Top 100 American Speeches of the 20th Century provides primary sources of the highest rated speeches for students' access during personal investigations.

**http://highered.mcgraw-hill.com/sites/dl/free/007256296x/77464/top100_only.html**

---

PA Publishing as well as Bertie Kingore do not have control or assume responsibility for third-party websites and their content. At the time of this book's publication, all facts and figures cited within are the most current available. All telephone numbers, addresses, and website URLs are accurate and active; all publications, organizations, websites, and other resources exist as described in this book; and all have been verified as of September 2012. If you find any errors or believe that a website listed here is not as described, please contact PA Publishing.

Kingore, B. (2013). *Rigor and Engagement for Growing Minds.* Austin, TX: PA Publishing.

# REFERENCES

Allington, R. (2008). *What really matters in response to intervention: Research-based designs.* Boston: Allyn & Bacon.

Anderson, L. & Krathwohl, D. (Eds.). (2001). *Taxonomy for learning, teaching, and assessing: A revision of Bloom's taxonomy of educational objectives.* New York: Longman.

Association for Supervision & Curriculum Development (ASCD). (2008). *Formative assessment in content areas: Middle school* (DVD). Alexandria, VA: Association for Supervision & Curriculum Development.

ASCD, Marzano, R., Gaddy, B., Foseid, M. C., Foseid, M. P., & Marzano, J. (2008). *Handbook for classroom management that works.* Upper Saddle River, NJ: Prentice Hall.

Authentic Intellectual Work (AIW). (2012). *Criteria and standards for authentic pedagogy and student work.* The Center for Authentic Intellectual Work. Retrieved from http://centerforaiw.com

Barrie, J. (1987). *Peter Pan: 100th anniversary edition.* New York: Henry Holt & Co.

Bergmann, J. & Sams, A. (2011). How the flipped classroom is radically transforming learning. Retrieved April 15, 2012, from http://www.thedailyriff.com/articles/how-the-flipped-classroom-is-radically-transforming-learning-536.php

Bergmann, J. & Sams, A. (2012). *Flip your classroom: Reach every student in every class every day.* Eugene, OR: International Society for Technology in Education (ISTE).

Betts, G. & Kercher, J. (1999). *Autonomous learner model: Optimizing ability.* Greeley, CO: ALPS Publishing.

Brulles, D., Saunders, R., & Cohn, S. (2010). Improving performance for gifted students in a cluster grouping model. *Journal for the Education of the Gifted, 34*(2), 327-500.

Burnett, F. (1911). *The secret garden.* Harlow, UK: Heinemann.

Carmichael, D. & Martens, R. (2012). Midwestern magic: Iowa's statewide initiative engages teachers, encourages leadership, and energizes student learning. *Journal of Staff Development, 33*(3), 22-26.

Carter, K. & Doyle, W. (1987). Teachers' knowledge structures and comprehension processes. In J. Calderhead (Ed.), *Exploring teacher thinking* (pp.147-160). London: Cassell.

Center for the Improvement of Early Reading Achievement (CIERA). (2001). *Put reading first: Research building blocks for teaching children to read.* Jessup, MD: National Institute for Literacy at ED Pubs.

Charlip, R. (1993). *Fortunately.* NY: Aladdin Paperbacks.

Chiao, T. (2011). Spotlight on common sense media. National Writing Project. Retrieved from http://www.nwp.org/cs/public/print/resource/3727

Colangelo, N., Assouline, S., & Gross, M. (2004). *A nation deceived: How schools hold back America's brightest students.*

Iowa City, IA: Belin & Blank International Center for Gifted Education and Talent Development.

Common Core State Standards (CCSS). (2010). *Common core state standards for English language arts and literacy in history/social studies, science, and technical subjects.* Washington, D.C. National Governors Association Center for Best Practices, Council of Chief State School Officers.

Common Core State Standards (CCSS). (2010). *Common core state standards for Mathematics.* Washington, D.C. National Governors Association Center for Best Practices, Council of Chief State School Officers.

Cooper, J., Kiger, N., Robinson, M., & Slansky, J. (2011). *Literacy: Helping students construct meaning (8th ed.).* Belmont, CA: Wadsworth Publishing.

Costa, A., & Kallick, B. (1992). Reassessing assessment. In A. Costa, J. Bellanca, & R. Fogarty (Eds.), *If minds matter: A foreword to the future* (pp. 275-280). Palatine, IL: IRI/Skylight.

Cousins, N. (2005). *Anatomy of an illness as perceived by the patient: Reflections on healing and regeneration.* New York: W. W. Norton & Company.

Crockett, L., Jukes, I., & Churches, A. (2011). *Literacy is not enough: 21st century fluencies for the digital age.* Thousand Oaks, CA: Corwin Press.

Csikszentmihalyi, M. (1990). *Flow: The psychology of optimal experience.* New York: Harper and Row.

Csikszentmihalyi, M. (1993). *The evolving self: A psychology for the third millennium.* New York: HarperCollins.

Csikszentmihalyi, M. (2002). Motivating people to learn. [Interview]. Retrieved from http://www.edutopia.org/mihaly-csikszentmihalyi-motivating-people-learn

Daggett, W. (2007). *The education challenge: Preparing students for a changing world.* Rexford, NY: International Center for Leadership in Education.

Daniels, H. & Bizar, M. (2005). *Teaching the best practice way: Methods that matter, K-12.* Portland, ME: Stenhouse Publishers.

De Frondeville, T. (2009). Ten steps to better student engagement. Retrieved from http://www.edutopia.org/project-learning-teaching-strategies

Dean, C., Hubbell, E., Pitler, H., & Stone, B. (2012). *Classroom instruction that works: Research-based strategies for increasing student achievement (2nd ed.).* Alexandria, VA: Association for Supervision & Curriculum Development.

Deans, T. (2000). *Writing partnerships: Service-learning in composition.* Urbana, IL: National Council of Teachers of English.

Duke, N. (2000). 3.6 minutes per day: The scarcity of informational texts in first grade. *Reading Research Quarterly, 35,* 202-224.

Duke, N. (2004). The case for informational text. *Educational Leadership, 61*(6), 40-44.

Dweck, C. (2006). *Mindset: The new psychology of success.* New York: Random House.

Dweck, C. (2007). The perils and promises of praise. *Educational Leadership, 65*(2), 34-39.

Dweck, C. (2010). Giving students meaningful work: Even geniuses work hard. *Educational Leadership, 68*(1), 16-20.

Edwards, J. (2010). *Inviting students to learn: 100 tips for talking effectively with your students*. Alexandria, VA: Association for Supervision & Curriculum Development.

Egan, K. (2009). *Learning in depth.* In M. Scherer (Ed.), *Engaging the whole child: Reflections on best practices in learning, teaching, and leadership* (pp.133-142). Alexandria, VA: Association for Supervision & Curriculum Development.

Elias, M. (2012). SEL and whole child education: An essential partnership. Social-Emotional Learning Lab. Retrieved February 17, 2012, from http://www.edutopia.org

Erickson, L. (2007). *Concept-based curriculum and instruction for the thinking classroom.* Thousand Oaks, CA: Corwin Press.

Ferguson, R. (2010). Student perceptions of teaching effectiveness. [Discussion Brief]. National Center for Teacher Effectiveness and the Achievement Gap Initiative, Harvard University. Retrieved October 14, 2010, from http://Ronald_Ferguson@Harvard.edu

Flynn, P. (2012, February 10). School arts = higher scores: The developing reading education with arts methods. *San Diego Union-Tribune.*

Ford, D. & Harris, J. (1999). *Multicultural gifted education.* New York: Teachers College Press.

Galbraith, J. & Delisle, J. (2011). *The gifted teen survival guide: Smart, sharp, and ready for almost anything.* Minneapolis, MN: Free Spirit Publishing.

Gerwertz, C. (2012). Districts gear up for shift to informational texts. *Education Week, 31*(24), 1, 14-15.

Gifford, M. & Gore, S. (2008). *The effects of focused academic vocabulary instruction on underperforming math students.* [Research Report]. Alexandria, VA: Association for Supervision & Curriculum Development.

Gillies, R. & Boyle, M. (2008). Teachers' discourse during cooperative learning and their perceptions of this pedagogical practice. *Teaching and Teacher Education: An International Journal of Research and Studies, 24,* 1333–1348.

Ginsburg, D. (2012). Formative assessment efficiency, summative assessment proficiency. [Blog]. Retrieved January 23, 2012, from http://blogs.edweek.org/teachers/coach_gs_teaching_tips/2012/01/formative_assessment_efficiency_summative_assessment_proficiency.html

Graves, D. & Hansen, J. (1983). The author's chair. *Language Arts, 60*(2), 176-183.

Guskey, T. & Anderman, E. (2009). Students at bat. In M. Scherer (Ed.), *Engaging the whole child: Reflections on best practices in learning, teaching and leadership* (pp.155-165). Alexandria, VA: Association for Supervision & Curriculum Development.

Harrison, B. (2004). *Writing across the curriculum guide.* The Northern Nevada Writing Project. Retrieved from http://writingfix.com/WAC/Exit_Tickets.htm

Harste, J. (1994). Literacy as curricular conversations about knowledge, inquiry, and morality. In R. Ruddell, M. Ruddell, and H. Singer (Eds.), *Theoretical model and processes of reading (4th ed.* pp.

1220-1242). Newark, DE: International Reading Association.

Hattie, J. & Timperley, H. (2007). The power of feedback. *Review of Educational Research, 77*(1), 81-112

Himmele, P. & Himmele, W. (2011). *Total participation techniques: Making every student an active learner.* Alexandria, VA: Association for Supervision & Curriculum Development.

International Baccalaureate Organization (IBO). (2007). *Primary years programme.* Cardiff, Wales GB: IBO

Johnston, P. (2012). *Opening minds: Using language to change lives.* Portland, ME: Stenhouse Publishers.

Jones, R. (2008). *Strengthening student engagement.* Rexford, NY: International Center for Leadership in Education.

Jones, R. (2010). *Rigor and relevance handbook (2nd ed.).* Rexford, NY: International Center for Leadership in Education.

Kaplan, S. & Cannon, M. (2000). *Curriculum starter cards: Developing differentiated lessons for gifted students.* Austin, TX: Texas Association for the Gifted and Talented.

Kingore, B. (2007a). *Assessment: Timesaving procedures for busy teachers (4th ed.).* Austin, TX: Professional Associates Publishing.

Kingore, B. (2007b). *Assessment: Interactive CD ROM.* Austin, TX: Professional Associates Publishing.

Kingore, B. (2007c). *Reaching all learners: Making differentiation work.* Austin, TX: Professional Associates Publishing.

Kingore, B. (2008). *Teaching without nonsense: Translating research into effective practice (2nd ed.).* Austin, TX: Professional Associates Publishing.

Kingore, B. (2011). *Tiered learning stations in minutes: Increasing achievement, high-level thinking, and the joy of learning.* Austin, TX: P A Publishing.

Kipling, R. (1902). *Just so stories.* New York: Doubleday.

Konigsburg, E. (2000). *Silent to the bone.* New York: Aladdin.

Leana, C. (2011). The missing link in school reform. *Stanford Social Innovation Review,* Fall, 30-35.

Levy, S. (2008). The power of audience. *Educational Leadership, 66*(3), 75-79.

Lionni, L. (1969). *Alexander and the wind-up mouse.* New York: Dragonfly Books.

Lucas, S. & Medhurst, M. (2008). *Words of a century: The top 100 American speeches, 1900-1999.* New York: Oxford University Press.

Macaulay, D. (1979). *Motel of the mysteries.* Boston: Houghton Mifflin.

MacLachlan, P. (1985). *Sarah, plain and tall.* New York: HarperCollins.

Marzano, R. (2006). *Preliminary report on the 2004-2005 evaluation study of the ASCD program for building academic vocabulary.* Alexandria, VA: Association for Supervision & Curriculum Development.

Marzano, R. (2010a). Meeting students where they are: Using games to enhance student achievement. *Educational Leadership 67*(5), 71-72.

Marzano, R. (2010b). Representing knowledge nonlinguistically. *Educational Leadership, 67*(8), 84-86.

Marzano, R. & Pickering, D. (2005). *Building academic vocabulary: Teacher's manual.*

Alexandria, VA: Association for Supervision & Curriculum Development.

McTighe, J. & O'Connor, K. (2005). *Seven practices for effective learning. Educational Leadership, 63*(3), 10-17.

Measures of Effective Teaching Project (MET). (2012). *Gathering feedback for teaching: Combining high-quality observations with student surveys and achievement gains.* Seattle, WA: Bill & Melinda Gates Foundation.

Medina, J. (2009). *Brain rules: 12 principles for surviving and thriving at work, home, and school.* Seattle, WA: Pear Press.

Moline, S. (2011). *I see what you mean: Visual literacy (2nd ed.).* Portland, ME: Stenhouse Publishers.

National Association for Gifted Children (NAGC). (2010). Redefining giftedness for a new century: Shifting the paradigm. [Position Paper]. May. Washington, D.C.: NAGC.

Neill, M. (2010). A better way to assess students and evaluate schools. *Education Week Online, 29(36).* Retrieved from http://www.fairtest.org/better-way-assess-students-and-evaluate-schools

Noddings, N. (2009). All our students thinking. In M. Scherer (Ed.), *Engaging the whole child: Reflections on best practices in learning, teaching and leadership* (pp. 91-100). Alexandria, VA: Association for Supervision & Curriculum Development.

Northern Nevada Writing Project. (2011). Writing about reading: Constructed response. The Northern Nevada Writing Project. Retrieved from http://writingfix.com/RICA/Constructed_Response.htm

Novak, J. (1991). Clarify with concept maps: A tool for students and teachers alike. *The Science Teacher, 58*(7), 45-49.

Novak, J. (1998). *Learning, creating, and using knowledge: Concept maps as facilitative tools for schools and corporations.* Mahwah, NJ: Lawrence Erlbaum & Assoc.

Ogle, D. (1986). K-W-L: A teaching model that develops active reading of expository text. *The Reading Teacher, 39,* 564-570.

Otoski, K. (2008). *One.* San Rafael, CA: KO Kids Books.

Paul, R. & Elder, L. (2004). *The thinker's guide to the nature and functions of critical and creative thinking.* Santa Rosa, CA: Foundation for Critical Thinking.

Pink, D. (2005). *A whole new mind: Moving from the information age to the conceptual age.* New York: Riverhead Books.

Pink, D. (2010, September 12). Think tank: Flip-thinking—The new buzz word sweeping the US. [Newspaper article]. *The Telegraph.* Retrieved from http://www.telegraph.co.uk/finance/businessclub/7996379/Daniel-Pinks-Think-Tank-Flip-thinking-the-new-buzz-word-sweeping-the-US.html

Plucker, J., Burroughs, N., & Song, R. (2010). *Mind the (other) gap! The growing excellence gap in K–12 education.* Bloomington, IN: Indiana University, Center for Evaluation & Education Policy.

Reeves, D. (2012). What is "good reading" anyway? *ASCD Express, 7* (11), 1-4.

Reis, S., Burns, D., & Renzulli, J. (1992). *Curriculum compacting: The complete guide to modifying the regular curriculum for high ability students.* Mansfield Center, CT: Creative Learning Press.

Reis, S. & Renzulli, J. (2005). *Curriculum compacting: An easy start to differentiating for high potential students.* Waco, TX: Prufrock Press.

Renzulli, J. (1997). *The interest-a-lyzer.* Mansfield Center, CT: Creative Learning Press.

Rogers, K. (2007). Lessons learned about educating the gifted and talented: Synthesis of the research on educational practice. *Gifted Child Quarterly, 51*(4), 382-396.

Sagor, R. (2009). Cultivating optimism in the classroom. In M. Scherer (Ed.), *Engaging the whole child: Reflections on best practices in learning, teaching and leadership* (pp. 45-54). Alexandria, VA: Association for Supervision & Curriculum Development.

Scholastic & the Bill & Melinda Gates Foundation. (2012). Primary sources 2012: America's teachers on the teaching profession. [Research Report]. Retrieved from www.scholastic.com/primarysources

Seuss, T. & Prelutsky, J. (1998). *Hooray for Diffendoofer Day.* New York: Knopf Books for Young Readers.

Sheets, K. (2010). Thinking historically, teaching historically: Perspectives on the professional development of teachers from a teaching American history grant. *History Teacher, 43*(3), 455–461.

Shepard, L. (1997). *Measuring achievement: What does it mean to test for robust understanding?* Princeton, NJ: Educational Testing Service.

Siegle, D. (2011). Gifted children's bill of rights. In J. Galbraith & J. Delisle, *The gifted teen survival guide: Smart, sharp and ready for almost anything (4th ed.).*

Minneapolis, MN: Free Spirit Publishing.

Silverman, L. (2002). *Upside-down brilliance: The visual spatial learner.* Austin, TX: DeLeon Publishing.

Slocumb, P. & Payne, R. (2011). *Removing the mask: How to identify and develop giftedness in students from poverty (2nd ed.).* Highlands, TX: Aha! Process, Inc.

Sousa, D. (2009). *How the gifted brain learns (2nd ed.).* Thousand Oaks, CA: Corwin Press.

Sousa, D. (2010). *Mind, brain, & education: Neuroscience implications for the classroom.* Bloomington, IN: Solution Tree Press.

Sousa, D. & Tomlinson, C. (2010). *Differentiation and the brain: How neuroscience supports the learner-friendly classroom.* Bloomington, IN: Solution Tree Press.

Stiggins, R. & Chappuis, J. (2011). *An introduction to student-involved assessment for learning (6th ed.).* Boston, MA: Pearson Education.

Stronge, J. (2012). *Qualities of effective teachers (2nd ed.).* Alexandria VA: Association for Supervision & Curriculum Development.

Sullo, B. (2009). *The motivated student: Unlocking the enthusiasm for learning.* Alexandria, VA: Association for Supervision & Curriculum Development.

Sword, L. (2001). Psycho-social needs: Understanding the emotional, intellectual, and social uniqueness of growing up gifted. Gifted & Creative Services Australia. Retrieved from www.giftedservices.com.au

Thompson, M. (2001). The verbal option: How can we challenge gifted students with classical literature, enriched vocabulary, and the study of grammar? *Understanding Our Gifted, 14,* 7-10.

Toffler, A. (1984). *The third wave.* New York: Bantam.

Tokuhama-Espinosa, T. (2010). *Mind, brain, and education science: The new brain-based learning.* New York: W.W. Norton.

Tomlinson, C. (2001). Differentiated instruction in the regular classroom: What does it mean? How does it look? *Understanding Our Gifted, 14*, 3-6.

Tomlinson, C. (2003). *Fulfilling the promise of the differentiated classroom: Strategies and tools for responsive teaching.* Alexandria VA: Association for Supervision & Curriculum Development.

Tomlinson, C. (2011). A week in a differentiated classroom: Inside the mind of a teacher planning for differentiation. Boston, MA: ASCD Professional Development Institutes Conferences. [PowerPoint]. Retrieved from http://caroltomlinson.com/index.html

Tomlinson, C. (2012). Educators at work differentiating instruction. London, England. American School of London Learning Institute. [Powerpoint]. Retrieved from http://caroltomlinson.com/index.html

Vygotsky, L. (1962). *Thought and language.* Cambridge: MIT Press.

Wagner, T. (2010). *The global achievement gap: Why even our best schools don't teach the new survival skills our children need—and what we can do about it.* New York: Basic Books.

Washor, E. & Mojkowski, C. (2007). What do you mean by rigor? *Educational Leadership, 64,* 84-87.

Wiggins, G. & McTighe, J. (2005). *Design for understanding.* Alexandria, VA: Association for Supervision & Curriculum Development.

Willis, J. (2006). *Research-based strategies to ignite student learning: Insights from a neurologist and classroom teacher.* Alexandria, VA: Association for Supervision & Curriculum Development.

Willis, J. (2007a). *Brain-friendly strategies for the inclusion classroom.* Alexandria, VA: Association for Supervision & Curriculum Development.

Willis, J. (2007b). The neuroscience of joyful education. *Engaging the Whole Child, 64,* Summer.

Willis, J. (2009). *Inspiring middle school minds: Gifted, creative, & challenging.* Scottsdale, AZ: Great Potential Press.

Willis, J. (2010). The current impact of neuroscience on teaching and learning. In D. Sousa, *Mind, brain, & education: Neuroscience implications for the classroom (pp. 45-68).* Bloomington, IN: Solution Tree Press.

Willis, J. (2011, April 14). Big thinkers: Judy Willis on the science of learning. [Video]. Retrieved from http://www.edutopia.org/big-thinkers-judy-willis-neuroscience-learning-video

Winebrenner, S. & Brulles, D. (2008). *Cluster grouping handbook: How to challenge gifted students and improve achievement for all.* Minneapolis, MN: Free Spirit Publishing.

Winebrenner, S. & Brulles, D. (2012). *Teaching gifted kids in today's classroom: Strategies and techniques every teacher can use.* Minneapolis, MN: Free Spirit Publishing.

Wolfe, P. (2010). *Brain matters: Translating research into classroom practice (2nd ed.).* Alexandria, VA: Association for Supervision & Curriculum Development.

Wolk, S. (2009). Joy in school. In M. Scherer (Ed.), *Engaging the whole child: Reflections on best practices in learning, teaching and leadership* (pp. 3-14). Alexandria, VA: Association for Supervision & Curriculum Development.

Wormeli, R. (2005). *Summarization in any subject.* Alexandria, VA: Association for Supervision & Curriculum Development.

Wormeli, R. (2006). *Fair isn't always equal: Assessing and grading in the differentiated classroom.* Portland, ME: Stenhouse Publishers.

Zwiers, J. & Crawford, M. (2011). *Academic conversations: Classroom talk that fosters critical thinking and content understandings.* Portland, ME: Stenhouse Publishers.

# INDEX

A page number followed by *f*
indicates a reference to a figure.

# ABOUT THE AUTHOR

**DR. BERTIE KINGORE** is an international consultant, a visiting professor and speaker at numerous universities, as well as an award-winning author of twenty-six books, ten customizable CDs, numerous articles, and instructional aids. Her motivational and informative sessions make her a respected and popular speaker at national and international conferences. She has received many honors including the Legacy Award as the author of the 2005 Educator Book of the Year, the TAGT President's Award, the Outstanding Alumnus Award from the University of North Texas, and the Texas Gifted Educator of the Year Award.

A former classroom teacher, she has worked in classrooms from preschool through graduate school. She continues to inspire best practices and master teaching through her classroom demonstrations and co-teaching at school sites. Teachers are eager to implement her effective and simpler-to-prepare ideas and techniques.

Dr. Kingore lives in Austin, Texas with her husband, Richard. They are the parents of three gifted sons who fuel her dedication to education and continuous learning for all students.

Visit Bertie at her website:
http://www.bertiekingore.com.

## Recognizing Gifted Potential:
### Planned Experiences with the KOI

Grades: K - 6

Binder of instructional materials, CD-ROM, and site license

232 pages of Planned Experiences

168 pages of the *Kingore Observation Inventory (KOI),* 2nd ed.

ISBN: 0-9787042-2-3 and 978-0-9787042-2-3

*Dr. Kingore's identification process culminating from 20 years of research and field application*

**Planned experiences are particularly responsive to under-represented populations and enable more childr** **of diversity or lower SES to demonstrate gifted potential.** They are high-level, open-ended activities designed elicit and diagnose gifted behaviors. Districts have requested this set of activities that elementary teachers comple with every student to provide **equal opportunities** for advanced behaviors to emerge. They have been nationally fie tested and revised with hundreds of classroom teachers to enrich all children and identify gifted potential.

Each planned experience includes a description of the objectives and KOI categories it can elicit as well as co plete, simple-to-implement procedures. Each also provides evaluation guidelines explaining how to interpret ea child's performance. All required forms or visual aids are included.

The planned experiences are designed to be developmentally appropriate to a specific grade level and integra seamlessly with daily instruction. Each uses simple and readily available materials; several planned experiences a based on literature for children because quality literature has multiple high-level applications. The purchase include a site license providing life-time duplication within one school.

## Recognizing Gifted Potential:
### Professional Development Presentation

Grades: K - 8

Binder of instructional materials and two CD-ROMs

114 pages of the trainer's guide

232 pages of Planned Experiences

168 pages of the *Kingore Observation Inventory (KOI),* 2nd ed.

ISBN: 0-9787042-6-6 and 978-0-9787042-6-1

*Train your staff using Dr. Kingore's own presentation materials!*

*Over 700 slides provide two or more full days of training.*

*Explore student samples, interactive activities for participants, handout masters, articles, and guiding notes.* Responding to requests from administrators responsible for staff development, this professional development guide with full-color, complex, professional-level graphics provides everything needed for training staff to implement the *Kingore Observation Inventory (KOI),* planned experiences, and differentiated learning experiences.

For more information about these and many other internationally acclaimed publications by Dr. Kingore and to order, contact

**PA Publishing** • PO Box 28056 • Austin, Texas 78755-8056          Phone/Fax: 866-335-1460 • E-mail: info@kingore.com

Or visit us online at **www.kingore.com**

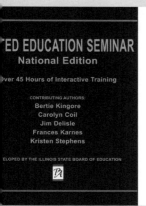

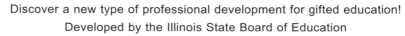

## GIFTED EDUCATION SEMINAR

Grades: K - 12

**Flash drive including over 45 hours of interactive training**

A copy of *Differentiation: Simplified, Realistic, and Effective*

A copy of *Differentiation Interactive CD-ROM*

ISBN: 978-0-9885255-2-8

Discover a new type of professional development for gifted education!

Developed by the Illinois State Board of Education

**Experience an economical means to train teachers to instruct gifted students!**

Gifted Education Seminar is designed to provide all teachers a solid foundation in gifted education as well as an exceptional launching point for further studies. This computer-based training has been carefully constructed to create a unique experience with interactive learning activities and authentic audio and video resources from gifted experts, including Bertie Kingore, Carolyn Coil, Jim Delisle, Frances Karnes, and Kristen Stephens.

### Modules:

**Perspectives**

Topics: the definition of gifted, facts and misconceptions, landmark studies, and brain research on gifted learners

**Knowing the Gifted**

Topics: characteristics of gifted learners, social and emotional needs, special populations, as well as instruments and procedures

**Differentiation**

Topics: targeting, the learning environment, content, process, and products

**Curriculum and Program**

Topics: five models designed for gifted education and one model modified for gifted education

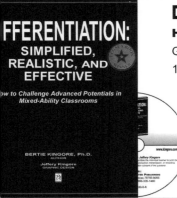

## DIFFERENTIATION: SIMPLIFIED, REALISTIC, AND EFFECTIVE

**How to Challenge Advanced Potential in Mixed-Ability Classrooms**

Grades: K - 12

192 pages

ISBN: 0-9716233-3-3 and 978-0-9716233-3-0

### Differentiation Interactive CD-ROM

Grades: K - 12

Over 65 customizable reproducible forms

ISBN: 0-9716233-6-8

This best-selling and award-winning book is being used as a book study by groups across the nation! Teachers view differentiation as important but continue to experience frustration at the vastness of the task. Management questions repeat themselves in district after district. This book simplifies the implementation of differentiation. Explore the included strategies and examples to simplify the planning and implementation process of differentiated instruction.

- Instructional Strategies that Impact Differentiation
- Understanding and Accommodating Advanced Potential
- Grouping to Enhance Differentiation
- Assessment Strategies that Impact Differentiation
- Eliciting Advanced Achievement
- Tiered Instruction
- Management Strategies
- Integrating Learning Standards

**BINDER:**

## RIGOR AND ENGAGEMENT FOR GROWING MINDS:
### PROFESSIONAL DEVELOPMENT PRESENTATION

Grades: K - 12

Binder of instructional materials and a CD-ROM with 1,010 professional development slide

228 pages of *Rigor and Engagement for Growing Minds*

CD-ROM from *Rigor and Engagement for Growing Minds*

ISBN: 978-0-9787042-9-2

*Train your staff using Dr. Kingore's personal presentation materials*
*Experience how to integrate the Common Core with intellectual integr*

Over 1,000 slides provide opportunities for you to select from more than a dozen hours of training information
engagement applications. The full-color, professional slides feature evidence- and research-based content.

- How to implement rigor and engagement
- Interactive learning experiences for participants
- Facilitator's notes and guides

- Student samples
- Templates for customizing new slides
- References

## RIGOR AND ENGAGEMENT FOR GROWING MINDS:
### FACILITATOR'S GUIDE FOR A BOOK STUDY

ISBN: 978-0-9885255-1-1

A complimentary Facilitator's Guide is available to any school or group using this book for a school-wide book st
The guide is designed to develop a common, shared language of rigor and engagement as it enhances understan
and application of the information and learning experiences. It includes recommendations for a productive book st
introduction experiences, guiding and probing questions, interactive learning tasks, graphic organizers, reflecti
and assessment experiences to enhance implementation of these success-filled applications.

## RIGOR AND ENGAGEMENT FOR GROWING MINDS:
### UNIVERSITY COURSE GUIDE

Grades: K - 12

Guide book and customizable CD-ROM

ISBN: 978-0-9885255-0-4

**A complimentary *University Course Guide* is available**
**when this book is ordered as a class text.**

The customizable CD-ROM provides ease in customizing and duplicating
class copies of the provided syllabus, tests, and class learning experience

This guide facilitates collaborative management, critical thinking, and deeper understanding of rigor and enga
ment. It provides sample tests, rubrics, and other assessment tools. Each chapter is organized with introduct
experiences, guiding and probing questions, small group engagement experiences, graphic organizers, reflecti
and interactive projects or tasks to enhance understanding and application.